Sunset

Orient
TRAVEL GUIDE

By the Editors
of Sunset Books
and
Sunset Magazine

LANE PUBLISHING CO. Menlo Park, California

Acknowledgments

We are grateful to the many individuals and organizations that helped in the preparation of this travel guide. We particularly wish to acknowledge the assistance and cooperation of the Hong Kong Tourist Association, Macau Tourist Information Bureau, and Cathay Pacific Airways Ltd.

For assistance in the gathering of information and manuscript checking, we extend special thanks to the Hong Kong Tourist Association; Japan National Tourist Organization; Korea National Tourism Corporation; Macau Tourist Information Bureau; Taiwan Visitors Association; Tourism Bureau, Republic of China; U.S. China Travel Service, Inc.; and Judy Jacobs of *AsiaPacific Travel*.

Research & Text: Joan Beth Erickson

Coordinating Editor: Deborah Thomas Kramer

Design: **Joe di Chiarro**

Illustrations & full-color map: **H. Tom Kamifuji**

Maps: **Joe Seney**

Photographers

Jack Cannon: 46, 91 right. **Sharon Chester:** 75 top. **Glenn Christiansen:** 139, 142 right, 147 bottom, 150 top, 155 top. **Betty Crowell:** 142 left. **David DeRoche:** 22 right. **Joan Beth Erickson:** 27 top. **Lynn Ferrin:** 43 bottom. **Shirley Fockler:** 134 top. **James Gebbie:** 70 top, 94 top, 158. **Hong Kong Tourist Association:** 107, 110 top. **Japan National Tourist Organization:** 30, 35, 43 top, 51, 54 top. **Korea National Tourism Corporation:** 75 bottom, 99 top. **Russell Lamb:** 78 top, 99 bottom right. **Esther Litton:** 150 bottom. **Macau Tourism Department:** 131. **Tim Ord:** 123 bottom left. **Dick Rowan:** 19 top, 27 bottom. **David Ryan:** 14 top, 22 left, 59, 91 left, 94 bottom, 110 bottom. **Teri Sandison:** 14 bottom, 19 bottom, 38, 78 bottom left. **Ron Sanford:** 11, 62, 147 top, 155 bottom. **Joan Storey:** 115, 118. **Ted Streshinsky:** 67, 70 bottom, 78 bottom right, 83, 99 bottom left, 123 top, 126, 134 bottom. **Taiwan Visitors Association:** 3, 86. **Tourism Bureau, Republic of China:** 123 bottom right. **Marie Ueda:** 54 bottom, 102.

Cover: Traditional Chinese fishing junk, its familiar bat-winged sails silhouetted against the setting sun, journeys homeward to Hong Kong. Photographed by the Hong Kong Tourist Association.

Sunset Books
  Editor: David E. Clark
  Managing Editor: Elizabeth L. Hogan

First printing August 1988

CONTENTS

SPECIAL FEATURES

Fearsome dragon *and tiger guard pagodas on Lotus Lake near Kaohsiung in southern Taiwan.*

THE ORIENT

A region of incomparable fascination for travelers:
exotic lands of rugged terrain, manicured gardens,
stunning art treasures, timeless traditions, and—from
village to metropolis—friendly people

In many ways, the countries of the Orient are alike, but some striking geographical, ethnic, and cultural differences provide a fascinating array of sights and experiences—images of the Orient, one of the world's most complex and intriguing regions.

GEOGRAPHIC PARTICULARS

The Orient stretches over the southeastern half of Asia, across the huge expanse of China to the islands of the north Pacific. Almost all of the region's mainland portion is taken up by China; Macau and Hong Kong cover only a tiny area at its southern border. The Korean peninsula extends from China's northeast side; off the mainland's east coast lie Taiwan and the island chain of Japan.

The land's development

Much of the present Asian land mass was under water until about a million years ago, when the vast prehistoric sea began to retreat. Huge areas of present-day India, Tibet, Turkey, and Iran were exposed; the waters separating Europe from Africa and Asia receded. During this period, mountain ranges took shape—the Alps, Andes, Rockies, and Himalayas (ocean sediments have been found in Tibet at 6,096 meters/20,000 feet above sea level). Volcanoes also formed at this time; they're especially numerous—and still active—in Japan, part of the Pacific's "circle of fire."

As the mountains rose, broad areas next to them became depressed, and these depressions are now vast deserts, like China's famous Gobi, which stretches about 1,609 km/1,000 miles from east to west and for some 966 km/600 miles from north to south.

A look at plants and animals

Forests once covered large areas of eastern Asia in the lowlands of the Yangtze and Yellow rivers and in the smaller river valleys. Modern Korea, Japan, and Taiwan are still heavily forested with spruce, fir, beech, and oak; common in the Orient's southern reaches are palms and bamboo, mixed with stands of pine and cedar.

The area's animal life is no longer as varied or as abundant as it once was, but native animals—varieties of deer, wild boar, monkey, bear, fox, and badger—still roam in mountainous and forested areas.

Some of the world's richest fishing grounds are found in the Sea of Japan and the East China Sea, which together form the body of water separating Japan and Taiwan from the Asian mainland. The Yellow Sea, partly enclosed by the Korean peninsula, is also rich in marine life.

ENDURING CIVILIZATIONS

The Orient has a long history. In a cave near Beijing, fossilized remains of early man were discovered, dating back more than 350,000 years. A highly developed civilization evolved on the mainland at least 1,000 years before Christ; over the millennia, it spread eastward to influence the cultures of Korea and Japan.

Although civil and regional wars have swept the area countless times, the cultures of China, Korea, and Japan have endured; they are among the oldest continuing civilizations on earth.

Cultural origins

The Chinese culture was the Orient's mother culture: the fertile lands near the Yellow River in north China are considered one of the four birthplaces of civilization (the other three were India, Mesopotamia, and Egypt).

Surrounded by mountains and plains to the north and west, and by oceans to the east and south, the Orient's original inhabitants existed for thousands of years in almost total isolation. In this isolation, a settled agricultural society evolved that contributed to China's early development.

Archeologists believe that agriculture originated in the Near East during the 7th or 8th century B.C. and moved eastward. Rice farming developed in China's fertile valleys about the 2nd century B.C.; it then spread southward to Southeast Asia and eastward to Japan. In central and western China, both rice and wheat were cultivated. Agriculture provided a stable food supply, which led to a high population growth rate and permitted culture to develop at an incredible pace.

As China's culture flourished, it spread eastward, influencing the development of both the Korean and the Japanese cultures. The Japanese began adopting Chinese ideas and practices—Confucianism, Buddhism, the study of history, calligraphy, Chinese administrative structure—in the 6th or 7th century; at this time, the Chinese civilization was already 2,000 years old.

Western influences

Until Portuguese, Spanish, and Dutch mariners arrived in the Orient during the 16th century, the Oriental people were largely ignorant of western culture. Westerners were similarly ignorant of the Asian nations' long history; nor did their chief concern lie in understanding and appreciating these ancient cultures. To the missionaries, the Orient seemed ripe for Christianity; traders and merchants saw in it the promise of great wealth. To European governments, the Asian countries offered a means of augmenting their holdings—and increasing their power—abroad. Several western nations soon established colonies in the Orient.

The western attitude toward the Orient did little to build a harmonious and lasting relationship. Instead, the European presence aroused mistrust, fear, and even hatred—feelings that have taken centuries to fade.

Western scientific knowledge, industrialization, economic prosperity, and military power seemed to pose a direct threat to the Orient. Ironically, though, these

were the western world's greatest contribution to the region, contributions that enabled China, Korea, and Japan to acquire their own power and wealth. Western ideas triggered changes in government and encouraged industrialization and commerce.

Japan provides a good example of development due to western influence. The Portuguese, Spanish, and French introduced the country to western military technology, medicine, and science; by the 1800s, the Japanese realized that science was the key to the West's power. By studying the sciences, Japan learned western industrial techniques, setting the stage for great economic strides in the 20th century.

LIFESTYLES

About 20 percent of the more than one billion people who live in Japan, Korea, Taiwan, Hong Kong, Macau, and China dwell in the Orient's major cities, which are among the largest in the world. Shanghai has a population of 11 million and Tokyo 11.5 million; Beijing's residents number 9.3 million and Seoul's exceed 10 million. Much of Hong Kong's population of 5.5 million live in the metropolitan area. The rest of the Orient's population lives in smaller cities, towns, villages, or farming communities.

Religion, a dominant theme

Religious practices are threaded into the daily life of most of the Orient's population. Impressive edifices—Buddhist temples, Shinto shrines, Muslim mosques, Christian churches, Confucian memorial houses, animist spirit houses—dot the cities and countryside.

Buddhism is the predominant faith in many areas, but often a person follows more than one religion. It's not uncommon for a Taoist or a Christian to have a Buddhist burial. In the next paragraphs, you'll find a brief description of the eastern religions practiced in the Orient.

Buddhism. Buddhists believe in reincarnation. The goal of all devout Buddhists is nirvana—the total release from earthly pain, sorrow, and desire. Though nirvana is seldom reached in just one lifetime, Buddhists believe that it can eventually be gained by right living, right believing, and peace of mind through meditation. When attained, nirvana releases man from the trial of repeated earthly existences.

Shintoism. The Japanese Shinto religion is concerned more with life in this world than with life in the world to come. Its ideal—purity of body and spirit—is accomplished through prayer and ritual. Unlike Buddhist temples, which can be very ornate, Shinto shrines are typically very simple. Usually constructed from unpainted timber, they blend into the natural landscape.

Others. Confucianism follows the teachings of Confucius, who emphasized devotion to parents, family, and friends. Taoism, based on the doctrine of Lao Zi (Lao-tzu), advocates simplicity and selflessness.

Many Orientals also practice animism (the belief that inanimate objects and natural forces have spirits) and ancestor worship, often in combination with one of the other religions.

Oriental philosophies

Traveling in the Orient, you'll discover that the countries share some common philosophies.

A love of beauty and tranquility. The upturned curve of a tiled roof, a vermilion *torii* framed in evergreens, lily-covered ponds brightened by colorful fish, a shady tree-lined path, the peaceful confines of a Shinto shrine, a raked sand garden set with distinctive stones—these are all elements of Oriental beauty.

An appreciation of tranquility and esthetic harmony is an integral part of Oriental culture. As you discover this harmony in unexpected places, it will add a fresh dimension to your travels.

Respect for age. The reverence of the Chinese for their ancestors and for culture and education have had a profound influence on all the nations of the Orient.

For centuries, Chinese relationships were based on the family; children learned from their elders. Respect for age was reinforced by ancestor worship; the living depended on their deceased relatives to intercede with the gods.

Importance of education. From the days of the scholar-officials, the Chinese stressed education as a way to develop ability. Education and philosophy were focused on organizing human beings into a harmonious and peaceful society.

The Japanese and Koreans adopted Chinese concepts of education, but were also receptive to western ideas. In addition to traditional subjects, they studied applied science, recognizing it as the basis for future development.

Festivals and events

Past and present mingle in the Orient. Each country celebrates its special days, many commemorating historical or legendary events with colorful festivities. Often a special deity is honored. (Since the dates of many festivals are determined according to the lunar calendar, these celebrations occur on different dates each year.)

A number of these celebrations are associated with popular eastern religions. Families living in various countries of the Orient celebrate many of the same festival days. In addition, countries have special celebrations that are uniquely their own.

Below are notes on some of the festivals and events celebrated in a similar manner in more than one country. Additional celebrations are listed in each chapter. For a current calendar of events, check with the government tourist office in advance or upon arrival.

New Year's Day. On the first day of the western calendar, you can see ceremonial dragons, lions, or unicorns—all beasts of happiness and goodwill—dancing in public parks in Hong Kong and Korea. In Japan, families customarily make early-morning visits to shrines at the beginning of the year. Arrangements of pine twigs and bamboo stalks decorate house doors to bring good luck; women wear their most colorful kimonos.

Chinese New Year. In late January or early February, the streets resound with greetings as the Chinese wish their friends and relatives prosperity in the New Year. Though the New Year festivities officially last only two or three days, they don't really end until Yuen Siu (Lantern Festival) 15 days later. Traditionally, the Chinese New Year is a time for family reunions, lavish feasting, visiting friends, giving gifts, making offerings to ancestors and the gods, paying debts, and getting the year off to a good start.

Yuen Siu (Lantern Festival). Held 15 days after the start of the New Year celebration, this event marks the end of the New Year period in Hong Kong, Macau, and Taiwan. Shops are stocked with a tremendous selection of fancifully shaped lanterns. Streets and houses are bedecked in lanterns, many of them illuminated at night.

Seafarers' festivals. In April or May, fishing communities honor the goddess of fishermen or the sea (Tin Hau in Hong Kong, A-Ma in Macau, and Ma-Tsu in Taiwan) with temple celebrations and decorated fishing boats.

Birthday of Lord Buddha. In May, religious ceremonies at Buddhist temples and monasteries commemorate Buddha's birth, enlightenment, and attainment of nirvana. In some places Buddha's images are sprinkled with water and paraded through the streets.

Dragon Boat Festival. This celebration honors the exiled scholar-official Ch'u Yuen, who drowned himself in the Milo River in China's Hunan Province in protest against government reforms. Legend says that fishermen raced out in their "dragon boats" to save him. In Hong Kong, Macau, and Taiwan, dragon boat races are held in his honor in May or June.

Yue Lan (Festival of Hungry Ghosts). According to legend, wandering souls return to earth one day a year and must be fed by their descendants. Buddhists and Taoists celebrate this festival in August or September.

Confucius's Birthday. Ceremonies commemorate China's famous teacher and philosopher in late September or October at Hong Kong's Confucius Temple in Causeway Bay, Taipei's Confucius Temple, and other Confucius temples throughout Taiwan.

Mid-autumn Festival (also called Moon Cake Festival). In September or October, when the moon is at its most beautiful, Chinese families travel to scenic viewpoints to watch the moonrise. Golden brown delicacies called moon cakes are traditionally eaten during the festival. In Korea this occasion also celebrates the autumn harvest, and many people visit the tombs of their ancestors.

Christmas. December 25 is a special day for Christians in the Orient, as it is for those in the West.

SOMETHING FOR EVERYONE

For those with a fondness for new experiences, the Orient offers a host of ideas: you can take an all-night hike up a sacred mountain, then watch the sunrise from the top; search for antiques or crafts in the colorful confusion of a local bazaar; journey by ferry to islands that receive few western visitors; or discover local specialties in native restaurants and food stalls. Old and new cities invite exploration; quiet villages inspire leisurely strolls. It's all part of the Orient.

Ancient and modern cities

Despite the antiquity of the Oriental cultures, many of the region's architectural treasures—historic temples, palaces, gardens, shrines, and tombs—date from relatively recent times.

In Korea, the Silla Dynasty's period of greatest achievement was between A.D. 600 and 800. Nara served as the royal capital of Japan during the 8th century, followed by Kyoto from the 8th to the 19th centuries and Tokyo in modern times. Though Beijing was founded in the 10th century, its splendors date from the Ming Dynasty (1368–1644). Not until the 20th century did Hong Kong and Taiwan experience any great growth.

Except for Korea, where stone was used extensively, most "ancient" structures are actually reconstructed buildings. In Japan many wooden temples and shrines have been periodically rebuilt, with techniques and materials similar to those used in the original construction.

Remnants of the past often coexist with modern skyscrapers. Cities have expanded far beyond their original walled confines, but often gates and portions of the old walls remain. Centuries-old gardens have become peaceful refuges in the center of busy cities. Visit Kyoto and Nara in Japan, Kyongju in Korea, Beijing in China, and sections of Tokyo, Taipei, Hong Kong, and Macau, and you'll pass from the modern to the old world at the turn of a corner.

You'll come upon small streets lined with dim shops

and food stalls, people dressed in traditional clothing, quiet gardens with paths for strolling, houses constructed and furnished in ways unfamiliar to the western visitor, and shops selling unusual masks, jade articles, Chinese calligraphy, and paintings done on scrolls and bamboo.

What's outdoors?

Fresh-air enthusiasts will find a wealth of activities and sights. Trekkers can hike Japan's Mount Fuji or backpack through the Japan Alps, roam Hong Kong's outer islands, walk through Taiwan's Taroko Gorge, or enjoy the autumn color in Korea's Mount Sorak National Park. You can bask on the beaches in Hong Kong and Korea, and go skin diving in the tropical waters off southern Taiwan. And if your tired muscles begin to complain, you can soak away your aches and pains in a wonderful Japanese hot spring.

Shopping at its best

The Orient is truly a shopper's paradise. Electronic products, cameras, binoculars, transistor radios, tape recorders, watches, and clocks are all widely available, often at discount prices, in Hong Kong, Taipei, and Tokyo. But the real shopping discoveries are the handicrafts. So many well-crafted, locally produced items invite inspection that you'll have a difficult time choosing which to buy. In many cases, you can watch the craftspeople at work.

Things to buy. The list is almost endless. Delicate silk fabrics, carpets, embroidered linens, woodblock prints, lacquerware, chinaware and pottery, handpainted scrolls, carved jade, and paper lanterns are just a few of the handcrafted products.

What not to buy. The United States restricts the import of products made from animals and plants it has officially listed as endangered or threatened. This includes tortoise-shell jewelry; items made from the skins or fur of certain animals including the cheetah, jaguar, ocelot, leopard, and tiger; products carved from elephant ivory or whale's teeth; and items made from crocodile and sea turtle, including shoes, handbags, belts, wallets, and luggage.

The fact that you can buy these items abroad doesn't mean that you'll be allowed to bring them into the United States. If you are in doubt about a purchase, check with the local United States embassy or consular office. The vendors' assurances may not always be correct. There is no refund for purchases confiscated by the United States customs or wildlife inspector; there may even be a fine.

Only a few of the restricted items have been listed here. For a more complete listing, write to the Fish and Wildlife Service District Law Enforcement Office in your area.

Culinary pleasures

Esthetic qualities are important in Oriental cuisine. For hundreds of years, people of the Orient have studied the elements that make foods appetizing and tasty. Food must be perfectly cooked, and served at the right temperature; it must also meet certain standards of color, texture, size, and shape.

Oriental chefs have learned to combine crisp vegetables, tender meat, fresh fish and shellfish, rice, and noodles in hundreds of dishes that are delicious to eat and beautiful to behold. Often food is prepared ahead and then cooked quickly. Nearly all Oriental cooking is done over a single, all-purpose heat source. Hundreds of dishes, including breads and pastries, are prepared by steaming, pan-frying, or deep-frying, or by assembling precooked ingredients.

Palate-pleasing dishes can vary from mild to spicy hot; each region has its own specialties. You can sample China's regional cuisines in Taiwan and Hong Kong as well as in China, dine on piquant Peking duck, spicy chile prawns, or delicately seasoned stir-fried noodles. Japanese gourmet treats include *tempura* (vegetables and seafood lightly coated with batter and deep-fried), and *yakitori* (grilled chicken on a skewer). Korean cooking is never bland; popular flavor enhancers include garlic, red peppers, sesame oil, and soy sauce. *Kimchi* (pickled cabbage) accompanies most meals. Portuguese influence is evident in Macau's country-style cooking; here you can sample *bacalhau* (a dish prepared with a local cod), *caldo verde* (a soup with meat, vegetables, and olive oil), and other dishes.

TRAVEL TIPS

Modern transportation has made the Orient easily accessible to the traveler. International airlines and cruise ships transport visitors to the major cities; guided tours on air-conditioned buses follow established sightseeing routes to the most popular destinations. Hotels, restaurants, and other tourist facilities in the big cities and resort areas are among the world's best.

Since the Orient offers such a variety of destinations, accommodations, and transportation, prospective travelers should consult a knowledgeable travel agent when planning a trip.

Climates vary from region to region. The more southerly countries of Taiwan, Hong Kong, Macau, and southern China and Japan are subtropical. It can get chilly in Hong Kong and Macau during the winter, though. Korea, central and northern Japan, and northern China have more seasonal weather, including freezing temperatures and snow during the winter. Summer in the Orient is hot, humid, and rainy.

For more information on each country's weather, see the "Know Before You Go" special feature in each chapter.

JAPAN

A graceful land blending serenity and activity, the
traditional and the modern: feudal castles and
soaring skyscrapers, silk kimonos and Paris fashions,
cobbled lanes and neon-lit thoroughfares

For every traveler, the complex character of Japan evokes many different associations. Particular images that come to mind are startling in their diversity: a land of serene, pastoral retreats, where ancient folkways still play a significant role in the daily life of a contemporary society; a nation of tremendous modern business and industrial power, respected throughout the world.

Separated from the Asian mainland by the Sea of Japan and the East China Sea, the string of islands that composes this prosperous country hums with activity. Its thriving industries support more than 117 million residents who live in a mountainous land slightly smaller than the state of California.

Reflecting a theme common to much of the Orient, Japan is a country of striking contrasts: the serenity of a traditional inn exists not far from the bustle of a modern skyscraper hotel; sleek bullet trains speed through hand-tended rice fields; television antennas rise above weathered tile roofs; immense factories produce sophisticated consumer products, while small shops are home to artisans who practice skills handed down over the centuries.

For many visitors, a surface fascination with Japan gradually evolves into something deeper. As they develop an understanding of and appreciation for the Japanese people, culture, and traditions, most travelers find the country exerts an increasingly strong appeal. One sophisticated world traveler tells us: "If I went to Japan once a year and stayed for 6 months, I could go for 100 years and never see the same thing twice. There's an array of national, cultural, religious, mythological, and political displays to be found in no other part of the world."

AN ISLAND NATION

Japan's chain of islands forms a long, narrow, irregular crescent. It's 2,993 km/1,860 miles from Hokkaido in the north to the Ryukyus in the southwest. Exceeding 3,900 in number, the islands lie in the North Pacific Ocean, east of Korea and China.

Honshu, the largest of the islands, is almost 1,287 km/800 miles long. Smallest of the big islands is Shikoku, only about 96 km/60 miles wide by 160 km/100 miles long. Other main islands include Kyushu and Hokkaido. Off these islands lie a multitude of lesser islands. Hundreds of them dot the quiet, misty waters of the Inland Sea, a protected waterway stretching for 402 km/250 miles between Honshu and Shikoku.

Mountainous terrain

An irregular coastline, towering mountains (topped by 3,776-meter/12,388-foot Mount Fuji), and deeply indented valleys dominate the landscape of Japan. Approximately 70 percent of the land is mountainous, though broad alluvial plains stretch out beside the country's rivers and narrow coastal plains border the island's shores.

Geologically, Japan is a young country, part of the Pacific's great "circle of fire." Many of its 150 volcanoes are still active (about 40 have erupted this century). Mineral hot springs are a popular feature at many resorts. Earthquakes are such a common occurrence that the Japanese consider them part of their normal experience.

Rain-washed rail *adds spot of color to Omogokei Gorge overlook on Shikoku Island, an area noted for meandering streams, splashy autumn foliage.*

Plants and animals

Vast forests cover more than two-thirds of Japan—hardy spruce and fir on Hokkaido, beech and oak on Honshu, palm trees in southern Shikoku and Kyushu. Pine, cedar, and bamboo thrive throughout the archipelago. More than 160 varieties of trees and 2,700 kinds of vegetation grow here, composing one of the most diverse collections of plants to be found anywhere.

You'll find apple orchards in the north, and citrus and stone fruits throughout central and southern Honshu. Tea grows in the southern areas.

Animal life is prolific. Native animals include varieties of deer, wild boar, bear, monkeys, weasels, martens, foxes, and badgers—the latter two often found as characters in Japanese folklore.

HISTORICAL NOTES

Man arrived to settle the Japanese archipelago during the Stone Age. These early inhabitants migrated from continental Asia and the southern islands. Anthropologists believe one large group of early settlers, the Ainu, gradually interbred with Mongols and Malays to form the ancestral Japanese.

Strongly influenced in its early centuries by immigrants from China and Korea, Japan's culture swiftly changed from that of a society of hunters to one firmly grounded in the Bronze and Iron Ages. Chinese calligraphy and the Chinese calendar were introduced in the 6th century. Two hundred years later, Buddhism arrived—a religion that was to have a profound influence on the country.

Imperial rule

By the 4th century, Japan had become unified by the ancestors of the Imperial family, and in the early 8th century Nara was established as the seat of government. Though the Nara Period lasted only 84 years, it flourished as the golden age of Japanese art and an era when Buddhism prospered. During this period the huge bronze *Daibutsu* or Great Buddha of Nara was cast. Elements of the Chinese administrative system and of China's art and architecture were adopted.

Birth of Kyoto. In 794, Nara ceased to serve as Japan's capital; a new capital was established at Heian-kyo (now the city of Kyoto). This town was to remain the nation's capital until 1868. During the Heian Period, a Japanese writing system came into being, and painting, sculpture, and architecture began to show more distinctly Japanese characteristics.

An extended period of unrest began in the early 9th century as a succession of emperors and rival families battled for power. Between 823 and 1338, Japan had 44 emperors, 23 of whom abdicated or were deposed.

The shoguns. In 1192, control of the country was taken over by the Minamoto clan, the first in a line of military families that ruled Japan for nearly 700 years. The leader of each family was called the *shogun.*

Shogun rule strengthened the country (repulsing two attempted invasions by Kublai Khan), encouraged the development of arts and crafts, and resulted in the construction of some of Japan's finest castles (Osaka and Himeji among them). During this period the tea ceremony became enshrined as a noble national tradition and the Japanese drama *kabuki* emerged.

Seclusion. Trade between Japan and Europe gained momentum in the 16th century and was soon followed by the arrival of Portuguese and Spanish missionaries, who introduced Christianity to Japan. The first two leaders of the Tokugawa shogunate accepted and even encouraged Christianity. But in the mid-17th century, a later Tokugawa shogun enforced a strict ban on Christian literature, persecuted the Christians, and closed the country to all foreigners, with the exception of one Dutch ship a year.

Cut off from the rest of the world, Japan lived in a state of cultural immobility for more than 200 years. During this time, known as the Edo Period, great scientific discoveries and political revolutions were taking place in Europe and America—events that were unknown in Japan. In the 1850s the major world powers secured new treaty concessions from Japan, bringing the long period of isolation to an end.

Reform and modernization. In 1868 the imperial court regained control of the country. Emperor Meiji initiated a series of reforms that paved the way for a modern Japan. Tokyo became the seat of the government, a new constitution was promulgated, a parliamentary system was introduced with the first National Diet meeting in 1890, and an administrative system was adopted to replace one that had been in effect since 645.

Modern science, political thought, economic theory, and industrial technology were studied and implemented with incredible speed. Suddenly, Japan had electricity, the telegraph, a railway network, and other modern improvements. The country's strong, young army and navy enabled the Japanese to defeat the Chinese in 1894–1895 in a battle over Korean territory and, a decade later, to get Manchuria.

Territorial expansion and war. Early in the 20th century, Japan began reaching out for the riches present in other Asian lands. Korea was annexed in 1910. Japan occupied Manchuria in 1931. By the late 1930s, vast portions of China were under Japanese control. In 1941 Japanese armed forces occupied Indochina, setting the scene in the Pacific for World War II.

Following its attack on the U.S. fleet at Pearl Harbor in December 1941, Japan scored one military victory after another. The country's conquests stretched from the Solomon Islands in the South Pacific to the Aleutian chain

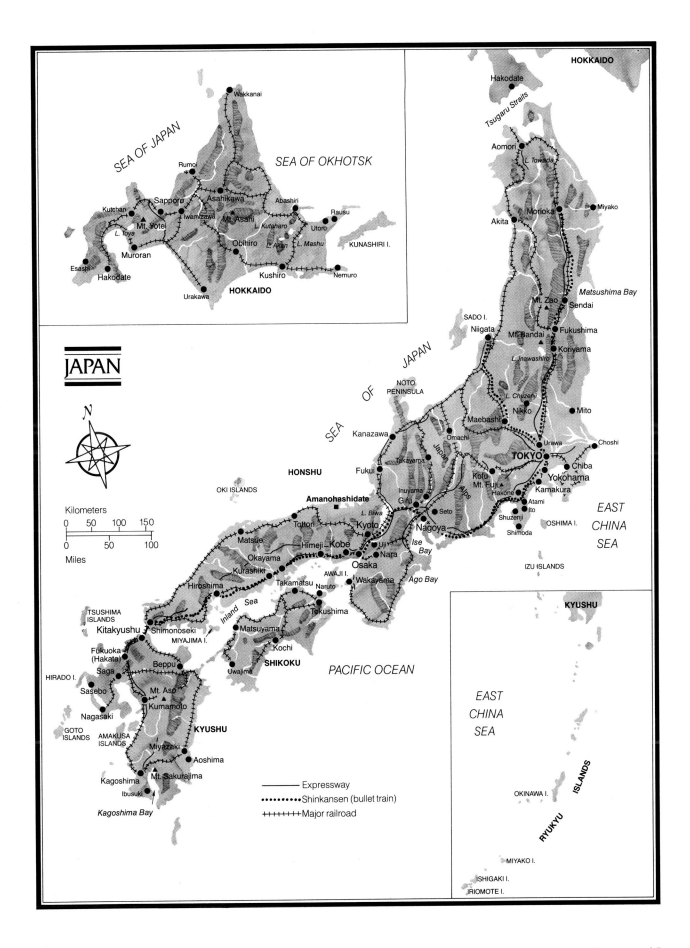

JAPAN

HOKKAIDO

SEA OF JAPAN

SEA OF OKHOTSK

Wakkanai

Rumoi

Kutchan · Sapporo · Asahikawa · Abashiri
Mt. Yotei · Iwamizawa · Mt. Asahi · Rausu
L. Toya · · L. Kutcharo · Utoro
Muroran · Obihiro · L. Akan · L. Mashu
Esashi · · · KUNASHIRI I.
Hakodate · Kushiro · Nemuro
Urakawa

HOKKAIDO

N

Kilometers
0   50   100   150
0   50   100
Miles

Hakodate

Tsugaru Straits

Aomori
L. Towada

Akita · Morioka · Miyako

Mt. Zao · Sendai · *Matsushima Bay*
SADO I. · Mt. Bandai · Fukushima
Niigata · · Koriyama
L. Inawashiro

NOTO
PENINSULA · L. Chuzenji · Mito
Maebashi · Nikko
Kanazawa · Omachi · Urawa · Choshi
Takayama · **TOKYO** · Chiba
Fukui · Kofu · Yokohama
HONSHU · Mt. Fuji · Kamakura
OKI ISLANDS · Inuyama · Hakone · Atami
Amanohashidate · Gifu · Seto · Ito
L. Biwa · Nagoya · Shuzenji · Shimoda
Tottori · Kyoto · Ise · OSHIMA I.
Matsue · Himeji — Kobe · Uji · Bay
Okayama · Nara · IZU ISLANDS
Kurashiki · Osaka
Hiroshima · Takamatsu · Naruto · Wakayama · *Ago Bay*
TSUSHIMA · Tokushima
ISLANDS · Inland · AWAJI I.
Kitakyushu · Shimonoseki · Sea
Fukuoka · MIYAJIMA I. · Matsuyama
(Hakata) · Beppu · Kochi
Saga · **SHIKOKU**
HIRADO I. · Uwajima
Sasebo · Mt. Aso · **PACIFIC OCEAN**
Nagasaki · Kumamoto
GOTO · **KYUSHU**
ISLANDS · AMAKUSA
ISLANDS · Miyazaki
Kagoshima · Aoshima
Ibusuki · Mt. Sakurajima
Kagoshima Bay

SEA OF JAPAN

Japan Alps

ALPS

*EAST
CHINA
SEA*

KYUSHU

*EAST
CHINA
SEA*

RYUKYU ISLANDS

OKINAWA I.

MIYAKO I.

ISHIGAKI I.
IRIOMOTE I.

——— Expressway
••••••••• Shinkansen (bullet train)
++++++++ Major railroad

Rectilinear lines *of Mitsui Plaza add new dimension to Tokyo's skyline. Shinjuku District's building cluster contains offices, shops, theaters, high-rise restaurants with grand city views.*

East meets West *as modishly attired women survey traditionally garbed mannequins in Ginza store window. District is Tokyo's most important shopping and entertainment area.*

near Alaska. But reversals began to occur in mid-1942. These were followed by American landings in the Marianas and air raids on Tokyo and other industrial centers. Peace finally came in August 1945.

Postwar years

At the end of the war, American forces under the command of General Douglas MacArthur occupied Japan. Occupation policy was to demilitarize the government and rebuild the country under peaceful and democratic guidelines. Between 1945 and 1952 General MacArthur instituted many reforms, established new freedoms, attempted to dissipate the strength of the *zaibatsu* (Japan's industrial giants), reorganized the educational and agricultural systems, and restructured the National Diet. The emperor relinquished his status as a divine being and became a symbol of the state.

A nation rebuilds. Devastated at the end of the war, Japan was put on its feet by financial aid from its victors and the hard work and talents of its people. In relatively few years the nation was rebuilt, its economy stronger than ever. Today Japan is one of the world's great economic powers.

Constitutional democracy. Japan's postwar constitution created independent legislative, executive, and judicial branches. The legislative body is the National Diet, consisting of the House of Representatives with 512 seats and the House of Councillors with 252 seats. The country's chief executive is the prime minister, chosen by the Diet from among its members and appointed by the emperor.

JAPAN'S PEOPLE

Most of the nation's 121 million people are descendants of successive waves of early Asian immigrants, long since melded into a single race. The gentle-mannered Ainu people, members of an aboriginal culture living on Hokkaido, are an important minority ethnic group.

Lifestyles

Though urban Japanese have adopted many western ideas, the country's underlying character is strongly Japanese. During the daytime, office workers may favor western dress. But upon returning home in the evening, some shed the western exterior for the comfort of a traditional kimono. Shoes are left at the door. Even in modern apartments, there's usually one *tatami*-matted room, and the bath is a Japanese-style *ofuro* (a deep bathtub designed for soaking).

Deep-rooted traditions. The family remains a strong unit, often with several generations living under the same roof. Family elders are respected and family laws obeyed.

Industrious and polite, the Japanese are conditioned to living close together. Courtesy and formality involve one's personal honor; to lose his temper or show strong emotion would cause a Japanese to lose face—though he may push and shove strangers in the scramble for seats on a crowded train.

Traditions and beliefs have been deeply ingrained for generations. The Japanese show an appreciation for harmony and beauty (especially in small and subtle details), a deep love of nature, and a strong devotion to cultural traditions—music, drama, architecture, crafts, and festivals.

Dress. Outside the home, most Japanese now wear western dress (*yofuku*) rather than traditional Japanese dress (*wafuku* or *kimono*). But at Japanese inns and hot springs resorts, both men and women don the *yukata*, the comfortable, loose-fitting cotton kimono provided by the inns for guests. Traditional footwear include *geta* (wooden clogs), *zori* (loose-fitting sandals), and *tabi*, (ankle socks split for the sandal thong).

Japan's women don traditional kimonos for weddings and other special occasions. At a Shinto shrine or in a large hotel, you may encounter a wedding party, the bride enfolded in her stiff brocade kimono and heavy headdress, the groom and other men dignified in tails. Older women will be wearing their best kimonos—black with colorful embroidery and sashed with an embroidered brocade *obi* (midsection wrapping). Unmarried women dress in kimonos that rival the rainbow.

Religions. Japan's two principal religions, Shinto and Buddhism, have become closely interrelated. Shinto enters into many areas of everyday life; Buddhism dominates the spiritual life. Weddings are generally Shinto ceremonies; burials are Buddhist rites.

You'll find Shinto shrines, dedicated to a great pantheon of gods, everywhere in Japan. A *torii*, or high gate, stands before each Shinto shrine; to walk beneath it is the first step in purification.

Buddhism's ascetic philosophy provides a system of ethics by which the individual seeks to live in harmony with nature and find eventual enlightenment. Like Shintoism, it has no set services, but worshipers constantly visit the temples. Wherever you go, the graceful, curving roof corners of Buddhist temples and pagodas stand out against the Japanese skyline.

Visiting a Japanese family

Foreign visitors can arrange to spend an hour or two at home with a Japanese family in Tokyo, Sapporo, Narita, Yokohama, Nagoya, Kyoto, Osaka, Otsu, Kagoshima, Hiroshima, Kobe, Kanagawa, Okayama, Kurashiki, Fukuoka, Nagasaki, and Miyazaki. To make arrangements for a visit, contact the city's tourist information office.

Visitors should apply at least a day in advance. Your host family will show you the house and garden, converse with you, and perhaps entertain you with music. Most visits are planned for around 7:30 P.M., after the evening meal; small groups—no more than five visitors—are preferred. Visits are free except for the services of an interpreter, when needed.

TRIP PLANNING AIDS

Japan lies about 10,139 km/6,300 miles west of the United States. Nonstop travel time from California to Tokyo is about 10 hours.

Many international airlines—including the country's own Japan Air Lines and All Nippon Airways—serve New Tokyo International Airport (Narita), located 40 miles northeast of the city. Eleven other airports in Japan also handle international flights.

Several steamship lines offer passenger service between the U.S. West Coast and Japan.

Where to stay

Excellent western-style hotels are found in all of Japan's large cities and leading tourist resorts. Amenities at these first-class hotels include Japanese and western-style restaurants, coffee shops, cocktail lounges, nightclubs—not to mention your own yukata (cotton kimono), slippers, and toothbrush. Some of these hotels have a limited number of Japanese-style guest rooms.

Less expensive than first-class hotels are Japan's business hotels. Rooms with baths are small, but comfortable. You'll need to take your own robe and toothbrush. These hotels usually have no restaurants, but they're centrally located in cities.

Traditional inns. *Ryokan* (Japanese-style inns) provide a delightful sample of Japanese life for adventurous travelers (see page 36). Many of these inns qualify as luxury accommodations and are very expensive, but you can also stay at a less expensive, less impressive ryokan.

Another way to get to know the real Japan is to stay in a *minshuku* (family-style guest house). Considerably lower than at a ryokan, the price you'll be charged at a minshuku includes two meals, often eaten communally. During peak tourist seasons, you may have to share your room with others. You should carry a good Japanese/English phrase book because innkeepers generally know little English.

The bath ritual. If your visit to Japan includes a stay at a country resort, a hot springs hotel, ryokan, or minshuku, you'll probably have the opportunity to try one of Japan's famous communal baths. Many hotels and inns provide separate bathing facilities for men and women, but some still offer mixed bathing (usually with separate dressing areas).

The ofuro (bath) in Japan is ritual, intended as a prolonged relaxing and socializing period at the end of the day. In a large communal bath, small groups sit gossiping, laughing, and talking over business matters; others tranquilly soak away the day's tensions.

You must remember one important rule of Japanese-style bathing: no soap is used in the tub. Though some hotels and inns provide hot showers, the usual system is to sit on a small wooden stool on the tiled bathroom floor, soap yourself, and then rinse with warm water you dip from the big tub with a small wooden bucket. As tub water is not changed for each bather, scrubbing yourself clean before soaking is obviously an important courtesy.

When thoroughly rinsed, you climb into the deep tubful of hot water. Step in gingerly, for the Japanese like it very hot indeed.

Helpful guides. The Japan National Tourist Organization (addresses on page 65) issues several helpful accommodation guides including *Reasonable Accommodations*, *Japan Ryokan Guide*, and *Youth Hostels in Japan*. A listing of minshuku is also available.

Make reservations well in advance (up to 6 months ahead) for hotel space during the height of the tourist season—usually April through May and August through October. Choice hotel space is difficult to find during this period, particularly in Tokyo and Kyoto. The best ryokan are generally heavily booked.

Transportation tips

Japan's excellent transportation network connects all areas of the country by air, rail, and road. Cruises on the Inland Sea and smaller bodies of water provide a pleasing change of pace.

Air travel. Airline service is provided to the major cities and islands by Japan Air Lines, All Nippon Airways, and Toa Domestic Airlines.

Riding the rails. Stylish, punctual, and economical, Japan's trains provide the most popular means of public transportation. The Japanese Railways Group, composed of six passenger companies and one freight company, operates a 21,296-km/13,233-mile rail network serving the entire country. Both standard and Green Car (first-class) services are offered.

The *Shinkansen* (bullet train) provides high-speed service between Tokyo and Hakata on Kyushu Island, passing through Nagoya, Kyoto, Osaka, Okayama, and Hiroshima. There's also bullet train service between Tokyo and Niigata and Tokyo and Morioka in northern Honshu.

A Japan Rail Pass good for unlimited travel on the Japanese Railways Group system (including trains, buses, and ferries) is available for visitors. Sold in the U.S. and Canada, the passes are good for 7, 14, or 21 days. You can purchase passes for either ordinary or Green Car class.

The Japan National Tourist Organization publishes a *Condensed Railway Timetable* in English. Baggage on most trains is restricted to two small bags that can be stored on the overhead rack. Three additional suitcases can be shipped through a day ahead. It's advisable to travel light. Trains stop only briefly at each station, and porters are hard to find.

City transportation. Tokyo, Osaka, Nagoya, Yokohama, Kyoto, Fukuoka, and Sapporo all have subways that are a vital part of the urban transport system. Extensive bus systems also help in city commutes. One-day transportation passes good for unlimited travel are available in Tokyo, Kyoto, and Osaka.

Taxi drivers usually don't speak English. Have directions to your destination written in Japanese before you start out; carry the hotel's card or a packet of matches with the address to aid on the return trip.

Bus tours and hired cars. Several companies operate scheduled coach tours escorted by English-speaking guides or driver-guides. These excursions range from half-day sightseeing trips to multi-day tours. Each major city offers local excursions.

For a more individualized tour, you can hire a car with an English-speaking driver-guide. Rental cars are also available, but are not recommended since road signs are in Japanese.

Water travel. Several steamship companies operate cruises on the Inland Sea. Hydrofoil and hovercraft service covers more than 30 short water routes.

Dining opportunities

You can dine on Japanese, Asian, or western cuisine while in Japan. Put Japanese cooking high on your list and relish the fact that the art of food presentation is as important as the art of preparation.

Japanese favorites. Most travelers have heard of *sukiyaki*, probably the best known of Japanese dishes. Thinly sliced beef and various vegetables are first prepared on a tray and then cooked at your table. A soy-flavored sauce adds extra flavor.

Another popular method of Japanese cooking is *tempura*. Prawns or fish and a variety of vegetables are dipped in a batter and deep fried—usually while you sit at a tempura counter and watch. Before you eat a piece of tempura, you dip it into a special soy sauce mixed with grated radish and a touch of grated ginger.

Sushi, a less familiar dish, is a popular Japanese snack. Fish and shellfish—generally served raw—are attractively prepared with rice and vegetables. Raw fish (*sashimi*) cut into dainty slices tops vinegar-flavored rice patties, or is rolled inside a sheet of seaweed along with flavored rice or prepared vegetables. Sashimi, accompanied by a dab of green horseradish and thinly sliced white radish, is also popular as an appetizer.

Among other delicious Japanese dishes are *mizutaki* (chicken or beef and vegetables simmered in broth in a pot at your table, Mongolian barbecue, and *yakitori* (grilled chicken on a skewer). For an inexpensive meal, try a bowl of *soba* (buckwheat noodles) or *udon* (wheat-flour noodles). These are served in a broth with green onions, fried bean curd, slices of fish cake, and bits of meat and vegetables. *Bento,* Japan's version of the box lunch, includes rice, fish, and vegetables.

Meals featuring beef are expensive. In fact, beef is so costly that the Japanese buy it by the gram, not the pound. If you're willing to pay the price, try Japanese beef from either the Kobe or Matsuzaka district. It's excellent, the product of contented cows that are fed special grain, given a ration of beer to drink, and systematically massaged with *sake*.

Warm sake, a slightly sweet rice wine, is served throughout many Japanese meals. You pour it from a narrow-necked pottery flask into tiny cups. A number of Japanese beers and distilled whiskies are also available. Most restaurants serve green tea at no charge.

Where to eat. In major cities you'll find restaurants serving all types of cuisine. In smaller towns, Japanese restaurants predominate.

To eat without straining your budget, you may wish to seek out restaurants catering to local trade. These include department store dining rooms, restaurants in office buildings 'avoid the noon to 1 P.M. rush hour), shopping center eateries (including fast-food establishments), and tiny restaurants on side streets off main thoroughfares. In this category, you'll find tempura, sushi, and yakitori bars, and noodle shops.

Menus may not be in English, but plastic food replicas, usually displayed in a glass case in front of the restaurant, will help you make a choice. Prices are usually in Arabic numerals.

Your choice of entertainment

In Japan's main cities, a colorful world comes to life each evening in theater-restaurants, nightclubs, cabarets, bars, hotel cocktail lounges, teashops, coffee houses, and discos. Activity begins early—around 6:30 or 7 P.M.—peaks early, and is relatively quiet by midnight.

Where to go. The cost of nightclubbing can be a shock, even to western business travelers geared to expense account entertainment. The high prices reflect the extensive expense accounts of Japanese executives. Along with drinks and entertainment, nightclubs and cabarets often feature hostesses who pour drinks and make polite conversation. For food, drinks, and entertainment without the additional expense of hostesses, try a theater-restaurant.

Less expensive drinking establishments favored by locals include beer halls, beer gardens (summertime rooftop establishments), wine pubs, and hotel cocktail lounges. Japan's youth prefer discos for drinks and lively entertainment.

Traditional Japanese theater—kabuki, *noh*, and *bunraku*—is performed in major cities (see page 21). At the other end of the entertainment spectrum are lavish dance revues in Tokyo and at Takarazuka. Colorful and spectacular, these elegant vaudeville shows feature hundreds of beautifully costumed precision dancers, accompanied by sizable orchestras.

The talented geisha. Though fewer young women choose to enter geisha training today than once did, the geisha remains an important part of Japan's entertainment scene. A versatile and respected entertainer, she fills a unique role.

At geisha parties, she acts as hostess, interested listener, witty conversationalist, attentive waitress (who serves the food and keeps the sake cups filled), dancer, musician, and singer. Her music will be on the guitarlike *shamisen* and drum; her dancing will use traditional steps; her costume will be the brilliant kimono and elaborate coiffure of the geisha of three centuries ago.

The two main geisha schools are in Kyoto—the Gion-machi and Pontocho. Near the schools you often see the geisha—especially in the evening—costumed in elaborate kimonos, special hairdos, and elevated wooden clogs.

Tea and flowers. Two Japanese art forms, *ikebana* (flower arranging) and *sado* (tea ceremony) can add flavor to your stay in Japan. Many department stores and some hotels feature demonstrations of both.

Ikebana's guiding principle is simplicity. Flowers are arranged in ways that make them appear to be alive and growing. Students of ikebana learn patience, gracefulness, tranquility, and self-control while refining their arranging skills.

The rigorous training of the tea ceremony leads to mental composure and inner harmony. Because all the aspects of etiquette important to cultured Japanese are employed in the tea ceremony, brides-to-be are encouraged to master it. For more information, see the special feature on page 52.

The shopping scene

Japan offers the traveler marvelous shopping. The country has long been famous for its cultured pearls. Electronic products—cameras, binoculars, transistor radios, stereos, tape recorders, watches, and clocks—are also immensely popular. Japanese arts and crafts and fine art items make yet another good investment. These include silks and brocades, china and pottery, red and black lacquerware, cloisonné, woodblock prints, handpainted fans, damascene, hanging scroll paintings, and traditionally dressed dolls. Other distinctively Japanese products you can buy are kimonos, happicoats, and cotton yukata; lanterns and parasols; noh masks (worn by the actors in noh plays); an infinite variety of toys made of paper, wood, and lacquer; bamboo ware; wooden clogs and straw slippers; and *origami* (folded paper art).

Japan's various regions produce a wealth of native crafts. Visitors to Tokyo can preview regional products in showrooms maintained by various prefectures of Japan. Most of these showrooms are located in or near the Tokyo Central Station (see page 23).

A talent bank. To help preserve Japan's ancient arts and crafts, the country has established a unique talent bank. Officially known as "Holders of Important Intangible Cultural Properties," 70 individuals have been designated as "living national treasures." They continue to follow ancient and time-honored processes in producing some of Japan's finest traditional arts and crafts.

Great craftspersons produce pottery, puppets, hand-dyed fabrics, handwoven textiles, hand-forged swords, lacquerware, metal arts, wood and bamboo crafts, dolls, and handmade paper. Members of the performing arts field—actors, musicians, dancers—preserve the ancient traditions of Japanese music and drama, especially noh, kabuki, and bunraku. The artists and artisans who make up this talent bank possess more than talent and skill. They are guided by a code of ethics that encourages constant striving for perfection.

The superiority of the artists' work has a tangible and lasting effect on much of the handcrafted work produced throughout Japan. The piece of lacquerware you buy, for instance, may be an object created in a small studio by an artisan who has trained under one of the "Holders of Important Intangible Cultural Properties."

Tax-free shopping. Visitors can purchase quality souvenirs free of Japanese taxes in hundreds of stores in Japan's main cities; these stores display an identifying sign in English. For a list of tax-free items, write to the Japan National Tourist Organization (see page 65).

At the time of purchase, you must present your passport. The shop attaches a card, "Record of Purchase of Commodities Tax-Exempt for Export," to your passport. When you leave the country, you must take all these listed purchases with you. Customs officials check them against the card at the time of your departure.

Store hours. Stores are open every day of the week, including Sundays (the busiest shopping day) and holidays. Stores open around 10 A.M. and usually close about 6 P.M., though many shops in downtown arcades stay open until 9. Most department stores close on one day during the week, most often Monday or Thursday. Fixed prices prevail; bargaining is not customary.

What not to buy. The United States restricts the import of products made from animals and plants it has officially listed as endangered or threatened. The fact that these items are sold abroad doesn't mean they'll be allowed into the United States. For more information on restrictions, see page 9.

Solemnity and pageantry combine in traditional Japanese wedding. Heavily embroidered bridal kimonos of brilliantly dyed silk are costly; most brides rent outfit.

Tokyo's National Museum in Ueno Park houses Japan's largest Oriental art collection. Park, popular site for viewing cherry blossoms, contains other important galleries as well.

Recreational pursuits

Baseball heads the list of spectator sports, drawing extremely enthusiastic crowds to every game during its April-to-October season.

Several million Japanese practice *judo*, a system of self-defense in which an opponent's strength is used against him. Other traditional Japanese sports include *karate*, the unique art of combat in which the participant's hands play the role of weapons, and *kendo*, a form of Japanese fencing in which two contestants fight with bamboo swords.

Enthusiastic crowds watch massive *sumo* wrestlers perform in vast arenas. Japan's ancient wrestling combines colorful pageantry and ritual with plenty of action. Often weighing more than 300 pounds, sumo wrestlers dress in belted loincloths and wear their hair in medieval topknots.

Another national pastime. *Pachinko* is a Japanese game of chance that has become something of a national pastime. Despite its exotic name, pachinko is merely a Japanese version of pinball. The main difference between pachinko and its American counterpart is a cosmetic one. In Japan, the playing machines are designed to fit against a wall vertically rather than horizontally.

To play pachinko the player first buys 25 steel balls for about ¥100. At each pull of a spring-loaded lever, one ball after another is shot onto the pachinko board. When a ball drops into one of the holes on the board, the player wins a certain number of steel balls. When finished, he takes all the steel balls (both those bought and those won) to the payoff counter. If he's been lucky, he redeems them for prizes—food, cigarettes, and candies. (Gambling that involves direct payoffs in money is prohibited in Japan, except in horse and bicycle racing.)

Other sports. On the less traditional side, you'll find Japan offers opportunities for skiing (from late November through March), bicycling (on a network of well-kept cycle paths), fishing, and golf. Most of Japan's golf courses are private, very costly, and crowded. Visitors who wish to golf should play at their hotel golf course. The country also has some 3,000 golf driving ranges, many of them tiered so that several players can practice their drives at the same time.

TOKYO, HUB OF JAPAN

Sprawling along the shore of glittering Tokyo Bay at the mouth of the Sumida River, 20th century Tokyo is an intriguing composite of East and West.

Modern towers of steel and glass now jut above its relatively low skyline (restricted in height until recent years because of the area's susceptibility to earthquakes). Sleek expressways slice the city's irregular web of narrow streets.

Younger than the classic cities of Nara and Kyoto, Tokyo—originally called Edo—dates from 1457, when a feudal lord built a castle on the present site of the Imperial Palace. In 1590 the Tokugawa shoguns made it their headquarters. When imperial rule was restored in 1868, Emperor Meiji moved the imperial capital from Kyoto to Edo, which he renamed Tokyo (meaning "eastern capital").

One of the largest cities in the world, metropolitan Tokyo now boasts a population exceeding 11½ million crowded into an area of about 2,486 square km/960 square miles.

Bringing Tokyo into focus

Like other large cities, Tokyo is composed of many districts, each with a character of its own. Because Tokyo is such a sprawling city, it's best to explore it district by district.

The Imperial Palace and its carefully landscaped grounds mark the tranquil heart of the city. To the east lie the bustling business, shopping, and entertainment districts of Hibiya, Marunouchi, Yurakucho, Nihombashi, Ginza, and Shimbashi. South of the palace is Kasumigaseki, the political center; industrial districts stretch along the waterfront.

Northern districts include Kanda, the site of several universities; the Asakusa amusement area; Ueno Park and its many attractions; the Korakuen sports center; and several outstanding gardens.

The lively subcity of Shinjuku dominates western Tokyo. Other attractions include the Meiji Shrine and gardens; Shibuya and Harajuku, fashionable districts; Roppongi, with restaurants featuring international cuisine; and Akasaka, a hilly district of sophisticated entertainment and intriguing lanes, where you can still discover the old Japan in modern Tokyo.

For bird's-eye views of the city, visit the observation platforms of 333-meter/1,093-foot Tokyo Tower. The tower also houses Japan's largest aquarium and a wax museum.

Searching out a particular address is not as easy as it might seem. People generally locate particular destinations by the district name and major cross streets. In an address, *ku* indicates the district where a building is located, *cho* means the precinct, and *chome* the block.

Imperial Palace, a tranquil spot

As you walk through the landscaped grounds toward the Imperial Palace, you are instantly aware of the paradoxical location of this peaceful 101-hectare/250-acre retreat in the heart of one of the world's largest cities. Noisy traffic swirls around the perimeter of the palace grounds. But swans glide silently across the still waters of the moat, and gnarled pine boughs frame your view of the palace.

The palace itself—residence of Japan's emperor

TRY TRADITIONAL JAPANESE THEATER

To add a new dimension to your trip, plan to attend a performance of traditional Japanese theater: *kabuki, noh,* or *bunraku.*

Kabuki. Kabuki, the Japanese theatrical form most familiar to westerners, combines intricate plots, lavish costumes, bizarre make-up, and plenty of action. Men perform all the parts.

A kabuki program generally comprises three or four plays, and a theater usually offers two programs daily. Though the performances often last for hours, you needn't stay for the entire program—people come and go throughout the performance. You can see kabuki performances in Tokyo, Kyoto, and Osaka.

Noh plays. The classical drama of the early aristocrats, noh dates back to the 12th century. Stylized and highly symbolic, it is especially interesting to students of serious drama. The slow-paced drama with musical background is performed on a bare stage; a huge pine tree is painted on the backdrop. The main performers wear masks depicting the characters they portray, and they speak in strangely raucous, falsetto voices.

Performances last from 3 to 6 hours, depending on the number of plays presented. There are noh stages in Tokyo, Kyoto, and Osaka.

Bunraku. Japan's puppet plays, known as bunraku, may not sound exciting, but they're considered one of the country's finest theatrical arts. The plays are really kabuki in miniature, specializing in heroic tales of *samurai,* the fierce warriors who fought under various warlords.

The puppets—nearly life-size, wonderfully mobile

creatures that even change their facial expressions— are manipulated by dexterous puppeteers garbed in dark kimonos. Three operators sometimes manage one puppet.

Like kabuki and noh, bunraku is performed in Tokyo, Kyoto, and Osaka.

and his household—is surrounded by a broad moat, high stone walls, ancient pine trees, and gardens. It occupies the site of Edo Castle, built more than 500 years ago, and for 265 years the residence of the Tokugawa shoguns. It became the royal residence when Emperor Meiji moved the capital from Kyoto to Tokyo in 1868. The old palace was heavily damaged in an air raid in 1945; the new palace buildings were completed in 1968.

You can stroll across the plaza at the southeast end of the palace to the double-arched bridge—the Nijubashi—and gaze through the feudal gates. From the bridge, you look up at the tile-roofed palace. The general public is allowed to visit the palace grounds only twice a year—on the emperor's birthday and January 2 during the new year celebrations. But you can visit the Imperial Palace East Garden daily (except Mondays and Fridays) from 9:30 A.M. to 3 P.M. Designed over 300 years ago, this garden includes varieties of trees representing each of Japan's prefectures (states).

Kasumigaseki, the political center

South and west of the Imperial Palace is the Kasumigaseki district, Japan's political center, where the National Diet Building dominates a complex of white modern government buildings.

Joyful woman *flings food in bird-choked courtyard at Asakusa Kannon Temple. Appropriately, this place of worship is dedicated to goddess of mercy.*

Fans' rainbow array *brightens store windows in Tokyo's Asakusa District, crowded shopping area of crosshatched alleyways and covered passages.*

National Diet Building. Completed in 1936, the National Diet Building is constructed of native materials and took nearly 17 years to build. It houses the House of Councillors and the House of Representatives. When the Diet is in session, visitors may watch the proceedings from the gallery; you simply sign your name at the information office near the entrance.

National Theater. To the north is the National Theater, its two halls used for kabuki, *gagaku* (court music), Japanese music and dance performances, bunraku (puppet drama), *kyogen* (farce), and noh. Check for current performances.

The fabled Ginza

The pulse of Tokyo beats strongly in the Ginza, the capital's foremost shopping district. The word *ginza* means "silver mint"; the district acquired its name when the Tokugawa shoguns minted coins in the area. Major stores and specialty shops line an 8-block section of the Ginza's Chuo-dori Avenue. Side streets and narrow alleys invite further exploration. You'll find restaurants here, too.

Strolling the Ginza. The color, activity, bright neon lights, and stimulating atmosphere of one of Japan's most cosmopolitan communities act as a magnet, drawing both Japanese and foreign visitors. Innovative stores, restaurants, nightclubs, boutiques, art galleries, bars, coffee houses—you'll find them all here. Willow trees add a graceful note to the district's surroundings.

On Saturdays, Sundays, and holidays the Ginza becomes a pedestrian's paradise: the wide main street is closed to motor traffic. Shop owners put out sidewalk displays and provide stools for weary walkers, restaurateurs set up stalls in the middle of the street, and vendors sell snacks and beverages from decorated carts.

Shimbashi on its way up. Activity spills southward into the Shimbashi district, once a rowdy, workingmen's area, now a mosaic of restaurants, sake bars, and small cabarets. It's liveliest here between 8 and 11 P.M. The little sake bars are usually in basements.

Businesslike Marunouchi

North of the Ginza and just east of the Imperial Palace is the Marunouchi district, a glass-and-steel forest of elegant office buildings. This is the heart of Tokyo—a district of finance, business, airline offices, restaurants, shopping arcades, and the central post office.

Tokyo Central Station. One million passengers pass through this Marunouchi landmark daily. The giant station also provides access to the world's largest underground town—five levels, several blocks of shopping malls, restaurants, coffee shops, and the huge Daimaru department store.

Hibiya Park. Located south of Marunouchi across the moat from the palace plaza, this 16-hectare/40-acre park is a green oasis for office workers during the summer. You can enjoy summer pops concerts in its outdoor theater on weekend afternoons and Tuesday evenings. The park has more than 200 species of trees. In November some of the city's finest displays of chrysanthemums flourish here.

Nearby Nihombashi. East of Marunouchi, the neighboring Nihombashi district is less crowded and touristy than Ginza. An older district, it is recommended by local residents for its quality stores and fine restaurants.

Two fine museums in the Nihombashi area are the Yamatane Museum of Art in the Yamatane Building, featuring a collection of contemporary Japanese paintings; and the Bridgestone Museum of Art at 1 Kyobashi, housing paintings and sculpture by Japanese and western artists of the 18th and 19th centuries.

Kanda, an education center

North of Marunouchi and Nihombashi is Kanda, home of several universities (Chuo, Hosei, Meiji, and Nihon are the best known) and numerous bookstores. The district's main thoroughfare is Yasukuni-dori.

Publishing center. Kanda contains dozens of small publishing houses and printing establishments; its streets are lined with small shops where new books, old books, foreign books, translations, rare editions, and old prints may be purchased at reasonable prices. One of the best stocks of foreign books will be found at Katazawa.

Shrines. Area shrines include Kanda Myojin Shrine, just north of the Kanda district, and Yasukuni Shrine in western Kanda across from Kitanomaru Park. The Kanda Myojin Shinto Shrine dates from the middle of the 8th century. Its imposing vermilion main building provides the background for Kanda Matsuri, a popular festival held in mid-May during odd-numbered years.

Yasukuni Shrine has one of Tokyo's largest torii gates—nearly 22 meters/72 feet high. Surrounding gardens are noted for their cherry blossoms and chrysanthemums. Festivals are held here on April 22 and October 18.

Kitanomaru Park. Located in western Kanda in the northern part of the Imperial Palace complex, the park contains Tokyo's largest indoor auditorium, Nippon Budokan Hall, built for the 1964 Olympic Games and seating 15,000 spectators.

The National Museum of Modern Art occupies a handsome three-story structure, open in design. Frequent exhibits feature the work of a specific school or period in Japanese art. In the museum collection are more than a thousand paintings, sculptures, woodblocks, copper-plate prints, and lithographs.

Ueno Park for culture

North of Kanda is Ueno Park, at 85 hectares/210 acres, Tokyo's largest. Originally the garden of the Kaneiji Temple, today the park is Tokyo's cultural center, where you'll find many of the city's outstanding museums. Other park attractions include a zoo and a shrine. Musical events take place in the Tokyo Metropolitan Festival Hall.

Museums. Ueno Park's superb museums house many of the country's national treasures. The National Museum, largest in the country, holds some 36,000 items representing the history and fine arts of Japan and the Orient.

Next door is the National Science Museum (in two buildings), and nearby is the National Museum of Western Art. Opened in 1959, the latter museum contains the Kojiro Matsukata collection of 19th and 20th century French paintings and sculpture.

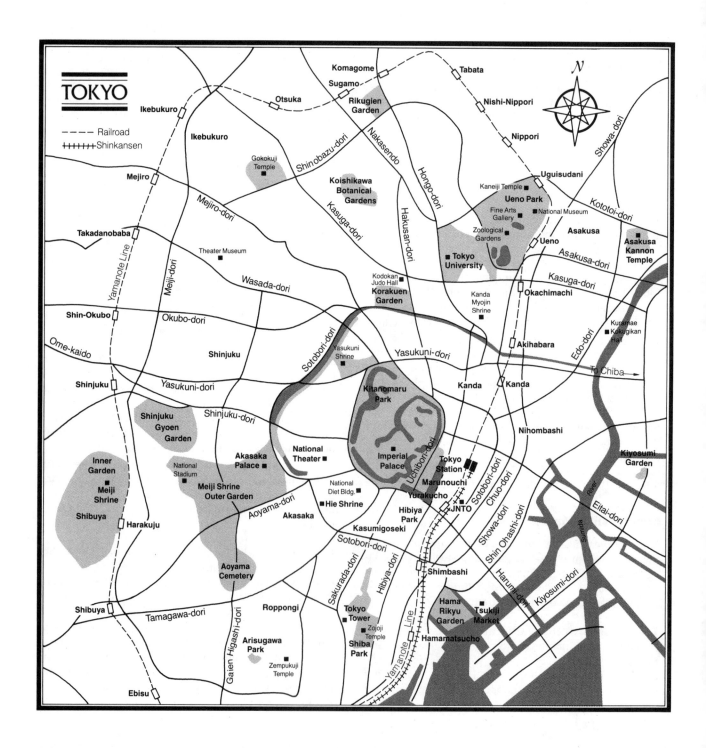

Travelers can easily have a comfortable—or even luxurious—stay in Tokyo, Japan's capital city.

Getting there

Tokyo is served by air, rail, and bus.

Air. International service to and from Tokyo is by Japan Air Lines (JAL), All Nippon Airways (ANA), and foreign flag carriers. Domestic flights on JAL, ANA, and Toa Domestic Airlines link Tokyo with other major Japanese destinations.

New Tokyo International Airport (Narita), located 64 km/40 miles northeast of the city, is Tokyo's major international airport. Haneda International Airport, 16 km/10 miles from town, handles domestic flights and some international flights. Buses and taxis transport travelers from New Tokyo International Airport to downtown Tokyo. The monorail runs between Haneda Airport and downtown Tokyo's Hamamatsucho Station; there's also bus service.

Rail and bus. Trains and express buses link Tokyo with Japan's other major cities.

Accommodations

Tokyo's numerous international-standard hotels provide cosmopolitan comforts for visitors.

Hotels in the heart of the city near the Imperial Palace and the Ginza include the Imperial, Shimbashi Dai-ichi, Ginza Dai-ichi, Ginza Nikko, Ginza Tobu, Ginza Tokyu, Hotel Seiyo, Tokyo Station Hotel, Kokusai Kanko, Marunouchi, Grand Palace, and Palace. In the Akasaka district, you'll find the Akasaka Prince, Akasaka Tokyu, ANA Hotel Tokyo, New Otani, Capitol Tokyu, and Hotel Okura.

In Shinjuku, one of Tokyo's eastern districts, major hotels include the Hotel Sunroute Tokyo, Keio Plaza, Tokyo Hilton, and Century Hyatt Tokyo. The Shiba Park and Tokyo Prince, overlooking Shiba Park, are in the southern part of the city. Among Shinagawa district hotels are the Miyako Hotel Tokyo, New Otani Inn, Takanawa, Takanawa Prince, Takanawa Tobu, Shinagawa Prince, and Pacific.

Hotels near Narita Airport include the Narita View, Nikko Narita, and Narita Holiday Inn. The Haneda Tokyu Hotel is near Haneda Airport.

Tokyo Disneyland area hotels include the Sheraton Grande Tokyo Bay, Hotel Castle, Tokyo Bay Hilton International, and Regent Park on Tokyo Bay.

Some of the western-style hotels listed above have a few Japanese-style rooms available; there are also Japanese inns *(ryokan)* within Tokyo city limits.

Getting around

Taxis, trains, and subways are all good forms of transportation in Tokyo. The city also has plenty of cruising taxis or you can find a row of waiting taxis at major hotels. Before venturing forth, ask your hotel desk clerk to write the name and address of your destination in Japanese. Carry the hotel's card or matchbox to simplify your return trip. Pay the driver the amount on the meter; no tipping is necessary.

An easy way to get from one district of Tokyo to another is by subway or electric train. Plan your excursion to avoid the crunch of commuter rush hour. Your hotel desk clerk can direct you to the nearest station and tell you which stop is closest to your destination. Station signs in English are posted at each stop.

Color-coded English maps are available at subway ticket windows; an outstretched hand and the word *chizu* (meaning "map") will convey your request. A special one-day subway pass, sold at major subway stations, is valid for unlimited rides on seven of Tokyo's ten subway lines including those serving Tokyo's major sights.

Tours

Half- and full-day tours take in city sights, Kamakura (page 31), Hakone (32), Mount Fuji (32), Nikko (34), and Mashiko (34).

Dining out

Tokyo's restaurants, some 95,000 of them, are renowned both for international cuisine and for Japanese specialties. You can dine on delicious dishes from China, Indonesia, India, France, Italy, Germany, and many other countries, as well as on Japanese fare (see page 17).

Entertainment

The city boasts a staggering variety of after-dark entertainment: ballet, symphony, opera, legitimate theater, motion pictures, bowling, hotel dancing, elegant or intimate restaurants for dining. Nightclubs, cabarets, and small bars abound.

English-language newspapers—the *Asahi Evening News*, the *Mainichi*, the *Japan Times*, and the *Yomiuri*—list current attractions. *Tour Companion*, available in your hotel, includes a listing of night life activities.

More information

Tokyo's Tourist Information Centers are located at the New Tokyo International Airport (Narita) in the central passenger terminal building, and on the 1st floor, Kotani Bldg., 6-6 Yuraku-cho, 1-chome, Chiyoda-ku.

The Metropolitan Fine Arts Gallery, part of the Tokyo University of Arts, features changing exhibits, the most distinguished of which are displayed in the autumn. Toyokan Museum, a later addition to Ueno Park, houses an outstanding collection of Oriental art and antiquities from the countries of Asia and the Middle East.

The Shitamachi Museum, on the banks of Ueno Park's Shinobazu Pond, houses a re-creation of an Edo-Period street, complete with wooden houses and shops.

Zoological Gardens. In the park's large zoo—a primary attraction—animals are kept in enclosures resembling their natural habitats.

Toshogu Shrine. Dedicated to Ieyasu, the 17th century founder of the Tokugawa Shogunate, this 300-year-old shrine is noted for its many stone and bronze lanterns, gifts of feudal lords.

A neighboring university. Tokyo University, Japan's most prestigious college, lies west of Ueno Park, its campus occupying the site of a former feudal mansion.

Asakusa, lively amusement center

Stretching east of Ueno Park along the Sumida River is Asakusa, with Asakusa Kannon Temple (Sensoji Temple) as its focal point. Surrounding the temple is one of Tokyo's largest downtown amusement areas featuring a melange of movie theaters, bars, restaurants, tea houses, and souvenir shops. Nearby stands Kuramae Kokugikan Hall, headquarters for Japanese sumo.

The main hall of impressive Asakusa Kannon Temple enshrines a tiny image of the goddess of mercy; a festival honors the goddess in May. Souvenir shops and colorful stalls line Nakamise, the long approach to the temple. Items for sale include Japanese toys, sweets, ceramics, and clothing.

Inviting Shinjuku

Shinjuku—the Greenwich Village of Tokyo—attracts the young with its relaxed atmosphere and lively night life. Less tourist-oriented and less expensive than the Ginza, it has all the city atmosphere of ultramodern skyscrapers, large department stores, fashionable specialty shops, restaurants, movie houses, bars, discos, and coffee shops.

The activity centers around busy Shinjuku Station, encircled by a huge complex of shops and restaurants. A fascinating maze of narrow, lantern-lined streets and alleys leads off Shinjuku-dori, the district's main street. The smell of cooking and charcoal smoke is everywhere. Many tiny restaurants and food stands sell tempura or morsels of charcoal-grilled chicken or cuttlefish. Interspersed are tiny stores, kimono shops, and pachinko parlors.

Every Sunday Shinjuku-dori becomes a pedestrian mall where the district's young people promenade.

Shinjuku Gyoen Garden. Within walking distance of the station is one of Tokyo's loveliest gardens. The cherry blossoms of Shinjuku Gyoen (National) Garden are so famous that the Prime Minister gives a cherry-viewing party there each spring. In autumn, crowds flock to see the chrysanthemums.

Neighboring entertainment center. North of Shinjuku is another growing Tokyo subcenter, Ikebukuro, with numerous shops, restaurants, and bars.

Korakuen—botany and baseball

The Korakuen district, southwest of Ueno Park, is named for little 17th century Korakuen Garden, one of the most celebrated landscape gardens in Tokyo. Winding paths encircle a small lake, and "half-moon" bridges arch above the water. Irises provide a big May display.

Adjoining the garden is a sports and amusement center, including the Korakuen Baseball Stadium (home of organized baseball), an ice palace, a bowling center, a cycle track, and a gymnasium. Nearby is Kodokan Judo Hall, where you can watch judo each afternoon.

North of the Korakuen district, another outstanding garden—Koishikawa Botanical Gardens—covers about 16 hectares/39 acres and contains more than 6,000 species of plants, including some fine old trees dating from the end of the 17th century. It is part of Tokyo University.

Gokokuji Temple, one of the city's largest Buddhist temples, lies just northwest of the botanical gardens. The 17th century temple's chief image, carved from amber, represents Kannon, goddess of mercy. The hillside cemetery behind the temple has, for the past century, served as a burial ground for the Imperial Family.

Harajuku—shrines and sports

The airy, attractive district of Harajuku lies south of Shinjuku. It encompasses both the Meiji Shrine and its Inner Garden and—across several boulevards—Meiji Shrine Outer Garden.

The Meiji Shrine, near Harajuku Station, is probably Tokyo's biggest tourist attraction. It's the site of many festive events. Within its Inner Garden are more than 200,000 trees, gifts of the people of Japan in 1920 when the shrine was constructed. The buildings of the main shrine express the classic beauty visitors associate with Japan. Paths, well-marked in English, meander through the heavily wooded 72-hectare/175-acre Inner Garden. An iris bed, containing more than a hundred varieties, draws flower lovers in May and June. In the south pond, water lilies bloom in late June or early July.

In Meiji Park (the Outer Garden) are the city's big sports arenas, dominated by the huge 85,000-seat National Athletic Stadium, designed by Architect Kenzo Tange for the 1964 Olympic Games. Other sports facilities include the Chichibu Rugby Ground, a 66,000-seat baseball stadium, and an Olympic-size pool.

Despite exposure to elements, *Kamakura's massive* Daibutsu *(Great Buddha) image presides serenely over countryside. Shelter was swept away by tidal wave in 1495.*

Adorned with scarlet capes *and hats, small stone statues (*jizos*) represent local gods.*

Shibuya and Aoyama

To the south of Meiji are Shibuya and Aoyama, the former a more compact and restrained version of youth-oriented Shinjuku. If you walk in the vicinity of the station, you'll find many small shops and medium-size stores. The area's two most famous shopping streets are Dogensaka-dori and Koen-dori.

Aoyama, a fashionable residential area, lies east of Shibuya. It's noted for sophisticated couturier shops and boutiques and the 100-year-old Aoyama Cemetery, where many leaders of the Meiji Restoration are buried.

The Nezu Art Museum, just south of the cemetery, holds an outstanding collection of ancient fine arts and handicrafts from Japan, Korea, and China. The Japan Traditional Craft Center at 3-1-1, Minami, Aoyama, displays and sells a variety of Japanese craft items.

Akasaka's varied attractions

Home of many of Tokyo's major hotels, this sophisticated district of gentle hills lies southwest of the Imperial Palace; its many side streets invite exploration. Area sightseeing attractions include the Akasaka Palace and the Hie Shrine.

The district's nightlife reputation is based on its plush and expensive nightclubs and restaurants. Here, too, are many small and lively cabarets, bars, and all-night coffee houses.

Akasaka Palace. This Versailles-style palace looks more European than Japanese. Built in 1909 for the Crown Prince, it has since been used intermittently as a provisional imperial chamber and to house a few government agencies; recently, though, it has been renovated and converted to accommodate important guests of the state. The walls of its luxurious rooms display paintings by French and Japanese artists.

Hie Shrine. Near the Capitol Tokyu Hotel sits Hie Shrine (also called Sanno-sama), the most popular shrine in the area during the Edo Period. Its June 1 festival is one of Tokyo's great events.

Roppongi and Azabu

Merging into the Aoyama and Akasaka districts is Roppongi, another pleasure center for young fashionables. Among its more than 600 restaurants are some of Tokyo's finest. Its nightclubs are usually going strong long after those in the Ginza and other areas close.

The greenest part of Tokyo is Azabu district, south of Aoyama. Foreign embassies line the streets, along with private mansions owned by important Japanese. High-rise apartments house members of the foreign community.

Near the little Arisugawa Park (nice for strolling) is Zempukuji Temple, with gardens laid out in the 18th century by Kobo Daishi.

Shiba's tower and temple

Focal point of the Shiba district, southeast of Roppongi is Shiba Park, dominated by Tokyo Tower. For an exciting view of the city and harbor, take the elevator to the upper observation platform 250 meters/820 feet above Tokyo's streets. Plan your visit for a weekday morning—it's crowded on weekends. Six of Japan's broadcasting stations transmit from the tower.

Shiba Park is a 26-hectare/50-acre wooded oasis surrounding Zojoji Temple, built in 1393 as the family temple for the Tokugawa shoguns. The massive temple gates are similar to those at Yomeimon in Nikko.

Along the bay

Along the bay east of Shiba Park are the less familiar areas of Tsukiji and Harumi. Here, the emphasis is on industry.

Tsukiji Fish Market. One of Tokyo's most unusual sights is its huge fish market, located on the Sumida River near Tokyo Bay. Action begins about dawn when large fish—tuna, swordfish, and sometimes sharks—are laid out in rows. Before the bidding begins, brokers scan the rows, chipping off tiny pieces of flesh to judge quality.

You'll also see a bewildering array of other seafood, including octopus, mackerel, cod, and shellfish of various kinds. Fish porters transport the large fish on iron hooks, pausing occasionally to warm their chilled hands over fires.

Hama Detached Palace Garden. A short distance south of the fish market is an uncrowded garden, noted for its lovely tidal lagoon spanned by three graceful bridges. Cherry trees bloom here in spring. River sightseeing boats depart nearby.

Discoveries for shoppers

Shopping is an adventure in Tokyo, with each alleyway and street promising new discoveries. Giant department stores offer an incredible variety of goods, from sushi to silks. Shopping arcades are everywhere. Downtown shopping areas include the Ginza, Nihombashi, Shinjuku, Shibuya, and Ikebukuro.

Department store shopping. Japanese department stores are a sightseeing attraction in themselves. You can spend hours inside, working your way down from the rooftop to the basement food market. There's usually at least one floor devoted to restaurants and at least one featuring special art displays. At many stores, you can pick up a printed store guide in English at the first-floor information desk. The Japan National Tourist Organization's Tokyo city map pinpoints the locations of the city's major department stores.

Main Ginza department stores include Matsuya,

Matsuzakaya, and Mitsukoshi. Nihombashi's two big stores are Takashimaya and Mitsukoshi. Hankyu and Seibu department stores are across from Yurakucho Station.

Busy Shinjuku (also known for discount camera stores) has several large department stores: Odakyu and Keio, both in the station building, and nearby Isetan. Shibuya shoppers head for the Tokyu and Seibu stores, and Ikebukuro has Seibu's large main store.

Shopping arcades. You'll find shopping arcades at all major hotels. Other arcades worth exploring include the Sukiyabashi Shopping Center and the International Arcade, both just a short walk east from the Imperial Hotel, and Nikkatsu Arcade, in the Hibiya Park Building on Harumi-dori Avenue.

Sporting events

Sumo wrestling, judo, baseball, and golf are all integral parts of the Tokyo sporting scene.

Thousands of people flock to Tokyo's three annual 15-day sumo tournaments, held in mid-January, mid-May, and mid-September at the Kuramae Kokugikan Hall near the Sumida River in the Asakusa district. These events sell out early. The sumo museum, adjacent to the hall, features exhibits relating to the history of Japanese sumo wrestling. (For more about sumo wrestling, see page 20.)

Judo students and experts work out every day at the Kodokan Judo Hall in Korakuen district. A stop at the big gymnasium—the world center of this defensive art—is a feature of many sightseeing bus tours.

JAPAN'S MIGHTY FORTRESSES

In days of old, when strong samurai warriors performed brave deeds and feudal lords ruled Japan, mighty castles—at one time, more than 150 of them—dominated the country's mountaintops, grassy knolls, and rolling plains. Today only a few remain: most of them, originally built of wood and plaster, were destroyed by military assault, earthquake, and fire. A few, however, have been rebuilt with sturdier materials and restored to their former splendor. Their highly ornamented donjons (watchtowers), with multitiered gables and curved roofs, will delight photographers.

Castle building reached its peak during the late 16th and early 17th centuries. Castles served not only as fortresses, but also as symbols of the ruling feudal lord's power. Because the buildings could easily be burned, a series of concentric moats and a number of stone walls were built to keep would-be invaders at a safe distance. And even if enemies advanced past the first moat and heavy iron-studded gate, it was hard to go farther: the second gate could be reached only by following a tortuous maze.

The inner castle stood at the heart of all these walls and moats; multistoried donjons dominated the area. Also within the inner circle were guardhouses, barracks for samurai on garrison duty, and courtyards edged with mansions for the lord.

Of the castles that remain today, perhaps the most impressive as well as best preserved is Himeji Castle (see page 55). Here you'll see an impressive five-story donjon (no trace of the residential quarters remains). At Nijo Castle in Kyoto, the donjon is gone, but a

beautifully preserved residential mansion remains (see page 47). Nijo, an excellent example of a flatland castle, is surrounded today by a modern metropolis.

Other castles worth a visit include Osaka Castle (see page 50), Nagoya Castle (see page 39), Hiroshima Castle (see page 55), and Kumamoto Castle (see page 58).

Fabled Mount Fuji's *snow-capped grandeur looms above Lake Ashi's blue waters.*

During baseball season (about the same months as in the U.S.), you can watch Japanese teams play at Korakuen Baseball Stadium. Sellout crowds of 50,000 are common.

If you want to play golf in the Tokyo area, inquire at the Japan National Tourist Organization's Tourist Information Center (see page 65). Courses are crowded and fees high. Most of the golf courses are private clubs, but often visitors may play them on weekdays if accompanied by a club member.

NEARBY EXCURSIONS

When you reach the point where you'd welcome a break from city sightseeing, plan to take day trips to a few of these neighboring attractions. All are easily reached by train from Tokyo, and as a bonus you'll see the Japanese countryside.

On Tokyo's outskirts

Not far from downtown Tokyo lie several attractions that point up the contrasts of Japan.

Tokyo Disneyland. This theme park, Disney's first outside the U.S., is located in Chiba Prefecture, 10 km/6 miles southeast of Tokyo. Take the Tozai subway line to Urayasu Station, then the Tokyo Disneyland shuttle bus to the park. Like its California counterpart, the park has five theme areas with entertainment, rides, shops, and restaurants.

Minka-en. One of the loveliest and least crowded places you can visit on Tokyo's fringes is Minka-en, an open-air folk museum in Kanagawa Prefecture, 18 km/11 miles south of the city. To get there, take the Odakyu electric train from Shinjuku Station to Mukogaoka-Yuenchi. Strolling the museum's paths, you'll return to a rural Japan of several centuries ago. Dotting the park are historic thatch-and-wood farmhouses from all parts of Japan. Reconstructed on the site, some of these buildings date back 200 to 300 years.

Takao Mountain. Another destination outside the city is Takao Mountain, just a 45-minute train ride west from Shinjuku Station. Take any *kyuko* (express) train on the Keio Line and ride to the end. After a 3-minute walk from the station, you choose your mode of transportation—cable car or open chair lift—up the mountain.

Mingei-kan. A small folkcraft museum called Mingei-kan is just a 5-minute walk from the Komaba Todai-mae Station stop on the Inokashira train line, which travels west from Shibuya Station. This museum attempts to preserve and chronicle Japan's folk arts through exhibits of pottery, furniture, cloth, and other artifacts.

Narita, a temple town

Just beyond the hectic scene at New Tokyo International Airport lies the tranquil 10th century town of Narita, site of famous Shinshoji Temple. Dedicated to Fudo, the god of fire, the temple was constructed in A.D. 940. Early worshippers made frequent pilgrimages to the temple. Soon a town was born. Today, Narita is still considered an important pilgrimage center, and each January Japanese flock to the area to pay their respects.

Behind the temple is a park of ponds, waterfalls, fountains, azaleas, and trees—maple, apricot, and cherry. Within the park is the Naritasan Historical Museum containing early treasures from the temple and surrounding area.

Yokohama, Japan's ocean gateway

Ocean liners from all parts of the world dock at Yokohama, an industrial city about 32 km/20 miles southwest of Tokyo.

Few travelers visit the port city unless they arrive by ship or have business. The country's second largest city, Yokohama is a trading center of some $2^3/_4$ million people.

Yokohama points of interest include Nogeyama Park, commanding a view of the city; Sankei-en Garden, with its 500-year-old pagoda; Birdpia, featuring tropical birds; and Chinatown. Main shopping areas are Isezakicho and Motomachi.

Kamakura, ancient feudal capital

The historic old city of Kamakura, 55 minutes southwest of Tokyo by train, has become one of the country's most popular beach resorts. Situated in an attractive valley bordered on three sides by hills, Kamakura was the feudal capital of Japan from 1192 to 1333. The city still has an impressive number of ancient shrines, temples; and artistic relics dating from the Kamakura Period, when it was the seat of shogunate government.

Finding your way around this city of about 160,000 is easy; from the train station in the center of town, a walk in any direction will lead to interesting sights.

The Great Buddha. The city is noted for its 700-year-old *Daibutsu* (Great Buddha), second in size (about 9 meters/30 feet high) to Japan's largest, the Buddha in Nara. But the Kamakura Buddha surpasses the other in artistic merit. Look for the sitting Buddha on the grounds of Kotokuin Temple, a few minutes by bus southwest of the train station.

Other ancient temples and shrines. Dozens of Buddhist temples and Shinto shrines are to be seen in the Kamakura area.

Dominating the city is Tsurugaoka Hachimangu Shrine, reached by a long stairway. Cherry trees shade the avenue approaching the temple; look for the enormous ginkgo tree to the left of the stone steps leading to the temple doors. Archery by costumed horsemen is featured during the shrine's annual festival on September 15 and 16.

Outstanding among the Five Great Zen Temples of Kamakura are Kenchoji and Engakuji temples, both located north of Kamakura. Kenchoji's lovely group of buildings (some dating from the 15th century) is surrounded by quiet gardens, shaded by a forest of tall cedars. Engakuji, near the Kita-Kamakura train station, was founded in 1282 and is a center for Zen meditation.

Shopping. On Kamakura's side streets you'll find numerous small antique and handicraft shops with excellent selections. Prices here are lower than in Tokyo or Kyoto. The local handicraft is *Kamakura-bori:* intricate carvings—flowers, mirror and picture frames, trays, and other objects—chiseled from hardwood, then heavily lacquered in black and vermilion.

A mountain playground

For high-country recreation, many Tokyo and Yokohama residents head for the mountains of Joshinetsu Kogen Highland National Park, about 4 hours northwest of the capital. From late spring to autumn, its varied terrain—wooded mountains, lakes and brooks, active volcanoes, and hot springs—attracts hikers and picnickers.

In early December, skiers take over. Activity centers on Shiga Heights, an alpine retreat on the slopes of 1,920-meter/6,300-foot Mount Shiga. From Maruike, the heart of the ski fields, cableways transport skiers to the high slopes; lifts interlink the area. Some ski schools have bilingual instructors.

FUJI–HAKONE–IZU NATIONAL PARK

Japan's most popular outdoor recreation area is Fuji–Hakone–Izu National Park, an all-season wonderland of verdant forests, deep blue lakes, tumbling waterfalls, steaming hot springs, and rushing rivers. Easily accessible by road or rail from Tokyo, this scenic region lures city dwellers to unwind and enjoy nature. Within the park they can camp, swim, water ski, boat, fish, hike, hunt and—during the winter months—ski and ice skate. Hot springs soothe overexerted muscles.

Dominating this varied region is the symmetrical cone of Mount Fuji, rising majestically over a handful of mountain lakes at its base. To the southeast lies the Hakone district, characterized by its hot springs and beautiful alpine scenery. The coastal villages and hot springs of the Izu Peninsula lie just beyond.

Tokyo-based tours take the Fuji–Hakone–Izu National Park area, as do trains and buses from Tokyo. For information on area accommodations, see page 41.

Legendary Mount Fuji

Magnificent *Fuji-san* occupies a special place in the hearts of the Japanese people not only for its supreme beauty but also for its spiritual significance. Snow-capped for much of the year, the country's highest peak rises 3,776 meters/12,388 feet above sea level to form one of the world's most perfect volcanic cones.

For thousands of years, Fuji has challenged the creative genius of Japan's poets and artists to depict its beauty and charm in literature, art, and song. Each year tens of thousands of pilgrims and nature lovers climb the dormant volcano.

Five beautiful lakes

At the forested northern base of Mount Fuji lie five mountain lakes—Yamanaka, Kawaguchi, Saiko, Shoji, and Motosu. Set in alpine splendor, they form the heart of a year-round vacation playground.

Seasonal splendors. In spring, when cherry trees and azaleas bloom, the area attracts hosts of nature enthusiasts. Summer brings vacationers to camp, hike, swim, boat, fish, and play tennis and golf. In autumn, visitors come to enjoy beautiful fall foliage. Hardy winter parkgoers ski or ice skate, or go duck hunting or ice fishing.

The Fuji Five Lakes area is considered the best area from which to view Mount Fuji. Crisp winter days bring the clearest air; on summer nights, a ribbon of lights is visible as climbers ascend the mountain's slopes.

Touring particulars. From Tokyo, the train trip to the lake region takes 2 hours. Most western travelers make their headquarters at one of the two larger lakes—Lake Kawaguchi or Lake Yamanaka.

A 160-km/100-mile road encircles the base of Mount Fuji, skirting the five lakes; by bus, the complete circuit takes 6 to 8 hours. The stretch of road between Kawaguchi and Motosu lakes is considered one of Japan's most scenic mountain dell roads. An expanse of virgin forest—known as the Sea of Trees—grows on the weathered lava of Mount Fuji's northwest slope.

Hakone's hot springs

The celebrated hot springs district of Hakone lies within the bowl of an ancient volcanic crater southeast of Mount Fuji. A dozen or so hot spring spas, Lake Ashi, beautiful mountain scenery, an open-air art museum, and views of Mount Fuji are the district's major attractions. Plum blossoms are spectacular in mid-February; cherry trees and azaleas bloom here in April.

From Odawara the road and railway twist up a narrow, wooded gorge to Miyanoshita, the largest and most popular of the hot springs resorts. Farther along are the spas of Gora and Kowakidani. You can reach the district from Tokyo in less than 2 hours by taking a train or bus.

Lake Ashi. Nestled 723 meters/2,372 feet above sea level, this splendid mountain lake (often called Lake Hakone) is famed for its magnificent reflection of Mount Fuji. Fishing for black bass and trout is almost as noteworthy.

Located 11 km/7 miles southwest of Miyanoshita, the lake offers a variety of water excursions—point-to-point transfers, as well as sightseeing trips. You can rent boats, too. Other sports and recreation facilities are available in Hakone-en lakeside park.

Mountain excursions. Woodsy walking trails crisscross the hills, leading to Fuji viewing points and several aerial ropeways that transport passengers up the mountains.

You can take a 10-minute cable car ride from Gora to Mount Sounzan, then transfer to another ropeway for a 33-minute descent to the north end of Lake Ashi. As the gondola sways along, you'll pass over Owakudani's sulphurous fumaroles and catch glimpses of Fuji.

Another long ropeway ascends 1,335-meter/4,379-foot Mount Komagatake on Ashi's east shore. Still another ride takes visitors to Togendai on Lake Ashi; en route, at Owakudani Station, you get a superb view of the Hakone area and Mount Fuji.

Hakone Open-air Museum. Built in a woodland setting of forested green hills, this museum displays the work of modern sculptors and painters in both indoor and outdoor galleries. Against a backdrop of wooded mountains and leafy glades stand the works of Rodin, Bourdelle, Moore, and Zadkine. Winding paths lead you past other portions of the museum's collection.

Scenic Izu Peninsula

Jutting out into the Pacific Ocean southwest of Tokyo, the Izu Peninsula is a marvelous piece of geography. Pine forests alternate with orange groves, stands of bamboo, orchards of plum trees, and small farms. Splendid coastal scenery, hot springs spas, and a mild climate combine to make this a prime vacation area. Hotels and inns abound.

At the head of the peninsula is Atami, about 105 km/65 miles and less than an hour from Tokyo by express train. From Atami, a branch rail line curves south along the scenic east coast for more than 64 km/40 miles to Shimoda at the peninsula's southern tip. Roads wind along the sea-eroded coastline and slice through the Amagi Range, the mountainous center of the peninsula. The coastal road, cut into cliffs high above the sea, offers views of Oshima and other offshore islands.

You can reach Ito on the east coast by rail from Tokyo in about 2 hours.

Atami, the unofficial capital. The seaside town of Atami is the unofficial capital of the area. A tangled mix of hotels, inns, and souvenir shops, Atami overflows in summer with Tokyo residents seeking relief from the city heat.

Among Atami's attractions is one of Japan's hottest natural springs (over 93° C/200° F). Called Oyu (Great Hot Water), this spring in the center of town was once a famous geyser, but the earthquake of 1923 reduced it to a bubbling spring. Its waters—considerably cooled—are piped to several local inns and bathhouses.

Shuzenji, a 9th century spa. In the mountains south and west of Atami, Shuzenji is one of the peninsula's oldest hot springs spas, known as a resort since the 9th century.

Located in the lovely wooded valley of the Katsura River, the little town is dominated by Shuzenji Temple, built in the early 800s. Nearby Shuzenji Park and Mount Daruma offer sweeping viewpoints. Orchid lovers shouldn't miss Izu Orchid Park.

Ito's attractions. Ito's more than 200 small hotels and inns cluster near the mouth of the Okawa River on the east coast—about 24 km/15 miles south of Atami.

William Adams, the first Englishman to set foot on Japanese soil, built Japan's first European-type ocean-going ships nearby in the early 1600s. A monument noting his achievements stands in Ito, and the town stages a William Adams Festival every August 10.

Shimoda, first U.S. consulate site. Busy Shimoda, about 48 km/30 miles south of Ito, a steamer port (for offshore islands) and fishing center, is the site of the first foreign consulate on Japanese soil.

Following the landing of Commodore Matthew Perry and the subsequent treaty between the United States and Japan in 1854, U.S. Consul Townsend Harris established his office in a nearby temple. The old consulate has been preserved much as Harris left it.

For the sports-minded. In addition to its beaches and many hot springs spas, the Izu Peninsula offers a number of other possibilities for outdoor recreation: stream fishing throughout the mountainous center; coastal fishing at Mito, Ajiro, Kawana, and Shimoda; hunting for wild boar in the Amagi Range; and hiking. Particularly popular are hikes from Amagi Pass to scenic Lake Hatcho on the upper slopes of Mount Amagi, from Ito to islet-dotted Lake Ippeki, and from Shuzenji up 3,200-foot Mount Daruma.

Volcanic Oshima Island. The smoking volcanic island of Oshima, in the Pacific Ocean east of Shimoda, is accessible by high-speed passenger ships from Atami (1 hour) or Inatori (40 minutes). Situated at the northern end of the Izu Islands chain, Oshima (considered part of the Tokyo metropolis) is noted for its active volcano, Mount Mihara.

Lush with vegetation, the island is noted for its camellias. Smoke trails from the volcano's crater, providing a landmark visible far out to sea. Hike the trail to the crater in about 45 minutes—or, if you prefer, you can rent a horse.

NIKKO NATIONAL PARK AREA

Nestled in a forested highland 150 km/93 miles north of Tokyo lies temple-dotted Nikko. Famed for its splendid shrines and temples, the city of Nikko is also home to Nikko Edo Mura Village, a restored samurai-era collection of 82 dwellings including a ninja house and kabuki theater. Nikko is also gateway to Nikko National Park, a mountainous park covering 1,406 square km/543 square miles of lakes, waterfalls, rivers, and hot springs.

There's daily train service from Tokyo (a 2-hour trip). Tokyo tour operators offer 1- and 2-day trips to the area, with transportation by bus or train. (The train is faster.) For information on Nikko accommodations, see page 41.

Beautiful Toshogu Shrine

Nikko's historic and architectural gem is Toshogu Shrine, mausoleum of the Tokugawa shogun Ieyasu, who founded the Tokugawa military dynasty. The shrine is considered the most outstanding existing example of old Japanese architecture. The finest craftsmen and artists of the day were taken to Nikko to build this lavishly decorated tribute, completed in 1636, 20 years after Ieyasu's death.

Thousands of majestic Japanese cedars, many of them more than 300 years old, line the approach to the shrine. The complex's architecture shows Buddhist and Shinto elements: a five-story pagoda, a torii gate, several storehouses, a stable, a belfry, and a drum tower.

Gilded and brightly painted, the shrine's major structures bear intricate carvings of legendary figures—lions, dragons, clouds, peonies. In the middle court, the Sacred Stable carvings include the original monkey trio depicting "Hear no evil, speak no evil, see no evil." Two-story Yomeimon Gate, at the entrance to the inner court, is renowned for its exquisite carvings.

Among other outstanding structures in the complex are Rinnoji Temple, containing three massive images; Yakushido, famed for its "crying dragon"; and Futarasan Shrine, the district's oldest building (1617).

The Toshogu Shrine Grand Festival, presented in May, is one of the most colorful in Japan (see page 60).

Nature's many attractions

Just 17 km/11 miles west of Nikko is Lake Chuzenji, formed behind a lava flow damming the Daiya River. From Umagaeshi, a well-engineered toll road climbs the slope of Mount Nantai in numerous hairpin curves.

From Akechidaira, the cable car terminal, you ride to a lookout point for superb views of the lake, 96-meter/316-foot Kegon Waterfall (the lake's outlet), and the surrounding area.

Chuzenji, a clear, fresh-water lake nestled at the foot of Mount Nantai, is almost a mile above sea level. Cherry blossoms line portions of the lake shore in mid-May; vibrant maples and birches form a brilliant border in autumn. Sightseeing boat rides leave from the resort.

Nikko National Park contains a number of other lakes—popular for boating and camping—and alpine plateaus, several ski slopes, skating rinks, and two golf courses. Fish abound in the lakes and streams, and hunting is excellent. Hiking trails cover varied terrain.

Mashiko for pottery

One of Japan's most important pottery-making towns, Mashiko, lies 48 km/30 miles southeast of Nikko. The region's unsigned folk pottery, usually glazed in brown or persimmon, features flecks of iron ore present in clay.

Pottery stores, open to the street, display diverse wares. Many of the potters work in rooms just behind the stores. You're welcome in both the stores and the potting sheds, where you'll see potters seated at their wheels throwing pots, as assistants and apprentices work at glazing and decorating.

The man responsible for the present flourishing state of this craft was potter Shoji Hamada, who moved to Mashiko several decades ago and devoted himself to strengthening the Japanese folk pottery tradition. In 1955 the Japanese government named Hamada a "Living National Treasure" (see page 18). He died in 1978.

One- and two-day bus tours of the Nikko area include a stop at Mashiko. If you prefer to make the trip on your own from Tokyo, take the train from Ueno Station to Utsunomiya, then a bus or taxi to Mashiko.

NORTHERN HONSHU

Few tourists venture beyond Nikko to the northeastern portions of Honshu. Those who do enjoy magnificent mountains, a rugged coastline, and uncluttered countryside. The region—called the Tohoku District—encompasses three outstanding national parks and seven quasi-national parks. It's also an area rich in hot spring spas.

If you time your visit for spring or autumn, you'll enjoy a profusion of blossoming trees in late April and early May and a tapestry of autumn foliage beginning in late September. The area's big festivals are held in early August. The *Tanabata* or Star Festival, held August 6 to 8 in Sendai, is one of the largest.

An excellent network of rail, air, and bus facilities serves the area; most destinations are 2 to 6 hours from Tokyo by express train. The district's major city, Sendai, is 45 minutes from Tokyo by plane, 2 hours by train. During summer months, Japanese tourists flock to Tohoku, and accommodations become scarce. For information on area accommodations, see page 41.

Traditional Tohoku crafts include regional lacquerware, copper and iron utensils, textiles, and dolls.

Takayama's *thatch-roofed, high-peaked homes provide rustic backdrop to field of summer daisies. Set among Japan Alps, old town includes homes where artisans work.*

Tea leaves *require hand picking. Conical-hatted women work amid tea plant hedges near Shizuoka in southern Japan. Area also noted for tangerine orchards.*

RELAX IN A RYOKAN

For many visitors to Japan, the highlight of the trip is a night or two in a *ryokan*, a Japanese inn. At the inn's entrance, you leave behind your western lifestyle (along with your shoes) to experience the world of Japanese living.

Your accommodations. Upon arrival, you'll be greeted with enthusiastic bowing and escorted along highly polished corridors to your room. You'll enter your room through sliding doors and probably look out sliding glass walls onto a serene Japanese garden. Rooms are sparsely furnished: *tatami* on the floor; a low table with *zabuton* (cushions) beside it; a *tokonoma* (an alcove with a scroll painting and a flower arrangement) set into the wall.

Before stepping into the tatami-matted room, it's customary to remove the backless slippers you put on at the front door. You'll be given a freshly laundered *yukata* (cotton kimono) to wear.

A leisurely pace. Soon after you arrive, a maid will bring you hot tea—your official welcome to the inn.

If you follow the routine of the ryokan, you'll try the honorable bath, a before-dinner ritual (see page 16). Many ryokan have private Japanese-style baths, but some will have a bath area to be used by several guests (it may also be used privately). Most ryokan today provide guests with private toilets, but in some of the finest older inns, you're likely to find such facilities down the hall.

Following your bath, dinner will be served in your room. Clad in a yukata, you'll sit on the zabuton beside the low table. A maid in a colorful kimono will ceremoniously serve a multicourse Japanese meal.

Later, your maid will move the table aside and pull *futon* (quilt mattresses) out of the closet, piling them on the floor in the center of the room. She will

cover them with a sheet and then lay one or two soft quilts on top. Next morning, the maid will put away the futon and serve your breakfast. If you're feeling adventurous, try a Japanese breakfast (including soup with bean curd, dried seaweed strips, hot boiled fish, and rice). Or you can order western-style ham and eggs, toast, and coffee the night before.

For more information. You'll find ryokan throughout Japan. Most of the best inns belong to the Japan Ryokan Association. The Japan National Tourist Organization (see page 65) publishes an annual ryokan guide.

Matsushima Bay's sea park

Endless *haiku* have been inspired by Matsushima's vast sea park, a protected bay sprinkled with hundreds of sea-eroded islands, most of them covered with gnarled pines. Many have tunnels and caves hollowed out by the waves. The area is considered one of Japan's three top scenic attractions, on a par with Itsukushima Island in Hiroshima Bay (see page 55) and Amanohashidate (page 49). Matsushima lies on Honshu's northeastern coast, a little less than 4 hours by express train from Tokyo via Sendai.

From Matsushima-Kaigan, sightseeing boats cruise among the islands, past oyster and seaweed beds. Some travelers consider this excursion Japan's most lovely sea voyage, its beauty surpassing the less varied (though more famous) trip through the Inland Sea.

The bayside village of Matsushima-Kaigan has numerous small hotels and ryokan, some with boating, swimming, and tennis facilities. Atop the rocky cliff near the village stands a moon-viewing pavilion dating from the 16th century. An hour's walk takes you to a series of small islands linked by charming red bridges that lead to ancient caves and old temples.

Coastal variety near Miyako

North of Sendai and Matsushima lies another area of scenic coastal beauty. Stretching for some 87 km/54 miles along the Pacific in the vicinity of Miyako is Rikuchu Coast National Park. Its changing coastline varies from rugged, rocky beaches through fiords to towering cliffs rising nearly 305 meters/1,000 feet out of the sea. Sightseeing boats depart from Miyako, offering passengers glimpses of grottoes, huge pillars of rock, and sea-eroded terraces and reefs—all backed by the greenery of thick pine forests. Rhododendrons grow wild throughout the area, adding brilliance to the countryside in late spring.

Aomori, port city

Honshu's northern tip is home to Aomori, a lumber town and active port. Walled off from the rest of the island by the Hakkoda Mountains, Aomori lies across the straits from Hokkaido. It's the southern terminal for ferries operating between Honshu and Hokkaido. Aomori is about 6½ hours from Tokyo by train and about 2 hours by air. From Sendai, anticipate a 3½-hour train trip.

The city is the starting point for excursions to Lake Towada and the Oirase Valley. Aomori is noted for its apples, grown primarily on the Tsugaru Plain.

The surrounding area is full of hot springs resorts. Some of the area's bathhouses are gigantic, accommodating as many as 800 bathers at one time. Nearby Asamushi Spa, facing a beautiful bay a few miles east of Aomori, is known as the Atami of the Tohoku region. Wild camellias bloom nearby in May and June.

Scenic Lake Towada

Mixed forests of evergreen and decidous trees rim the water-filled crater of Lake Towada, located in the northern part of Towada Hachimantai National Park, 64 km/40 miles south of Aomori. Attractive in any season, the lake is loveliest in autumn, when brilliant foliage—a dazzling blend of reds, yellows, and purples—contrasts with the blue waters of the lake and its pine-clad islets.

The village of Towadako is the terminus for buses from Aomori and the lake's launches. In the vicinity are several country inns, a youth hostel, and a hotel, along with souvenir shops and small restaurants. Often you'll see hikers off on a day's trek. Fishing is excellent—a small aquarium behind the Towada Science Museum displays native species. Lake trout is a breakfast standard at local hotels.

Best of the lake launch trips is an hour's cruise from Towadako to Nenokuchi, at the mouth of the Oirase River; along the way, passengers enjoy the lake's surrounding landscape—gentle hills, coves and inlets, rocky cliffs. From Nenokuchi, hike upstream along the tree-lined river, ablaze with bright foliage in autumn.

Ski country

In the alpine country west of Sendai rises Mount Zao, the center of Tohoku ski country. Cableways and chair lifts transport skiers to a variety of runs—from beginner to expert levels. Slopes are lighted for night skiing. Finally, a hot springs bath can top off a long day of skiing.

The small resort is also delightful for summer and autumn mountain excursions.

Bandai-Asahi—mountains and lakes

South of Mount Zao, Bandai-Asahi National Park holds further opportunities for outdoor recreation. High mountains and lovely Lake Inawashiro define the landscape of this park, which consists of four separate areas.

Second largest of Japan's national parks (topped only by Hokkaido's Daisetsuzan National Park), Bandai-Asahi covers nearly 200,000 hectares/500,000 acres, embracing not only the Lake Inawashiro and Mount Bandai area but also extending north to the Asahi Mountains and west into a primitive region around Mount Iide.

Spectacular Mount Bandai (1,818 meters/5,966 feet) erupted in 1888, blowing off about a third of its mass. Its northern slope is a sprawling plateau with more than 100 lakes, each a different color: indigo, cobalt, green, emerald, turquoise. Evidence of volcanic activity is visible throughout the area.

A few rail lines and roads provide access. The best is the 29-km/18-mile toll road (called the Bandai-Azuma Skyline) that follows the western slopes of 1,931-meter/6,336-foot Mount Azuma from Tsuchiyu to Takayu.

Mountainous Sado Island

Another trip that leads travelers through northern Honshu's beautiful mountain country is an excursion to Sado Island, off Honshu's west coast in the Sea of Japan. You reach Sado Island by taking a 1-hour jetfoil ferry ride from Niigata. From Tokyo, Niigata is accessible by air (55 minutes), by limited express train (about 4 hours), or Shinkansen express (about 2 hours).

An extensive plain of small rice farms divides Sado's parallel mountain chains. Your jetfoil docks at Ryotsu, the island's main town. The peaks of the Kimpoku Range rise above the city. You can tour the island easily in a day by bus or car. Part of Sado's appeal is the traditional dress of the island women: blue kimono and circular folded cane hat, originally worn when it was forbidden to gaze upon the emperor. You may want to buy some of the local red porcelain made at the village of Aikawa. Called *mumyoiyaki*, it's made from clay taken from old gold mines.

Centuries ago, Sado was a place of exile; many tales live on in melancholic island ballads. The old palace made of rough-hewn timbers at Izumi (about 6 miles from Ryotsu) is the site where exiled Emperor Juntoku lived for 22 years in the early 13th century.

Autumn *colors heavily forested hillside around Kiyomizu Temple. From temple veranda, visitors get good view of Kyoto.*

THE JAPAN ALPS

For more alpine scenery, travel south to the Japan Alps. This range of mountains cuts across the center of Honshu about halfway between Tokyo and Kyoto. You'll skirt the fringes of these mountains if you take the Shinkansen express (bullet train) between Tokyo and Kyoto.

In winter, trains are lively with ski-garbed Japanese on their way to the alpine ski country. In summer, young people dressed in jeans and hoisting knapsacks are headed for hiking trails that lace this lovely mountain country.

The town of Matsumoto, the gateway to Chubu-Sangaku (Japan Alps) National Park is accessible by train from either Tokyo (about 4 hours) or Nagoya ($3\frac{1}{2}$ hours). The area has western-style hotels and an abundance of delightful ryokan. For more on area accommodations, see page 41.

Alpine attractions

Known as "the roof of Japan," the Japan Alps are the country's highest mountains. Many peaks soar above 3,048 meters/10,000 feet. Mixed forests of evergreen and deciduous trees provide spectacular displays of autumn color.

In addition to hiking, horseback riding, swimming, boating, and other mountain activities, you'll find castles, temples, and shrines to explore. You can also ride the rapids through the gorge of the Tenryn River south of Matsumoto. Though not as well known as the Kiso River run (see page 40), it's an exciting but safe trip.

Skiing and climbing

Two of the most popular activities in the Japan Alps are skiing and mountain climbing.

Alpine skiing. Ski resorts are plentifully scattered throughout the Japan Alps, but the most celebrated is Happo-one, just north of Omachi. Judged to be the best alpine course in Japan, the resort has 20 lifts, a 1,829-meter/6,000-foot cableway, and night illumination.

Kamikochi, mountaineering base. Probably the best base from which to climb into the high mountains is Kamikochi, situated in a beautiful hidden valley due west of Matsumoto (about 3 hours by bus). Rugged peaks surround the Kamikochi Valley. The valley lies along the upper reaches of the Azusa River. From the Kamikochi area, trails lead up into the highlands. Some trails require 6 or 7 hours of tough climbing.

It's a relatively easy hike to the summit of 2,987-meter/9,800-foot Mount Norikura, a conical volcano with numerous small lakes near its summit. To reach the top, take a bus from Kamikochi to Norikura Hut. The hike to the summit is a little less than 3 km/2 miles and takes about $1\frac{1}{2}$ hours.

THE NAGOYA AREA

In the Nagoya area some 367 km/228 miles southwest of Tokyo, travelers can visit sacred shrines, tour pearl farms, watch porcelain items being made, shoot the rapids on the Kiso River, observe an interesting method of fishing using cormorants, and explore several old-world Japanese towns. Nagoya is the starting point for any of these trips.

Nagoya, a ceramics center

The superexpress trains on the Shinkansen (bullet train) Line link Tokyo with Nagoya, the nation's fourth largest city, in just 2 hours. A busy industrial center of wide, tree-lined streets, Nagoya is the hub of central Japan's transportation network, as well as the center of the country's porcelain industry. Lacquerware, cloisonné, and other craft specialties are also made here.

The city's commercial center is Nagoya Station; a network of underground passages lined by shops and restaurants connects many of the nearby business buildings. Hirokoji and Sakaemachi are other main shopping areas. But local attractions are not limited to shopping. Visits to castles, shrines, parks, and factories are part of the Nagoya touring scene.

Nagoya Castle. Originally constructed in 1612 by Ieyasu Tokugawa, founder of the Tokugawa Shogunate, Nagoya Castle was destroyed during World War II. Reconstruction of the castle—which bears a famous pair of golden dolphins—was completed in 1959. The castle grounds and the five-story inner tower are now open to the public.

Atsuta Shrine. Because it houses the *Kusanagi-no-Tsurugi* (Grass-mowing Sword), the shrine is one of the nation's Three Sacred Treasures. (The other two are the Sacred Mirror of Ise Grand Shrines and the Sacred Jewels at the Imperial Palace in Tokyo.) Atsuta Shrine is considered one of the most important sacred Shinto shrines in Japan, second only to Ise Jingu Shrine.

Higashiyama Park. One of the Orient's largest zoos is in Nagoya's Higashiyama Park; it has no fences to obstruct your view of the animals. The park also contains an extensive botanical garden displaying rare plants from all over the world.

Factory visits. Some local industries welcome foreign visitors. Since Nagoya is Japan's center of pottery, porcelain, and cloisonné manufacturing, a visit to one of these factories is fascinating. You can arrange to tour the Noritake china factory and Ando cloisonné company. Make arrangements through your travel agent, hotel, or the Nagoya Tourist Information Center in Nagoya City Hall.

Ise-Shima National Park

The beautiful scenery and seascapes of Ise-Shima National Park provide the perfect backdrop for Japan's most venerated Shinto shrines. Tucked into a grove of towering cedars, the shrine complex consists of two major shrines—the Outer Shrine (dedicated to the goddess of crops) and the Inner Shrine (honoring the sun goddess)—and 120 minor shrines.

The shrines are located near Ise City, a 1½-hour train ride southwest of Nagoya. Frequent trains leave Nagoya for the trip to Ujiyamada Station near Ise. The Outer Shrine, Geku, is only a short walk from the station. The Inner Shrine, Naiku, is about 6 km/4 miles away; buses connect the two shrines.

You approach each of the major shrines by passing under torii gates. The Sacred Mirror—said to have been given to the sun goddess when she came to reign on earth—reposes at the Inner Shrine.

In vivid contrast to the massive, ornately carved and decorated shrines found elsewhere in Japan, the two shrines are small, built of unpainted cypress with no ornamentation. Their classic simplicity represents a style predating the introduction of Chinese architecture into Japan in the 6th century. Originally built before the Iron Age, they were put together without nails or metal of any kind. According to tradition, the principal shrines are built anew every 20 years, and sacred relics are solemnly transferred to the new structures.

To this day, Japanese leaders visit this shrine to announce any important events or plans to the sun goddess. The general public is not permitted beyond the first fence at either shrine. Courtesy requires visitors to remove hats and coats in front of the shrines.

Pearl farming

Ago Bay and five other bays off Ise-Shima National Park are centers of Japan's famous cultured pearl industry. Toba, the rail terminus at Ise Bay, 15 minutes from Ise City, is the best place to learn about the pearl-growing process.

In 1893, Kokichi Mikimoto, son of a noodle maker, succeeded in artificially stimulating oysters to produce pearls. An irritant inserted inside the shell causes the oyster to secrete nacre, from which pearls are formed.

On Mikimoto Pearl Island, a footbridge-walk away from the Toba waterfront, you can view the pearl-making process—from "seeding" through harvesting and preparation for sale. You'll see women, clad in tight white cottton body suits, face masks, and caps, diving to collect the oysters. These are then seeded, placed in cages, and suspended from bamboo rafts. Pearls are harvested from 6 months to several years later, sorted and polished for use in jewelry.

Divers will make six or seven dives an hour into depths up to 30 meters/100 feet. Times are changing, though, and the demand for pearl divers is decreasing. Rather than have divers gather oysters for seeding, some pearl farms now raise their own oysters from eggs.

Mikimoto Pearl Museum exhibits reveal information about natural pearls, the history of cultured pearls, and the mechanics of pearl culture.

Besides the Ago Bay area, smaller centers of pearl production are located off the coast of Miyajima, Hiroshima, and Yamaguchi in western Honshu; off the Kii Peninsula; at Ushibuka on Amakusa-Shimo Island off Kyushu; and at several points around Shikoku.

Seto, the porcelain-making center

Seto, about 50 minutes east of Nagoya by local railway, has been one of the major centers of porcelain production in Japan since the 13th century. Skills originally brought from China have been handed down—with improvements and innovations—from generation to generation. Today the town has more than 900 factories.

Ancient and modern examples of locally produced porcelain are displayed (some are for sale) at the Ceramic Center near Seto's city hall. You can see one of the early masterpieces, the *Koma-inu* (lionlike dog), at Seto's Fukagawa Shrine.

Riding the Kiso River rapids

For a change of pace, take an exciting ride down the rapids of the Kiso River north of Nagoya. Several points of embarkation may be reached by train or bus from the city. Boats and experienced guides are available for hire from March through November. The trip covers a distance of 6 to 7½ miles, depending on where you embark.

At Inuyama, the terminus, a white feudal castle perches on a hill overlooking the rapids. Transportation is provided back to Nagoya.

Cormorant fishing and parasols at Gifu

On most nights from mid-May to mid-October, a curious spectacle—cormorant fishing—takes place on the Nagara River at Gifu. From a lantern-bedecked boat, you watch large tame birds, controlled by long leashes, retrieve *ayu* (a kind of river smelt) for their masters. The leashes fasten around the birds' necks preventing them from swallowing the fish. Fire baskets hang aboard fishing boats, attracting the fish and illuminating the scene.

The ancient industry of cormorant fishing continues at several sites in Japan, but Gifu—only 30 minutes by train north of Nagoya—is considered the best place to watch the performance.

Gifu's parasol factory is one of the few still active in Japan; its present prosperity is primarily due to export trade. The factory makes both paper parasols and silk parasols, each one individually painted. The production of bamboo parasol frames is a cottage industry, existing throughout the Gifu area. If you buy a *bangasa* (Japanese parasol) at the Gifu factory, it can be shipped to your home.

HOTEL TIPS/JAPAN

You'll find excellent western-style hotels in all of Japan's large cities and resort areas. The following is a limited list of hotels at major tourist destinations.

Fuji-Hakone area. In the lakes resort area you'll find the Fuji-View Hotel on the shore of Lake Kawaguchi, and the Hotel Mount Fuji and New Yamanakako Hotel near Lake Yamanaka. Hakone area hotels include the Fujiya (in Miyanoshita) and the Kowaki-en (in Kowakidani); the Gora Hotel at Gora; the Hakone Hotel and Hakone Prince Hotel on the shore of Lake Ashi; and the Fujiya's Sengoku Annex, Hakone Highland Hotel, Hakone Kanko Hotel, and Hotel Kagetsu-en, all north of Lake Ashi.

Nikko. Nikko's hotels include the Chuzenji Kanaya Hotel, Nikko Kanaya Hotel, Nikko Lakeside Hotel, and Nikko Prince Hotel.

Northern Honshu. You'll find accommodations in Aomori at the Hotel Aomori and Aomori Grand Hotel. In Sendai, you can stay at the Sendai Tokyu, Rich Sendai, Sendai, Sendai Plaza, Koyo Grand, or Sendai City Hotel.

Nagoya area. Western-style hotels in and around Nagoya include the International Nagoya, Meitetsu Grand, Nagoya Castle, Nagoya Kanko, Nagoya Miyako, Nagoya Terminal, and Nagoya Tokyu. In Takayama there's the Takayama Green or Hida hotels; in Kanazawa, try the Kanazawa Sky, New Kanazawa, Kanazawa Miyako, or Kanazawa New Grand.

Kyoto. Kyoto has a number of large western-style hotels, among them the ANA Kyoto, Fujita, Gimmond, Holiday Inn Kyoto, International, Keihan Kyoto, Kyoto Century, Kyoto Grand, Kyoto Park, Kyoto Prince, Kyoto Royal, Kyoto Tokyu, Kyoto Tower, Miyako, New Hankyu Kyoto, New Kyoto, New Miyako, Palaceside Kyoto, Sunroute Kyoto, and Takaragaike Prince. Nara has the Fujita Nara, Nara Hotel, and Hotel Yamatosanso.

Osaka. This city has a number of western-style hotels including the Do Sports Plaza, Echo Osaka, Hanshin, Holiday Inn Nankai, International Osaka, New Hankyu, New Otani, Nikko Osaka, Osaka Castle, Osaka Daiichi, Osaka Grand, Osaka Hilton International, Osaka Riverside, Osaka Terminal, Osaka Tokyu, Plaza, Royal, Tennoji Miyako, and Toyo.

Kobe. Downtown hotels include the Kobe Portopia, Kobe International, New Port, and Oriental. Atop Mount Rokko are the Rokko Oriental and the Rokkosan.

Inland sea area. Hotels in towns along the Inland Sea include the Himeji Castle (Himeji); New Okayama, Okayama Grand, Okayama Kokusai, Okayama Plaza, Okayama Royal (Okayama); Kurashiki Kokusai, Mizushima, Kokusai (Kurashiki); and ANA Hotel Hiroshima, Hiroshima City, Hiroshima Grand, Hiroshima Kokusai, Hiroshima River Side, Hiroshima Station, and New Hiroden (Hiroshima).

Shikoku. On the island of Shikoku you can stay at a number of hotels including the Keio Plaza Takamatsu, Rich Takamatsu, Takamatsu Grand, Takamatsu International (Takamatsu); ANA Matsuyama, Sunroute Matsuyama (Matsuyama); Kochi Dai-ichi (Kochi); or Awa Kanko, Oku-Dogo, or Tokushima Park (Tokushima).

Kyushu. This southern island has numerous hotels including the Kokura, Kokura Station, New Tagawa (Kitakyushu); ANA Hotel Hakata, Dai-ichi Fukuoka, Hakata Miyako, Hakata Tokyu, New Otani Hakata, Rich Hakata, Hakata Shiroyama, Nishitetsu Grand, Station Plaza, Takakura (Fukuoka); Nagasaki Grand, Nagasaki Tokyu, New Tanda, Parkside (Nagasaki); Matsukura (Sasebo); New Sky Kamamoto Castle, Kumamoto Kotsu Center (Kumamoto); Beppu New Grand, Hinago, Nippaku, Suginoi (Beppu); Miyazaki Washington, Phoenix, Plaza Miyazaki, Seaside Phoenix, Sun Phoenix (Miyazaki); Kagoshima Hayashida, Kagoshima Sun Royal, Kagoshima Tokyu, Shiroyama Kanko (Kagoshima); and Ibusuki Kanko and Ibusuki Royal (Ibusuki).

Hokkaido. Visitors to Sapporo, Hokkaido's major city, have many hotels to choose from; among them are the Alpha Sapporo, ANA Sapporo, Century Royal, Keio Plaza, New Otani, Sapporo Grand, Sapporo International, Sapporo Park, Sapporo Prince, Sapporo Royal, Sapporo Tokyu, and Fujiya Santus.

The Ryukyus. In the Okinawa area there's the Hyatt Regency-Manza Beach, Naha Tokyu, Okinawa Hilton, Okinawa Harbor View, Okinawa Grand Castle, Okinawa Miyako, Regent Okinawa, and Seibu Orion.

The flavor of old Japan

Within a day's trip of Nagoya are two towns that offer visitors a glimpse of the Japan of yesteryear. They are Takayama and Kanazawa.

Folklore at Takayama. Weathered 17th and 18th century wooden buildings fronted with simple latticework windows and sliding doors line the narrow streets of Takayama. An old castle city, it lies tucked in the Hida Mountains, a 3-hour train ride north of Nagoya.

That the people of Takayama want to protect their heritage is apparent in the number of folk museums and restored houses. The Kusakabe Folklore Museum, housed in the 18th century former home of a wealthy merchant, features old household items, lacquerware, and a tiny garden. Nearby, at the base of Mount Matsukura, stand the buildings of the Hida Minzoku-mura Folk Village. Within this complex is Hida-no-Sato Village, a model community of a dozen old private houses, craft workshops, and assorted cottages and huts. Here you'll see spinning and weaving tools, tableware, woodcarving, cypress hat making, and *Hidanuri* lacquering. Other town offerings of historical interest include a folk toy museum and several manor houses and temples.

During the town's spring and autumn festivals— Takayama Matsuri—ornate floats are wheeled through the streets. You can view some of these 18th century floats, noted for their intricate woodcarvings, at the Yatai Kaikan Museum.

Cross-island to Kanazawa. Quiet, uncrowded Kanazawa retains the flavor of old Japan. Its physical isolation—on the far side of the island, 5 hours by train from Nagoya— contributes to the atmosphere of times past. The city is known as the site of the outstanding Kenrokuen Garden and ancient samurai residences.

KYOTO, A LIVING MUSEUM

For many visitors, Kyoto's quiet, gentle ambience typifies the soul of Japan. Here, present and past coexist in remarkable harmony. Kyoto dates from 794, when Emperor Kammu built the village that has become the treasure house of the nation. Now a city of $1\frac{1}{2}$ million people, its central district is noisy and crowded. But beyond this area, you discover the quiet and peace of a living museum: palaces, temples, shrines, and gardens await you at every turn. Kyoto's reign as Japan's imperial capital remains strongly evident throughout the city.

Most travelers to Kyoto arrive from Tokyo by Shinkansen (bullet train) in less than 3 hours or by bus (overnight). You'll find a number of large, western-style hotels in Kyoto; many have Japanese-style rooms or separate cottages. Kyoto is also home to some of the country's finest ryokan. For a listing of Kyoto hotels, see page 41.

Getting settled

Kyoto offers a feast for the visitor—there's far too much to assimilate fully in limited time. With so many streets to wander, and splendid places to visit—more than 1,600 Buddhist temples, 300 Shinto shrines, and a dozen museums, plus many palaces and a number of outstanding gardens—most visitors find its cultural and esthetic richness overwhelming.

To survey the possibilities, many first-time visitors start with a local sightseeing tour. Once you've had an overview of the city's highlights, you can proceed to travel by train, subway, or taxi from point to point for an in-depth look at the sights that interest you most. Another rewarding way to get acquainted with Kyoto and to enjoy the juxtaposition of old and new is to explore the city on foot. Off main thoroughfares, narrow lanes lead you past simple houses of mellowed wood fronted by *shoji* (translucent screens) and topped by tiled roofs. A map, available from your hotel or the Tourist Information Center of the Japan National Tourist Organization, will help you locate the city's attractions.

Temples, shrines, and gardens galore

With so many significant places of worship in Kyoto, it's difficult to decide which ones merit a visit. This section describes a few of the major ones.

Kyoto provides the setting for some of the finest landscaped gardens in Japan; many occupy temple complexes. Among the most outstanding are the gardens at Daitokuji, Ginkakuji, Kinkakuji, Nanzenji, and Ryoanji temples.

Kiyomizu Temple. Mounted high on steep Higashiyama hillside in southeast Kyoto, Kiyomizu was originally established in 798, but most of the present buildings date from 1633. Mellow old pavilions with upturned eaves flank a wide, three-story pagoda. A massive trestle of timbers rises from the ravine below to support the veranda of the main hall.

Below you lies the city, a sea of tile roofs. Fascinating small streets lined with curio shops, old houses, and pottery workshops wind downhill from the temple complex.

Chionin Temple. North of Kiyomizu Temple, Kyoto's southeastern section holds another famous temple, one of the country's largest. Though fire has repeatedly plagued Chionin, several buildings dating back to 1633–39 remain intact. The imposing 24-meter/80-foot-high main gate dates from 1619.

The corridor behind the main hall is constructed so that a step on the floor triggers a sound resembling the song of the Japanese bush warbler. This architectural device, similar to one used in Nijo Castle, was designed to warn guards of approaching intruders.

Almost within sight of Chionin Temple is Kyoto's principal public park, Maruyama, famed for its display of

Vermilion torii *leads to Kyoto's Heian Shrine and tranquil garden noted for springtime cherry blossoms and autumn foliage.*

Sun's late rays *illuminate peaceful Nara Park, home for nearly 1,000 tame deer. At dusk, trumpet call summons them to pens.*

cherry trees, illuminated at night when in bloom. Adjoining the park is popular Yasaka Shrine, also called Gion Shrine. The Gion Festival is staged here in July (see page 60).

Nanzenji Temple. Northeast of Chionin Temple and off the usual tourist route, this quiet place of worship is noted for its main hall's 16th century paintings on sliding screens. The rock garden's classic design features rocks and white sand; compare it to Ryoanji Temple (see the listing below).

Ginkakuji Temple (Silver Pavilion). If you follow the pleasant cherry-tree-lined canal north from Nanzenji Temple, you'll eventually reach Ginkakuji, built in the 1400s as a villa for Shogun Yoshimasa Ashikaga. Original plans called for the villa's pavilion to be covered with silver leaf. Because the shogun died before the project was completed, the villa became a temple, silver in name only.

The temple's exceptional gardens, among the best-preserved of the era, are noted for their stone bridges, stone groupings, and waterfalls.

Heian Shrine. Northwest of Nanzenji Temple stands this 12-times-reduced replica of Kyoto's original Chinese-style Imperial Palace. Built in 1895 to commemorate the 1,100th anniversary of the founding of Kyoto, the shrine's impressive torii gate and simple vermilion and green buildings are set in magnificent gardens. Weeping cherry trees and azaleas bloom here in spring, and in autumn you'll see chrysanthemum displays. You're likely to glimpse a wedding party at the shrine, particularly in autumn; it's a favorite site for nuptials.

Nearby are the National Museum of Modern Art and neighboring Municipal Art Museum, city zoo, Kyoto Handicraft Center (see page 47), and Kanze Kaikan Hall, where noh (see "Try Traditional Japanese Theater," page 21) plays are performed.

Sanjusangendo Hall. Another southern Kyoto temple worth exploring is this Buddhist one. Built in 1266, Sanjusangendo Hall is noted for its wooden image of Kannon, who is flanked by 1,001 smaller, gilded Kannons, also of wood.

Higashi Honganji Temple. West of Sanjusangendo Hall and the Kamo River and a 10-minute walk north of Kyoto Station, this magnificent, massive-roofed structure is considered by some architects to be the country's best example of Buddhist architecture. The pavilion is occasionally used for the presentation of noh dramas.

Toji Temple. Located a 10-minute walk southwest of Kyoto Station, Toji Temple was established in 796 and is an important relic of the Heian Period. The temple's original buildings, largely destroyed during the 15th century civil wars, have been rebuilt. The main hall of the temple is one of the largest remaining buildings of the Momoyama Period (1573–1615). The temple's five-story pagoda, the highest in Japan, rises 56 meters/183 feet. The *azekura* (storehouse) is built entirely of wood assembled in a traditional method of building that does not use nails. It contains a large collection of art treasures unrivaled by any other Kyoto temple.

On the 21st of each month, a village of multicolored market stalls comes to life in the shadow of Toji's tall wooden pagoda. The lively Toji Flea Market operates from midmorning until late afternoon. Household and hardware items share display space with seaweed and baby chicks. Even crickets are for sale here, and sing from tiny bamboo cages.

Fushimi-Inari Shrine. Located in Kyoto's southeastern outskirts, this 8th century shrine is renowned for its more than 10,000 red-painted torii gates, which form a tunnel up to the mountaintop behind the shrine. Faithful worshipers donated the gates.

Kamo Shrines. Two of Kyoto's oldest shrines—believed to have been founded before the 6th century—are Kamikamo and Shimokamo, located in the northern part of Kyoto. The shrines' present buildings date from the 17th to 19th centuries. The Aoi Matsuri (Hollyhock Festival) held here every May 15 is one of Kyoto's major festivals (see page 60).

The city's Botanical Gardens, located south of Kamikamo Shrine on the bank of the Kamo River, date from 1923.

Daitokuji Temple. Northern Kyoto is also home to this historic Zen temple, founded in 1319. The complex's main building, erected in 1478, features beautifully painted sliding doors. The temple is also noted for its dry-landscape gardens featuring sculpted white gravel, stones, and background shrubbery.

Kinkakuji Temple (Golden Pavilion). Southwest of Daitokuji Temple is the Golden Pavilion. Gold foil covers the upper two stories of this striking three-story temple. Backed by forested hills, the pavilion was rebuilt in 1955 after fire destroyed the 1397 original. The present temple is an exact reproduction of the original. The pavilion first served as a shogun's villa. It became a Zen temple upon his death.

The Golden Pavilion's setting at the base of Kinugasa Hill is a lovely one. A landscaped garden surrounds the pavilion. Regarded as one of the finest in Japan, it features a brook running into a reflecting pond dotted with stone islands and edged by maples and pines.

Ryoanji Temple. Situated in the foothills a short distance southwest of Kinkakuji Temple, this 15th century temple is best known for its severely simple sand and rock garden, probably the most famous one in Japan. Though it was designed solely as a place for meditation, hordes of sightseers who descend upon the temple grounds often make this pursuit difficult.

DOING BUSINESS IN JAPAN

In Japan, as elsewhere in the world, establishing a good first impression plays an important role in successful business negotiations. However, western businessmen not versed in Japanese etiquette might make a poor first impression without realizing it.

Japanese culture is steeped in traditional customs. These rules dictate behavior and are designed to prevent embarrassment and maintain important surface harmony. Formality is the keynote.

This begins with the introduction. It is preferable to have a trusted common friend or business associate make the initial introduction. This will help pave the way for smoother business dealings.

Japanese generally bow one or more times upon meeting someone. It is a sign of respect to those being introduced. Not returning a bow is considered rude. If you feel awkward about bowing, you should at least bow slightly or nod your head.

Following the bow, you may shake hands. Handshakes are not customary in Japanese culture, but Japanese businessmen have come to expect them from their western counterparts.

Once introduced, address your host by his family (last) name plus the suffix *san*. In other words, "Mr. Fuji" would be addressed as "Fuji-san." First or given names are only used between close friends and family members.

The exchange of business cards is also an important part of the first meeting. Your calling card or *meishi* should be printed with your name, title, and company name and address in English on one side and in Japanese on the other. Present the Japanese side face-up. Your host will present his card English side face-up. Make sure you have enough business cards with you. They are an invaluable part of doing business in Japan.

Also essential to successful business dealings is a good interpreter who is familiar with the field you are discussing. This person should be well briefed on your plans prior to the first meeting.

However, even with an interpreter there can be misunderstanding. For example, when your host says *hai* ("yes") or nods his head, he may only mean he understands what you are saying, not that he is in agreement with it.

Similarly, direct answers may be avoided by your host. The Japanese have difficulty saying a direct "no" to proposals made. To say "no" is to imply that they are saying "no" to the person, not to his ideas. This would

cause embarrassment. There are a variety of euphemisms used to say "no" without saying it directly.

Patience is an important part of doing business in Japan. Your host may wish to spend time getting acquainted with you during the first few meetings, not discussing business initially. The development of a friendly business relationship and trust is more important at this stage.

Final decisions won't be made quickly, but will only come after many meetings. Politeness is key throughout the negotiations. Uncontrolled emotions are frowned upon. Periods of silence during the meetings are acceptable, and welcomed as a time to read others' reactions nonverbally and contemplate the proposals.

Remember that final decisions are made by the group involved, not an individual. Therefore, decisions will take longer. However, once they are made, plans will likely be implemented more quickly since all involved are in accord.

For more information on doing business in Japan, contact JETRO (Japan External Trade Organization), 360 Post Street, Suite 501, San Francisco, CA 94108.

Costumed geisha *share quiet moment in gardens of Kyoto inn. Rigorous training precedes geisha role as hostess, waitress, entertainer for business functions.*

A castle, palaces, and the National Museum

In addition to temples and gardens, Kyoto offers other important places to visit, including a castle, several palaces, and a national museum. Both the castle and the museum are open to the public. If you wish to visit the palaces, you must apply a few days in advance for a permit from the Office of the Imperial Household Agency, located in the northwest part of Kyoto Imperial Park.

Nijo Castle. Originally built in 1603 as a residence for Ieyasu, founder of the Tokugawa Shogunate, Nijo Castle now is owned by the city. Open to the public, it occupies six blocks of land just west of the heart of the city.

Stone walls enclose the 28-hectare/70-acre castle grounds. Most famous of the five buildings is the Ohiro-mai; it contains the Great Hall, decorated with paintings by Tanyu Kano (1602–74), official painter of the shogunate government and the most influential artist of his time. The Imperial Messenger's Chamber in the castle has a "bush warbler floor" similar to the one in Chionin Temple.

The castle's celebrated Ninomaru Garden was meticulously designed. It contains numerous fine stones and a reflecting pond.

Old Imperial Palace. Surrounded by high walls, the palace stands near the heart of Kyoto in the 89-hectare/220-acre Kyoto Imperial Park, northeast of Nijo Castle. Emperor Kammu, who founded Kyoto as the imperial capital in 794, built the original Imperial Palace; fire destroyed it and several replications. Though the existing palace dates only from 1855, it scrupulously follows the original design and is noted for its simplicity of line.

The landscaped gardens around the palace feature an appealing design incorporating large rocks, a pond, a waterfall, and an islet reached by stone bridges.

Shugakuin Detached Palace. The detached palace of Shugakuin Rikyu, or Imperial Villa, lies in Kyoto's northeastern outskirts at the foot of Mount Hiei. The spacious, parklike grounds are divided into three large gardens landscaped on different levels; each garden contains a villa (called *ochaya*). A high point on the palace grounds provides a superb view of the gardens, city, and surrounding hills.

Katsura Detached Palace. Situated in the city's southwestern suburbs facing the Katsura River, the palace and its outstanding gardens overlook the western hills. The simple and elegant stroll garden, laid out in the 1670s, is the masterpiece of Kobori Enshu. It has been preserved in its original state.

Kyoto National Museum. North of Sanjusangendo Hall, this museum is a repository for historical articles, fine art objects, and handcrafted treasures entrusted by Buddhist temples, Shinto shrines, and individuals.

Kyoto for handicrafts

A center for traditional crafts, Kyoto has many factories and workshops where you can watch craftspeople at work. Among Kyoto's local crafts are lacquerware, silk brocade, dyed cloth, ceramics, and woodblock prints. Other articles bearing the Kyoto stamp of tradition include delicately designed Kyoto fans, old folding screens, perfumed incense sachets, stone garden art, boxwood combs, and *Kyo-ningyo* (costumed dolls).

Craftspeople at work. An excellent place to observe and buy is the Kyoto Handicraft Center, Kumano Jinja Higashi, Sakyo-ku, across from Heian Shrine. Five floors of craft workshops offer visitors a splendid opportunity to watch craftspeople making damascene, woodblock prints, dolls, pottery, and Kiyomizu porcelain. Painters, weavers, and goldsmiths also work here. The center has a variety of craft items for sale.

Delicate Nishijin silk brocade is still handwoven in the old Nishijin district, where the sound of looms pervades the narrow back streets. You can see displays of the brocade at Nishijin Textile Museum at Omiya Imadegawa in Kamigyo-ku. The famous Nishimura Lacquerware Factory (established in 1657) at Okazaki Park, Sakyo-ku, welcomes visitors who want to watch lacquerware production and view displays of finished products. Other makers of cloisonné, damascene, and woodblock prints have similar open house policies.

Where to shop. Main shopping centers are Shijo-dori and the areas around Shinkyogoku and the Kyoto Station. Major department stores are Takashimaya, Daimaru, and Fujii Daimaru, all on Shijo-dori. Souvenir shops, theaters, pastry stalls, and restaurants line Shinkyogoku Arcade, a roofed amusement center paralleling busy Kawaramachi-dori. Among its varied shops are ones where you can purchase personal seals, house numbers chiseled from stone, and apothecary's medicinal herbs and potions.

Antique hunters should prowl Shinmonzen-dori, several blocks northwest of Yasaka Shrine. Here, handsome stores offer a fine selection of art objects and souvenirs. Where Teramachi-dori crosses Nijo-dori, investigate secondhand stores.

For a look at another side of Kyoto life, walk through the 400-year-old Nishiki Market, a block north of Shijo-dori on Nishiki-koji, where housewives and restaurant food buyers seek out fresh fruits and vegetables. Produce, poultry, and fish shops—as well as stalls holding groceries and dry goods—line the narrow street.

Dining—some Kyoto specialties

In comparison with Tokyo-style cooking, Kyoto's cuisine is less seasoned, less soy-colored, and more subtle in taste. Sampling authentic Kyoto dishes in the best restaurants is not inexpensive, but it provides a unique esthetic experience that transcends mere eating.

All of the more familiar Japanese dishes—sukiyaki, tempura, sashimi, sushi—are served in Kyoto, as is some of the best beef in the world. Kyotoites suggest that visitors not overlook the city's own local specialties. Typical is *kaiseki*, a mixture of fish—raw, baked, or steamed—with vegetables and special soups; *shojin ryori*, Zen-style vegetarian dishes in unbelievable variety; and *kyo bento*, a glorified box lunch in which fish, eggs, meat, and rice are prepared with special artistry and packaged in a lovely lacquerware box.

The entertainment scene

Though considerably more subdued than some of Tokyo's, Kyoto's entertainment district offers motion picture theaters, pachinko parlors, a multitude of small bars with hostesses, and a few nightclubs and cabarets. The three major nightclubs are the Gion, Osome, and Bel-Ami. They feature shows with international entertainers, music for dancing, and kimono-clad hostesses.

Gion Corner at Yasaka Kaikan in the Gion district gives visitors a chance to learn about various phases of traditional Japanese arts. Two evening shows illustrate the arts of *sado* (tea ceremony), ikebana (flower arrangement), bunraku (puppet play), *kyomai* (Kyoto-style dance), kyogen (Noh comic play), and gagaku (ancient court music and dance).

The colorful Cherry Dance is performed in Kyoto from early April to mid-May. You also can see geisha dances during this period at the following theaters: Pontocho Kaburenjo, the Kitano Kaikan, and the Gion Kaburenjo. Kabuki performances are presented at Minami-za and noh performances at Kanze Kaikan, Oe-Nogaku-do.

Unique to Kyoto is an evening exhibition of martial arts, a fast-moving, hour-long performance including expert demonstrations of karate, kendo, and judo. It is held at the Nihon Seibukan, the largest martial arts academy in the Orient.

Excursions from Kyoto

Kyoto makes an excellent base for exploring nearby points of interest. You can head west to take an exciting ride down the Hozu Rapids to Arashiyama. To the south are temples, green tea plantations, and the ancient capital of Nara (see page 49). To the north the scenic beauty of Lake Biwa, Mount Hiei, Ohara, and the northern coast beckons.

Rapid ride. A traditional excursion point since the Heian period, Arashiyama, west of Kyoto, boasts cherry blossoms in spring, mountain greenery in summer, colorful maples in autumn, and snow-covered hills in winter. From Kyoto, Arashiyama is a brief 25-minute train ride away.

Between March and November an exciting way to reach Arashiyama is by boat on the Hozu River. You take the train or drive to Kameoka and then ride the rapids in a flatboat to Arashiyama, a 10-km/6-mile trip of $1\frac{1}{2}$ hours. In spring and early summer, wild wisteria and azalea blossoms brighten the river banks; autumn voyagers view crimson foliage.

Uji. South of Kyoto on the road to Nara, this village is noted for its green tea and for the famous Byodoin Temple, Japan's best existing example of 11th century architecture. Originally a villa for the powerful Fujiwara family, it later became a Buddhist temple. Highlight of the temple complex is the Phoenix Hall, built in 1057 and housing Buddha statues.

To see how tea is graded and processed, stop at tea farms along the road to Uji. You can sample various blends of tea, buying the blend that suits your taste.

Lake Biwa. The huge body of water lying just east of Kyoto takes its name from the musical instrument it resembles in shape. With a surface area of 676 square km/261 square miles, Biwa is Japan's largest freshwater lake. You can travel around it by car, rail, bus, or steamboat. A unique paddle-wheel steamboat plies the lake's waters on both day and evening cruises.

In recent years the lake's western shore has been developed as a summer resort area for Kyoto residents, offering opportunities for hiking, camping, mountaineering, swimming, boating, and other water sports.

Daigoji Temple. Set in the mountains southeast of Kyoto on the way to Otsu, this temple is renowned both for its gardens and architecture. The gardens are among the area's finest for viewing cherry blossoms, and the red, five-story pavilion—dating from 951—is the oldest building in the Kyoto area. Richly textured, gold screen paintings decorate the temple walls.

Mount Hiei. A 50-minute drive northeast of Kyoto leads you to this 848-meter/2,782-foot mountain. From its summit, you get a panoramic view of the Kyoto basin, Lake Biwa, and the surrounding mountains. You can reach the top by way of a 457-meter/1,500-foot aerial ropeway. Enryakuji Temple, located in a grove of Japanese cypress trees on the summit, was built in 788 by Emperor Kammu to protect his new capital of Kyoto from evil spirits.

Ohara. Just north of Mount Hiei, this small town puts you in touch with rural Japan. It's a marvelous place for strolling. Easy walks lead to the small temple of Sanzenin—whose main hall dates from the 10th century—and to the hilltop's Jakkoin Nunnery, a small building with a tiny garden where you'll learn the sad story of a young empress dowager of the 12th century.

The garden is one of the best places around Kyoto for maple viewing. Maples cover the whole Ohara area; they're a glorious sight in early November.

The northern coast. Few foreigners visit the north coast of western Honshu, a beautiful area of quiet fishing villages, secluded inlets, rugged headlands, and sand dunes. Railways serve the north coast out of Kyoto and other cities.

For centuries Japanese have made trips to view Amanohashidate on Miyazu Bay. Classified as one of the country's "three great scenic attractions" (the other two are Miyajima and Matsushima), Amanohashidate or Bridge of Heaven is a long, narrow sand bar covered with fantastically shaped pine trees. From special viewing platforms, visitors traditionally take an upside-down look at the scene by observing it through their legs; presumably, this gives the effect of a bridge in the sky extending toward heaven. You reach the area— a fashionable resort for summering city folks—on a pleasant, 2-hour and 20-minute rail trip from Kyoto.

San-in Kaigan (Coast) National Park encompasses about 46 miles of coast from Kinosaki to Tottori. Northeast of Tottori a massive series of sand dunes stretches for about 16 km/10 miles. Dozens of hot springs spas with small hotels and ryokan provide comfortable accommodations.

QUIET, ANCIENT NARA

Founded in 709, historic Nara is even older than its sister city of Kyoto, 40 km/25 miles to the north. Nara served as Japan's capital from 710 to 794 and played an important role in Japan's early cultural development. During those years, influences from China, India, and Korea combined to form the singular culture of Japan, a culture that first flourished in Nara. Art, poetry, crafts, religion, and politics all flowered here.

Most visitors approach Nara from either Kyoto or Osaka. From Kyoto and Osaka, the quickest way is a 35-minute train ride. It takes about an hour to drive from either Kyoto or Osaka.

Taxis and tour buses are plentiful in Nara, or you can see the area's highlights on full-day bus excursions operating regularly out of Kyoto. But you may find a day's visit insufficient—the historical sites, temples, and museums in Nara and its vicinity demand more time. For accommodation information, see page 41.

Sightseeing in Nara

You'll absorb more of Nara's atmosphere and charm if you stroll, and since Nara means "flat" (the city is built on a flat plain), walking is easy. Most of the main temples and other places of interest are within walking distance of downtown. The Japan Travel Bureau, Jurakukaikan Building, near the Kintetsu Nara Station, is a handy information center for Nara visitors.

Though fire and time have taken their toll, many of Nara's structures and art treasures have changed little in 1,200 years. The attractions that follow are merely a sampling of this city's magnificent sights.

Nara Park. This woodsy expanse of huge Japanese cedars, oaks, and cypress is a good starting point for exploring Nara. Quiet paths wind through the trees and open meadows and alongside tranquil ponds. More than 1,000 tame deer (called "divine messengers") wander freely about the park during daytime hours. Don't be surprised if one of them nudges you for a handout. You can purchase deer food in the park.

The park's serenity comes as a pleasant contrast to its approach: busy Sanjo-dori, Nara's main street, runs east from the railway station to the park. The lovely willow-fringed lake to the right of the park entrance is Sarusawa Pond, with Kofukuji Temple reflected on its shimmering surface.

Kofukuji Temple. This temple's landmark is its famed five-story pagoda—50 meters/165 feet high—built in 1426. The temple's three-story pagoda dates from 1143. In the 8th century, Kofukuji Temple had almost 200 buildings. Fire after fire leveled them; now the pagodas and four halls are the only important buildings that remain.

Todaiji Temple. A few blocks north of Nara Park, this spacious temple houses the Daibutsu, or Great Buddha. The size of the temple is immediately impressive—especially if you approach the temple compound through the Nandaimon, or Great South Gate. Originally constructed in the 8th century, the Nandaimon blew down in a typhoon in 962 and was restored in 1199. Supported by 18 tall, red pillars, it is the largest such gate in Japan. It opens into a spacious enclosure surrounding the largest wooden building in the world.

As you enter the hall, the seated Great Buddha—16 meters/53½ feet high—looms before you, its head alone 5 meters/16 feet long and 3 meters/9½ feet wide. This is the largest bronze statue in the world and the most massive Buddha image in Japan.

Among other buildings of the Todaiji are the *Nigatsudo* (Second Month Hall), where the ancient Water Drawing Ceremony takes place on March 12, and the *Sangatsudo* (Third Month Hall), founded in 733 and oldest of all the temple structures. Its architecture illustrates the style of both the Nara and the later Kamakura periods.

Kasuga Grand Shrine. At the eastern border of Nara Park stands one of Japan's most celebrated Shinto shrines, founded in 768. If you walk beneath its two torii gates into the park, you'll approach the shrine along an avenue of stone lanterns. Some 3,000 lanterns are lighted during Kasuga's Mandoro Festival, held in early February and again in mid-August. Kasuga has four lovely small shrines, each dedicated to a separate deity.

Horyuji Temple. One of Japan's oldest wooden temples, revered Horyuji lies southwest of Nara, about 45 minutes by bus. The temple was founded in 607. Its five-story pagoda was rebuilt after World War II with the same timbers used in its original construction. The complex contains 40 buildings; those of chief importance are the Nandaimon or Great South Gate, the Kondo or Main Hall, the pagoda, the Daikodo or Lecture Hall (reconstructed in 990), and Yumedono or Hall of Dreams, an imposing octagonal structure built in 739.

Shopping around Nara

Nara-ningyo (carved wooden dolls) are a specialty of Nara; you'll find them in shops along Sanjo-dori. Other locally made items are ink sticks and writing brushes. Additional interesting shops dot Higashimuki and Mochi-Idono streets, which intersect Sanjo-dori. You can browse leisurely for dolls and other carved items, woodblock prints, and souvenirs and art objects.

OSAKA, CITY OF INDUSTRY

Japan's third largest city, Osaka, sprawls across the landscape at the point where the mouth of the Yodo River meets Osaka Bay, 554 km/344 miles southwest of Tokyo. Thanks to its role as a major eastern port on the Inland Sea, Osaka has long been the country's industrial and commercial center.

On the surface, Osaka exudes a modern cosmopolitan character. Glass and steel highrises glisten in the noonday sun. Busy freeways run beside and over a network of long-established canals that wind throughout the city. Approximately 1,700 bridges span these waterways. At night, neon signs reflected in the water turn the city into a mosaic of glowing color.

Frequent air service connects Tokyo and Osaka (a 55-minute flight), and Shinkansen (bullet trains) connect the two cities in 3 hours and 10 minutes. From Kyoto, 40 km/25 miles to the northeast, it's a 17-minute bullet train ride to Osaka. Local Osaka transportation includes taxis, subway trains, and half-day sightseeing tours. For accommodation information, see page 41.

Exploring Osaka

The nucleus of the city, aside from its residential areas, is divided into two main parts: the Kita or northern section, which includes the big shopping and amusement district around Osaka Station, and the Minami or southern part, containing the chief entertainment centers. Linking the two districts is a wide boulevard, Mido-suji. Lined with ginkgo and plane trees, Mido-suji is a pleasant place to stroll and window-shop.

A castle, shrines, and parks highlight Osaka's list of visitor attractions.

Osaka Castle. Dominating a hill overlooking the Yodo River, this famous Osaka landmark dates from the 16th century. Its massive, granite-walled fortress has been destroyed and reconstructed several times, most re-

cently following World War II. When the five-story building was originally built, warlord Hideyoshi assigned his generals the task of bringing him stones to build the castle's walls and foundation. Some of these enormous rocks are still in place; one called Higo-ishi is 14 meters/47$^1/_2$ feet long and more than 6 meters/19 feet high.

Today, the castle houses an exhibit of old weapons and costumes. From the castle's top floor you get a good view of Osaka and environs. Plum and cherry blossoms add springtime color to the parklands surrounding the castle.

Tennoji Park. The city's art museum, zoo, and botanical gardens are clustered in Tennoji Park in the southern part of the city. Here, too, is Keitakuen, one of the finest examples of a Japanese-style circular strolling garden. Paths circle a placid pond edged in cherry trees, azaleas, and other flowering plants.

Shitennoji Temple. The country's oldest temple, Shitennoji (founded in the 6th century) stands across from Tennoji Park. Most of its buildings have been reconstructed several times. Striking architectural accomplishments include a five-story pagoda. The torii gate dates from 1294.

Sumiyoshi Shrine. On the southern outskirts of the city, this popular Shinto shrine honors the guardian deity of the sea. Many stone lanterns, contributed by the faithful, line the approach path. The temple buildings are bright red and white. A high arched bridge graces the gardens.

Temmangu Shrine. This 10th century shrine in the northern part of the city is the scene of one of Japan's great festivals, the Tenjin Matsuri (see page 60), held annually on July 24–25.

Expo Memorial Park. The site of Expo '70, this park north of central Osaka offers visitors an ethnological museum and Japanese garden. Some futuristic pavilions also remain.

Hattori Park. In a green oasis west of Expo Memorial Park you'll find Osaka's Local House Museum, an open-air attraction featuring traditional houses from various districts in central Japan. Each house is equipped with traditional furniture and Japanese household goods.

Other diversions

Shopping, entertainment, and industrial tours add to the list of visitor activities you can sample in Osaka.

Shopping. Osaka is known for its underground shopping centers. The biggest and most popular is the multi-level Umeda Underground Shopping Center in the Osaka Station area in northern Osaka. There, more than

Old and new *appear to stand side by side in Osaka, where city's ornate 16th-century castle overlooks modern, high-rise buildings.*

Ice palaces *rise in the air during Sapporo Snow Festival. Site of 1972 Winter Olympics, area also offers good skiing.*

THE HONORABLE TEA CEREMONY

For the Japanese, the time-honored tradition of the tea ceremony offers a respite from the pressures of everyday life; inner peace and harmony are achieved through the stylized tea preparation and sipping.

Japan originally imported tea from China, then began its own plantations in the early 9th century. By the 15th century, Japan's tea masters—men who prepared ceremonial teas for the country's rulers—had established a formal ritual for making and serving tea. A number of tea ceremonial schools still exist. Though procedures vary to some extent, the basic steps of the ceremony are the same. A tea ceremony usually lasts about 40 minutes; visitors can see (and occasionally participate in) abbreviated versions at many hotels.

The ceremony begins when the host or hostess (the tea master or a student) enters the room carrying the ceremonial utensils—a tea bowl, tea caddy, teaspoon, bamboo whisk, water dipper, and cold water jar. The tea master kneels on the tatami floor opposite four or five kneeling guests, then arranges the utensils artistically next to the brazier holding the teakettle.

The tea master carefully wipes the utensils; then, using the teaspoon—a slender piece of bamboo curved at the tip—he scoops a small amount of powdered green tea from the caddy and places it in the tea bowl, which has been warmed and rinsed with hot water. Next, a little water is transferred with the bamboo dipper from teakettle to bowl; tea and water are then whipped to a froth with the bamboo whisk.

After placing the tea bowl on a *kobukusa* (small silk

napkin), the tea master hands it to one of the guests. The guest first compliments the tea master on the tea's frothiness, color, and aroma, then drinks the bowl's contents in several sips. The empty bowl is returned to the tea master, and the whole ceremony is repeated for the next guest.

---

200 shops and restaurants await the consumer. Above ground in the same area, you can do further shopping. South of Osaka Station is the city's other major shopping district, Shinsaibashi-suji, known for its many fine shops. Both districts have large department stores.

Entertainment. Highlights in Osaka are performances of bunraku and kabuki. The puppeteers perform at the Bunraku Theater, the national home of this 300-year-old art. The classical kabuki plays are given in the five-story Shin-Kabukiza, located on Mido-suji in the southern part of the city.

Japan's most famous women's opera, the Takarazuka troupe, presents its revue at the Takarazuka Grand Theater in Takarazuka City, 40 minutes by train from Osaka.

Industrial tours. Some of Osaka's local industries welcome visitors for tours of their plants. You can also visit the Osaka Stock Exchange and the Osaka International Trade Center, site of the mammoth biannual International Trade Fair.

KOBE, A HARBOR CITY

The thriving city of Kobe, Japan's seventh largest, spreads out along the shores of Osaka Bay for about 20 km/15 miles. To the north of this broad expanse of water rises the densely forested Rokko Range.

Kobe's wide harbor makes it one of Japan's major

ports. Thousands of ships from the Pacific Ocean and Inland Sea dock here annually. A large percentage of the country's exports (including steel, machinery, chemicals, and textiles) and imports are handled through the port of Kobe.

Situated 32 km/20 miles west of Osaka and 64 km/40 miles southwest of Kyoto, Kobe is a good starting point for tours and cruises on the Inland Sea. You can reach Kobe by road, rail, or air. For accommodation information, see page 41.

Kobe sightseeing

There are other sights to see in Kobe besides its busy port and industrial complex. Museum and gallery-going, shopping, and excursions to nearby woods and beaches are all worthwhile pursuits.

In-town exploring. Cultural points of interest in Kobe include the vermilion-painted Ikuta Shrine (near Sannomiya Station), the Kobe Municipal Art Museum, and the Hakutsuru Art Gallery. The observation deck of 109-meter/356-foot Port Tower is a great place from which to view the city and its harbor.

For shopping, explore the big department stores and the main shopping areas—like Motomachi Shopping Arcade and Santica Town—near the docks where steamers tie up. You should also try Sannomiya and Ikuta-Shimmichi streets, Tor Road, and the Shopping Nook at Kobe International House.

Waterfalls and beaches. In the hills behind the city, about $2^1/_2$ km/$1^1/_2$ miles from the port, you can visit a wooded area with two waterfalls (one dropping 45 meters/147 feet). Some 30 minutes west of Kobe by car are white sand beaches—Suma and Maiko—lined with dark green pines.

Akashi, about 21 km/13 miles west, has a planetarium; from Akashi, ferries transport travelers to Awaji Island, largest of the Inland Sea islands. At Awaji's southern end you can see the whirlpools of Naruto Straits (see page 56).

Viewpoints. Arching behind Kobe, the Rokko Range offers sweeping views of the city and harbor, of Awaji Island, and beyond to the Kii Peninsula stretching south of Osaka. You can reach the best viewpoints—the mountain tops of Rokko, Maya, and Futatabi—easily from Kobe. At night the view of Kobe Harbor resembles a small Hong Kong.

Hot springs. Arima Spa, located in a gorge at the base of Mount Rokko, is one of Japan's oldest hot springs resorts. Famous for its curative waters, the spa is also known for its surrounding wooded countryside. Cherry and maple trees provide seasonal color, and cascading streams brighten the landscape the year around. More than 30 ryokan, each equipped with its own hot spring bath, provide comfortable accommodations.

ALONG THE INLAND SEA

Stretching more than 483 km/300 miles east and west within the protecting arms of western Honshu and the islands of Shikoku and Kyushu, Japan's Inland Sea is one of the most scenic waterways in the world. It is actually a chain of five seas, linked together and connected to the Pacific Ocean by narrow, swift-flowing channels.

Much of the waterway is part of the Inland Sea National Park and offers abundant scenic beauty, including pine-studded islands, beautiful beaches, gently sloping farmlands, tiny fishing villages, and an occasional vermilion torii gate. Touring possibilities include water excursions and land trips along Honshu Island's southern shore.

Cruising the Inland Sea

Ships transport passengers along the waterway from Osaka to Beppu and crisscross the Inland Sea in many places. Depending on your route, you may board a 3,000-ton luxury cruise ship, a smaller cruise ship, a ferry boat, hydrofoil, or hovercraft. Ships cruise through an island-studded seascape, passing or stopping at villages that recall scenes from an antique Japanese print.

Daylight trip. Still the most popular excursion both for vacationing Japanese and for foreigners is the daylight trip departing Osaka at 8:30 A.M., stopping at Kobe, and arriving at Takamatsu, on Shikoku Island, at 2 P.M. The ship returns to Osaka by 8 P.M. Most passengers board the ship in Kobe.

Once you leave Kobe, your steamer joins an ongoing procession of coastal freighters, steamers, and open fishing boats. Docking at Takamatsu provides a wonderful mixture of dockside sights and sounds: noise, confusion, and emotions characterize the scene as passengers disembark and board. Cargo is thrown onto the dock, women vendors come alongside selling tangerines and souvenirs, and a wedding party may appear to bid goodbye to a bride and groom. For more information on Takamatsu, see page 56.

Still another excursion explores the western part of the Inland Sea by hydrofoil. The boat departs from Miyajima Island, stops at Hiroshima (where passengers can also board), then continues to Omishima for lunch and a visit to a shrine that has a 318-year-old stone torii gate. Another 20 minutes of cruising takes you to Ikuchijima and its ornately painted Kosanji Temple.

Night trip. An evening cruise operates three times a night from Osaka to Beppu. The best one leaves Osaka at 9 P.M., arriving in Beppu at 11:55 A.M., some 14 hours later.

Other water routes. Smaller steamships, ferries, hydrofoils, and hovercraft link various points on Honshu with several small port towns on Shikoku and other islands in

Willow-lined canals *meander through Kurashiki, an ancient walled town of narrow lanes and white granary buildings trimmed in black.*

Itsukushima Shinto Shrine's *torii gate appears to float above the bay near enchanting Miyajima. All shrine buildings extend over water.*

the Inland Sea. For information on routes and schedules, consult the Japan National Tourist Organization.

The land route

By rail or road, a Honshu Island trip along the shores of the Inland Sea offers a look at the gardens of Okayama, the old Edo-Period town of Kurashiki, Hiroshima, and the sacred island of Miyajima. For accommodation information, see page 41.

Himeji. A 25-minute ride northwest of Kobe on the superexpress Shinkansen (bullet train) takes you to Himeji, a city noted for its ancient feudal stronghold, Himeji Castle. Built atop tall rock ramparts, the great five-story structure—sometimes called the Egret Castle—is finished from top to bottom in white plaster. Its top levels offer a sweeping view of the countryside and the island-studded waters of the Inland Sea. In spring, apricot blossoms add delicate beauty to the garden.

Okayama. Less than an hour west of Kobe by train, Okayama is known for its Korakuen Gardens and its huge black castle. The gardens, among Japan's most beautiful, were designed in 1700 and feature graceful contours enhanced by carp-filled ponds, streams, waterfalls, and a variety of trees providing seasonal color. On a small hill overlooking the gardens stands Okayama Castle. Originally built in 1573 and reconstructed in 1966, it is often called Crow Castle because of its black exterior.

Kurashiki. Just west of Okayama, Kurashiki is a historic walled city. Now an important industrial center, it has managed to retain some of its original character, particularly in the old section, which remains a quiet haven of tiny winding streets, willow-lined canals, and old wooden rice granaries. During feudal times, Kurashiki served as an export center for rice produced in the region. Today there are museums, restaurants, tea and coffee houses, and shops in the white, two-story granary buildings trimmed in black tile.

Four old rice granaries have been converted into a Folkcraft Museum housing over 4,000 items, including rugs, textiles, pottery, wood and bamboo products, and other handicrafts. In another converted granary you'll find the Archeological Museum displaying relics unearthed from the surrounding countryside.

The Ohara Art Gallery, located in a neoclassical building built by a wealthy textile manufacturer, features one of Japan's best collections of western art, including works by El Greco, Renoir, Monet, Pissarro, and Degas. Japanese artists featured include Umehara, Yasui, and Fujita. The gallery also has a superb collection of Japanese pottery, woodblock prints, and stencil-dyeing.

Still other museums in Kurashiki's old town area include the Japanese Rural Toy Museum featuring fanciful antique creations for children, and the Historical Museum housing old weapons, musical instruments, and coins.

Hiroshima. Set beside a bay on the Inland Sea, Hiroshima is about a 2-hour bullet train ride west from Osaka or Kobe.

The first atomic bomb was dropped on Hiroshima in 1945. It was feared that the area would remain an atomic desert for 75 years, but Hiroshima has been rebuilt—mostly since 1955—into a busy, fully functioning city, its population surpassing the 400,000 of the preblast period.

Peace Boulevard (Heiwa O-dori) leads to the Atomic Bomb Explosion Center south of Peace Park. This center includes the Peace Tower and a museum containing mementos from the explosion. Many sobering photographs depict the bombed city and the trauma of its people.

Other city sights include Hiroshima Castle, built in 1589 and reconstructed after World War II, and, on a hill in the eastern part of the city, Hijiyama Park.

Miyajima and Itsukushima Shrine. One of the best reasons for going to Hiroshima is to visit the enchanting island of Miyajima and to see its famous Shinto shrine, Itsukushima. You reach the island by ferry from Miyajimaguchi, accessible from Hiroshima by train or sightseeing bus. Island and shrine have been famous for generations as one of Japan's most beautiful sights.

Itsukushima was founded by the Heike clan in the year 811. Most of its buildings have been rebuilt many times. The main shrine and several adjoining subsidiary shrines and galleries stand on stilts above the water. Offshore stands a tall vermilion torii.

For a splendid view of Hiroshima backed by distant mountains and of the Inland Sea and its islands and boats, take the ropeway from Momiji-dani Park behind the Itsukushima Shrine to the top of Mount Misen, the highest peak on the island. As a bonus, near the summit you can see Gumonjido Temple, built in the 9th century.

QUIET, RURAL SHIKOKU

Though scenic Shikoku—smallest of the four principal islands—marks the southern boundary of the well-known Inland Sea, it is off the main tourist routes of Japan. Relatively secluded, Shikoku retains much of the flavor of rural Japan, preserved in widespread ancient customs and folkways.

Shoppers will find bargains in bamboo products (carved and woven baskets and trays), decorated tissue paper and papier-mâché folk dolls, lanterns, mythological figurines and masks, paper streamers, kites, and earthy, unglazed pottery.

Getting there

You can reach Takamatsu by air from Osaka, by hovercraft from Uno (near Okayama), by steamer from Osaka and Kobe, and by hydrofoil from Kobe and Himeji. There's also air and boat service from Kochi, Matsuyama, and Tokushima. The 13-km/8-mile Seto Ohashi Bridge spans the Inland Sea linking Honshu and Shikoku, providing train and car access to the island. For accommodation information, see page 41.

Exploring the island

Shikoku has four major cities—Takamatsu, Tokushima, Kochi, and Matsuyama—each with a population exceeding 300,000. Your best means of transport around the island is by train. There are English-speaking guides in Takamatsu.

Shikoku visitor attractions range from celebrated gardens, ancient spas, and dramatic natural whirlpools to bullfights, long-tailed roosters, and fighting dogs.

Takamatsu. Originally laid out around a castle, the city is Shikoku's governmental center. A mile south of the station is lovely Ritsurin Park, one of the best strolling gardens in Japan. The park's landscaping harmonizes with its natural pine forest. Artisans display and sell local folk crafts in the garden's exhibition hall.

Matsuyama. West from Takamatsu is Shikoku's largest city, also a seaport and one of the oldest spa areas in Japan. In addition to numerous old inns, a major attraction is Matsuyama Castle, dating from 1603 and containing fine armor and weapons from Japan's feudal era.

On the outskirts is Dogo Spa, reputedly Japan's oldest spa and a favorite with Japanese visitors. The spa is located on a hillside northeast of the city. You can reach it by bus or streetcar.

Uwajima. This town on Shikoku's western coast is known for its bullfighting, in which two bulls are pitted against each other in a small open-air ring. Farmers enjoy the sport several times a year.

Hikers will enjoy the jagged-cliff headlands, fiord-like inlets, and natural woodlands of Ashizuri-Uwakai National Park, Japan's newest preserve.

Kochi. This southern seaport—about 161 km/100 miles from Takamatsu— is a marketing center for folk art. The city is noted for its handmade paper, its long-tailed roosters (birds sporting feather trains as long as 6 meters/20 feet), and its *Tosa* breed of fighting dogs. The mastiff-size dogs, traditionally bred and trained as bodyguards, are matched in ferocious fights.

Tokushima. The smallest of the island's four main cities is on the east coast, $1^1/_2$ hours by train from Takamatsu. Tokushima's annual 300-year-old Bon Dance festival (*Awa Odori*) attracts throngs of visitors to the area each August.

While in Tokushima, you should see the famous puppet plays performed in the area's shrines and temples. Bizan Park atop Bizan Hill, accessible by aerial cable car, is handsome in all seasons and provides a splendid view of the city and Kii Channel.

Naruto. A 45-minute train ride north from Tokushima takes you to Naruto, where you can see an unusual sight—the whirlpools of the Naruto Straits.

Twice a day, the waters of the Pacific roar through this narrow rocky channel—less than a mile wide—raging in swirls of angry foam. The extreme turbulence is caused by a difference in levels— as much as $1^1/_2$ meters/5 feet—between the Inland Sea and the ocean. An observation platform overlooks the channel, or you can take a boat trip for a closer look.

MOUNTAINOUS, MISTY KYUSHU

Kyushu, twice as big as the state of Hawaii, is the southernmost and third largest of Japan's four major islands. Its bubbling hot springs, volcanic mountains, dramatic coastlines, national parks, and other attractions—popular with Japanese vacationers—are fast being discovered by visitors from overseas.

Facing the East China Sea at the southwestern end of Japan's Inland Sea, Kyushu is the Japanese island closest to the Asian mainland. It has long been Japan's principal gateway to foreign culture and trade. Located on the island's northwestern coast, Nagasaki, the country's oldest international port, opened its harbor to foreign trading ships in 1571. When Japan's doors were closed to the outside world between the mid-17th and mid-19th centuries, Nagasaki was the only Japanese port to maintain contact with the west.

Much of Kyushu's scenery seems to come straight out of old woodblock prints: you'll see misty mountains and small coastal islands, farmhouses tucked into narrow green valleys, farm families tilling orderly fields, and fishermen poling sampans.

Though spring and autumn are the ideal seasons to visit, Kyushu has a mild climate for much of the year. Summer is less humid here than in other parts of Japan; on warm days, the cool mountains provide convenient relief. Winters can be severe; chilly winds sweep down from Siberia, and occasional snow falls as far south as Kagoshima.

Travel tips

You can travel to Kyushu by rail, ship, air, or road. Undersea rail and highway tunnels and a suspension bridge join Kyushu with Honshu. Shinkansen (bullet train) service connects Tokyo and Fukuoka—1,183 km/735 miles—in less than 7 hours, and a network of rail lines joins the island's main cities. Steamships of the Kansai Kisen Steamship Co. cruise the Inland Sea between Osaka/Kobe and Beppu. Domestic airline flights connect Tokyo and Osaka with Fukuoka and the island's other large cities. For information on accommodations, see page 41.

A complete tour of Kyushu, including the island's major cities and sights, will take about 8 to 10 days. In Kyushu's more remote areas, western tourists are still relatively rare. Beyond main city hotels, little English is spoken, and since most local tours are geared to Japanese tourists, you may want to arrange for an English-speaking guide through your hotel or a travel agency.

Consider the following possibilities as you plan your island tour itinerary. Kitakyushu, Fukuoka, and Hakata each offer you different views of Kyushu.

Kitakyushu—a tale of five cities

In 1963 five major industrial cities at the northern tip of Kyushu combined to form Kitakyushu, making it the largest city on the island (more than 1,050,000 people). Kitakyushu faces the narrowest stretch of Kammon Strait, which separates Kyushu from Honshu.

From Kitakyushu to Fukuoka you travel southwest along the coast through Genkai-Quasi National Park. Fantastic rock formations and green pine groves break long stretches of white sand beach.

Fukuoka

Straddling the Naka River, Fukuoka is a major industrial city, as well as the political, cultural, and communication center of Kyushu. An older portion of the city east of the river is known historically as Hakata, and Fukuoka's busy harbor bears this name as well. In modern times, the whole area—encompassing a population of about 1,163,000—has come to be called Fukuoka.

Area attractions include several shrines and parks. Fukuoka's many handicraft factories produce traditionally dressed Hakata dolls, silk textiles, and coral jewelry and carvings. Tenjincho Street, in the heart of the city, is Fukuoka's main business district.

Shrine touring. The city has its share of shrines and temples, dominated by restorations of Sumiyoshi and Hakozaki Hachiman shrines dating from the 16th and 17th centuries.

A 20-minute train ride from Fukuoka takes you to Dazaifu Temmangu Shrine. A 7th century bronze bell and attractively landscaped grounds featuring calm ponds and orange-painted, arched bridges distinguish the shrine.

A city of parks. Ohori Park, toward the west end of town, is a vast, open space surrounding a big tidewater lake created from the moat of the former castle. Bridges link the parkland with islands in the lake. Paths and playing fields attract strollers and sports enthusiasts. A forest and remnants of the old stone walls of Fukuoka Castle form a backdrop to the scene.

To the north is Nishi Park, reached by a cherry-lined avenue and stairway. At the foot of the stair is the workshop where Hakata's famous costumed dolls are made.

Nagasaki, Japan's first open door

One of Kyushu's most visually and historically interesting cities, Nagasaki curves around a busy port at the mouth of the Urakami River on the west coast of Kyushu, 153 km/95 miles southwest of Fukuoka.

Its European patina is immediately apparent: brick buildings, old forts, canals, and curving cobblestone streets are a legacy of the 16th century when the port was first opened to trade with the Portuguese and Dutch. In preceding centuries Nagasaki had been a major port for trade with Korea and China. Vestiges of this influence remain today in a famous Chinese temple, a large Chinese colony, and restaurants offering some of the finest Chinese cuisine in Japan.

Christianity was introduced into Japan at Nagasaki; it became firmly entrenched throughout Kyushu, only to be forced underground for some 200 years. Area monuments to martyred Christians are reminders of this period of Japanese history.

You can easily spend a day or more poking about the city, exploring its cobbled hillside streets, visiting its historic treasures, getting a closer look at the monumental Mitsubishi shipyards (where some of the largest ships in the world have been built), and trying some of Kyushu's fabled seafood.

Europe's influence. Glover Mansion, high on a hilltop at the south end of the city overlooking the bay, is typical of the fine homes built by wealthy European residents during the city's early trading days. Built in 1863, this mansion was the home of a British merchant.

Just down the hill from Glover Mansion, No. 16 House features a collection of European antiques and memorabilia.

A few blocks east of the mansion stands Oura Catholic Church, erected in 1865 in memory of 26 Japanese and foreign martyrs crucified in the 16th century. The wooden church is the oldest example of ecclesiastical Gothic architecture in Japan.

At the Dejima Traders Museum, you'll see relics of Nagasaki's early Dutch residents.

Other sights. You may also want to visit Nagasaki Park and adjoining Suwa Shrine with its imposing 10-meter/33-foot-high bronze torii gate. Sofukuji Temple, built in 1629, is an excellent example of Ming dynasty Chinese architecture. Peace Park marks the spot where the atomic bomb exploded in 1945.

North to Sasebo and Hirado

The 2-hour bus trip from Nagasaki north to the American naval base of Sasebo offers splendid scenery all the way. But the main objective of an excursion to Kyushu's northwestern corner is a visit to the island and town of Hirado. From Sasebo, it's about a $1^{1}/_{2}$-hour drive north to the bridge connecting Hirado Island and Kyushu.

The road to Sasebo. On your journey from Nagasaki north you'll catch glimpses of blue bays and tiny inlets, villages, farmhouses, and neat tobacco and rice fields.

The route crosses Saikai Bridge, spanning the spot where ebb and flow tides meet to create a great maelstrom during certain tidal periods. People come to watch the phenomenon from the bridge, from picnic spots on the hillsides, and from seafood restaurants near the water.

Sasebo has the charm of a miniature Nagasaki. It offers similar hillside vantage points, narrow curving streets, and attractive hillside homes.

Hirado Island. One of the largest of many islands stretching southward along this coastal area, Hirado gives you the feeling of having ventured pleasantly far off the beaten track. The small waterfront shops in the town of Hirado provide a charming ambience. The ramparts of Hirado Castle overlook the town and sea. Located in a hillside garden mansion, the town's small museum houses not only European relics and objects from the Christian "underground" but treasures from the region's feudal past.

A cruise around Hirado's neighboring scenic islands makes a satisfying excursion from Kyushu. Boats complete the Hirado-Kashimae (Sasebo) run in 55 minutes, steering a course through narrow inlets past misted, pine-forested islands and an occasional fishing sampan.

Unzen-Amakusa National Park

Southeast of Nagasaki lies Unzen-Amakusa National Park, offering hot springs, a mountain resort, and scenic islands. Mount Unzen, an inactive volcano soaring above the Shimabara Peninsula, is the park's central feature. A quiet resort town, Unzen, clings to the volcano's flanks. Unzen's small hotels, many with landscaped gardens, cluster about sulphurous, bubbling hot springs. An old-fashioned feeling pervades the town. The gaudiness that characterizes many such resorts is absent here. Panoramic views of the Shimabara Peninsula are spectacular at any time of year.

South of the Shimabara Peninsula are the Amakusa Islands, the most attractive of which are now linked by five bridges. The trip across all five bridges—sometimes called the Pearl Line route—offers some spectacular views. You'll see offshore oyster beds and a pearl showroom on one of the islands. The Five Bridges Route wends its way back to Misumi, about 32 km/20 miles southwest of Kumamoto.

You can also get to the Amakusa group by ferry from the peninsula port of Shimabara. The $1\frac{1}{2}$-hour trip through island-studded waters grants views of distant mountains.

Shimabara, a small harbor town, has a castle (Shimabara Castle, built in 1616) containing 17th-century Christian relics. Shimabara is a good stopover point for exploring the Mount Unzen area.

Kumamoto, a castle town

Kumamoto is a prefectural capital on Kyushu's central west coast, almost due east of Shimabara. You can reach Kumamoto from Shimabara by ferry and a 30-minute drive.

Kumamoto Castle, an exceptionally striking building rising above the center of the city, ranks as one of Japan's great castles. Built in 1607, it was burned by a rebel army in the 1800s and wasn't restored until the 1960s. Cherry trees line the walkway to the castle entrance. As you climb the castle's central stairway, you'll view displays of artifacts from the feudal period.

Suizenji Park, one of the most famous landscape gardens in Japan, is ideal for easy strolling. Designed in 1632, it reproduces some of the features of Honshu from the old Tokaido Road (Tokyo to Kyoto).

Mount Aso, an active volcano

A $1\frac{1}{2}$-hour ride by bus or taxi from Kumamoto takes you to towering, smoking Mount Aso—sentinel of Aso National Park, containing the largest crater cavity in the world. There's a toll road almost to the top, and you can approach the rim by foot or ropeway—except when access is closed by resident volcanologists.

Great spurts of white smoke and gases burst from fissures at the bottom of the crater. You may feel a rumbling beneath your feet. A number of concrete pillbox shelters, set back from the rim, provide cover in case the volcano becomes too active and begins spitting rocks along with the smoke and gas.

Beppu—the steam factory

From Aso you continue across the mountains to the eastern coastal resort of Beppu, Japan's leading hot springs spa and terminus of Inland Sea cruises.

Noted for its geothermal activity, at first glance Beppu looks like one vast steam factory. Clouds of steam escape from hillsides, gardens, backyards, cracks beside the road, even from beneath buildings. The hot springs of the city's eight spas produce 19,000 gallons of water per day. The Kannawa Spa is best known for its unusual "hells"—boiling ponds. One is steamy, another red ("Bloody Hell"), and still another has a geyserlike eruption every 20 minutes.

You'll find baths at nearly every hotel— hot baths, tepid baths, carbonated baths, iron baths, sulfur baths— as well as an enormous hot spring swimming pool. North of the ferry dock, there's a section of beach where Japanese hot sand enthusiasts bury themselves up to their necks in steaming, wet sand.

Miyazaki, the Hawaii of Japan

The road south from Beppu to Miyazaki traverses rural countryside along Kyushu's eastern coast. Nicknamed the "Hawaii of Japan," Miyazaki is a leisurely paced,

CHERRY BLOSSOM TIME

Springtime bursts forth in a superb show of color as millions of blossoms paint the landscape a delicate pink. It's cherry blossom time in Japan! For Japanese families, it's time for blossom viewing, a favorite pastime during the first two weeks in April when flowering is at its peak in many parts of the country. Visitors to Japan during this period can join in the celebration of nature's beauty by strolling through some of the many gardens in which cherry trees grow.

In the Tokyo area, the best display is in Ueno Park, where 1,500 trees—stretching for miles along an aqueduct—stand in full bloom. Other gardens for blossom touring include the Imperial Palace, Shinjuku Gyoen, Koganei, and Tama Cemetery.

More than 4,000 trees bloom at Mukogaoka Recreation Ground southwest of Tokyo, near the Mukogaoka-Yuen Station of the Odakyu Electric Railway. A grove of 10,000 trees bursts into flower at Higashi-Yamatoshi near Lake Tama, outside Tokyo.

In Kyoto, extensive groves turn things rosy in late April along the Oi River in the vicinity of Arashiyama Park. The trees here were transplanted from Yoshino in the 13th century. In Kyoto's Maruyama Park, night-time illumination adds to the display during blossom season.

Yoshino, an otherwise sleepy little town about an hour's trip southeast of Osaka, becomes the focus of sightseers from all over Japan each April when more than 50,000 cherry trees splash pink across the Yoshino hills in groves originally planted by a 7th century Buddhist priest.

On Hokkaido, Japan's northern island, cherry trees wait until early May to blossom. There are large groves at Goryokaku Park, near the city of Hakodate, and at Matsumae.

Below, children frolic beneath a lacy canopy of blossoms in Tokyo's Shinjuku Gyoen Garden.

FESTIVAL TIME IN JAPAN

The Japanese thrive on festivals, which satisfy both a social and religious need. Vast numbers of people gather for these celebrations—some lighthearted, some solemn. Costumes, colors, and decorations follow centuries-old traditions.

New Year Days. Shrine visits are made and greetings exchanged during the first 3 days of the year. Streets are festive with arrangements of pine twigs and bamboo stalks, believed to bring good luck. Women wear their most colorful kimonos at this festive time.

Snow Festival. Elaborate snow sculptures line Sapporo's main street in early February. Similar festivals are held elsewhere on Hokkaido.

Bean-throwing Festival. On February 3 or 4, people at temples and shrines throughout Japan drive out imaginary evil spirits by shouting and tossing beans about. The celebration marks the last day of winter (according to the old lunar calendar). Big celebrations take place at Ikegami Hommonji Temple in Tokyo and at the Narita Fudo Temple in Chiba Prefecture.

Mandoro Festival. On February 3 or 4 and again on August 15, more than 3,000 lighted lanterns line the avenue to Nara's lovely Kasuga Shrine and hang beneath the shrine's eaves.

Buddha's Birthday (Flower Festival). On April 8, children in festive costumes visit Buddhist temples throughout the country.

Hollyhock Festival. Costumed marchers parade through the streets of Kyoto on May 15 to pay homage at the shrines of Shimokamo and Kamikamo. The parade reenacts an ancient imperial procession.

Sanja Festival. Tokyo's Asakusa Shrine is the scene of a festival and parade of colorful palanquins on the third weekend in May.

Grand Festival of Toshogu Shrine. More than 1,000 marchers, clad in feudal costumes and armed with swords and spears, participate in Nikko's gala procession on May 17 and 18.

Sanno Festival. Colorful shrine palanquins are carried through Tokyo streets to the Hie Shrine on June 15 in one of the city's happiest festivals.

O-Bon Festival (Feast of the Dead or Feast of Lanterns). Buddhists throughout Japan honor the souls of ancestors during this July 13 to 16 celebration. Special dances, called *Bon Odori*, are held in many cities. Thousands of lighted paper lanterns are launched on rivers and lakes to carry back to heaven the spirits who returned to earth during this period. Nagasaki observes the festival from August 13 to 15; Okinawa celebrates in traditional style in late August.

Gion Festival of Yasaka Shrine. Kyoto is the site of one of Japan's biggest and most spectacular festivals; it dates back to the 9th century. On July 17, tall and beautifully decorated floats parade through city streets.

Tenjin Festival of Temmangu Shrine. On July 25, gaily decorated boats sail down Osaka's canals to the accompaniment of a fireworks display.

Nebuta Festival. Huge papier-mâché dummies (called *nebuta*) representing animals, birds, and men are placed on carriages and pulled through the city streets. The festival is celebrated August 1 to 7 in Hirosaki and from August 3 to 7 in Aomori City.

Kanto Festival. Costumed men balance *kanto* (long bamboo poles hung with many lighted lanterns) on their hands, foreheads, or shoulders. The festival is celebrated in Akita from August 5 to 7 to encourage a bountiful harvest.

Awa Odori Festival. The entire city of Tokushima celebrates August 12 to 15 with a parade through the city and 4 days of music and dancing.

Autumn Festival of Toshogu Shrine. A thousand Nikko townsmen, armed as in the days of feudal warlords, parade on October 17.

Festival of Eras. Kyoto's *Jidai Matsuri* is held on October 22 at Heian Shrine. Celebrants parade in historical costume to commemorate the founding of the city.

Daimyo Gyoretsu. On November 3, marchers in feudal dress wind in stately fashion around Hakone's various hot springs resorts.

Children's Shrine Visiting Day. During the *Shichigosan* (literally "seven-five-three") Festival on November 15, parents take children of these ages to their guardian shrines, including the Meiji Shrine in Tokyo.

sun-washed city of palm trees and tropical flowers, thanks to a semitropical climate.

Miyazaki is rich in history and legend. The home of the first emperor, Jimmu, before he set out to conquer Japan, the city is supposedly the site of the first imperial palace. Beautiful Miyazaki Shrine, dedicated to Jimmu, is another spot worth visiting.

Replicas of ancient terra cotta figures and artifacts dug from 2,000-year-old burial mounds are scattered throughout Miyazaki's Haniwa Garden. Saito, about 15 miles northwest of Miyazaki, is the site of the ancient burial mounds of Saitobaru. The group of 380 mounds is strikingly similar to the burial grounds of Kyongju in Korea (see page 79).

A spectacularly scenic road follows the Nichinan coast south of Miyazaki to Shibushi Bay. Luxuriant subtropical and tropical plants line the route. In February, blooming cherry trees add to the roadside color.

Betel-nut palms and other subtropical vegetation cover the tiny islet of Aoshima. When the tide ebbs, notice how the island's wave-eroded coastline resembles a corrugated washboard.

South to Kagoshima

Southern Kyushu's largest city occupies the western shore of beautiful Kagoshima Bay (also called Kinko Bay), an elongated inlet cutting deeply into the southern end of the island. Kagoshima, a pleasant city, is a good excursion base from which to explore nearby points of interest. The hillside vantage point of Shiroyama Park provides you with an overall view of the city. Smoking Mount Sakurajima dominates the horizon.

Mount Sakurajima. Kagoshima's major attraction is this active, 1,118-meter/3,700-foot volcano. Located just across the bay from the city, it can be easily reached by ferry. Once an island, Mount Sakurajima became a peninsula in 1914 when a massive lava flow blocked the channel and connected the island with the eastern shore of the bay. A good road traverses the lunarlike landscape of the lava fields. Nearby are several hot spring spas.

Iso Park. Near the north end of the city lies Iso Park, site of a seaside villa noted for its 300-year-old landscaped gardens. A mill-turned-museum adjacent to the park features displays of old guns and glassware.

Kirishima-Yaku National Park. Lying about 50 km/30 miles north of Kagoshima, this scenic area contains 23 volcanoes, 15 craters, and 10 crater lakes.

Ibusuki. You'll find the island's most popular seaside resort an easy 48 km/30 miles south of Kagoshima. Dominating the beachfront is the huge Ibusuki Kanko Hotel. Underwater springs along the coast warm the swimming beach; in special locations, attendants dig holes for kimono-clad bathers, who are then covered from chin to toe with hot sand.

In winter, spring-warmed sand baths are available indoors. Nearby, a huge greenhouse jungle bath provides hot-spring pool soaking amid lush tropical vegetation.

Area attractions include the crater lake of Ikeda and Mount Kaimon, a nearly perfect volcanic cone. Enroute to Ibusuki from Kagoshima, you can stop to explore the village of Chiran. During feudal times this town was home to many of the island's samurai warriors—look for their homes and beautiful walled gardens. A number are still intact.

RUGGED, VERDANT HOKKAIDO

Mountainous Hokkaido marks the northernmost end of the Japanese archipelago. The Tsugaru Straits separate it from Honshu.

Though it contains nearly one-fifth of Japan's total land area, only about 5 percent of the nation's population lives here. A rugged land of great natural beauty, Hokkaido offers its visitors plenty of rewarding territory to explore. Deep lakes and dense forests cover substantial portions of the island. Many active and inactive volcanic cones mark the island's central highlands, numerous hot springs dot its southwest region, and in the west-central area, the Ishikari River drains an extensive fertile plain.

Hokkaido's climate differs from that of Japan's other islands. Summers, shorter than on Honshu, arrive about a month later. Winters are severe; snow begins to fall in late autumn and covers the ground for 5 to 6 months, providing a long season for skiing and other winter sports.

Flowers—cherry blossoms, crocuses, primroses, irises, lilies of the valley—seem to burst out all at once in late May. In summer, you'll find good hiking and camping in clear mountain air, excellent lake swimming, good salmon and trout fishing, and numerous campgrounds with cabins and tents available for rent.

Autumn brings spectacular color in September and October; days are warm, evenings crisp and cool, particularly in the mountains.

Hokkaido sightseeing

Sapporo, Hokkaido's largest city, is a 1¹/₂-hour flight from Tokyo. You can reach Hakodate, the island's other entry point and port city, by ferry or plane from Aomori on Honshu.

Though you'll probably do most of your traveling around Hokkaido by train, bus, or guide-driven car, this is one place in Japan where you could feel relatively relaxed with a rental car. The roads are narrow, but well maintained. For information on accommodations, see page 41.

Lanterns lend colorful accents *to Kumamoto's back streets and alleyways on Kyushu, Japan's third largest island.*

Sapporo, capital city

Hokkaido's main city consists of a checkerboard of broad, tree-lined boulevards. Odori Promenade is the city's flower-lined central parkway, Tanukikoji its main shopping street.

Massive, intricately carved snow statues dominate Sapporo's landscape during the city's annual February Snow Festival. You can see smaller ones in the heart of Sapporo at Odori Park. Larger sculptures (including replicas of famous buildings) are displayed at Makomanai, a short subway ride away. Many of the sculptures feature snow slides, tunnels, and stairways; these quickly become children's playgrounds.

Hokkaido University. The vast campus of Hokkaido University lies north of Sapporo station. Including its experimental farms, it covers an area of about 67,611 hectares/167,000 acres. The Botanical Gardens contain a stand of virgin forest and some 5,000 species of plants from around the world.

Also in the Botanical Gardens is the Ainu Museum, displaying over 20,000 items relating to this primitive race. The Ainu, members of an aboriginal race whose origins scientists still debate, dwell on Hokkaido. Like other primitive peoples in the world, their numbers are rapidly dwindling. Fewer than 17,000 are left. Gentle, farmer-fisher folk, the Ainu, unlike other Asians, have Caucasian features, light skin, and hairy bodies. At the village of Shiraoi, near Noboribetsu Spa on Hokkaido's south coast, you can see Ainu and look at a typical Ainu grass house. Ainu tribespeople are also in Akan National Park.

Other sights. Maruyama Park, situated at the foot of Maruyama Hill in the western part of the city, is noted for spring-blooming cherry and plum trees, its zoo, and the extensive virgin forest adjoining the park. Smaller Nakajima Park surrounds a pond; it has extensive sports facilities. Hokkaido Shrine, dating from 1869, is another place to enjoy cherry blossoms in late May.

Skiing center. During the 1972 Winter Olympics, held on Hokkaido, ski buffs added two new names to their lists of top international ski areas: Teine, where the slalom races were held, and Eniwa, site of the downhill races. Both are in the beautiful, birch-forested mountains ringing Sapporo. Mount Moiwa, 30 minutes by bus southwest of the city, overlooks the capital and the Sea of Japan. Skiers enjoy its slopes in winter.

Most skiers stay in a Sapporo hotel and commute to the slopes as the locals do—by taxi (equipped with ski rack) or by bus.

A host of national parks

Hokkaido boasts some of Japan's most scenic national parks—beautiful wilderness areas dotted with volcanoes (many of them active), lakes, forests, and spas.

Shikotsu-Toya National Park. Covering 971 square km/375 square miles southwest of Sapporo, this park has volcanoes and caldera lakes, as well as forests, valleys, and hot springs. Of the volcanic mountains, 1,893-meter/6,209-foot Mount Yotei is celebrated for its graceful contour, while 1,042-meter/3,359-foot Mount Tarumae is renowned as a triple volcano.

Another principal feature of the park is Lake Toya, a caldera lake 43 km/27 miles in circumference. On its shores are hot springs and Toyako Spa, with numerous inns and hotels.

One of Hokkaido's best-known mountain resorts is Jozankei Spa in the thickly wooded gorge of the Toyohira River, a 45-minute bus ride from Sapporo.

Daisetsuzan National Park. Called the "roof of Hokkaido," this mountainous wilderness of 2,344 square km/905 square miles is the largest of Japan's national parks. It includes the island's highest mountains. You reach the park in central Hokkaido by train from Sapporo by way of Asahikawa.

One of the most beautiful Daisetsuzan touring routes skirts the northern edge of the park from Asahikawa eastward to Sounkyo Spa, a 2-hour trip by bus. The spa, tourist center of the district, is in the middle of Sounkyo Gorge, a defile flanked by unusual rock walls and waterfalls rising to 137 meters/450 feet.

Akan National Park. Located east of Daisetsuzan, this park contains 881 square km/340 square miles of volcanic mountains, primeval forests, and crater lakes. Growing in Lake Akan is a *marimo*, a strange spherical weed found only in two other places: in Switzerland and on the Russian island of Sakhalin. This unusual water plant absorbs oxygen from the water it lives in. It rises to the surface of the lake to release oxygen and sinks back into the water once the gas has been released.

Buses travel to the park from Bihoro, Obihiro, Kushiro, and other points. Not far from Kushiro is Kushiro Marshy National Park's vast swampy fields, home of red-crested white cranes.

Shiretoko National Park. This remote park lies on the narrow Shiretoko Peninsula on Hokkaido's northeastern tip. Though its topography is volcanic, some of its most dramatic features— rocks eroded by the sea and precipices hanging 183 meters/600 feet above the water—are best seen by sightseeing boat (available in summer at Utoro).

SOUTH TO THE RYUKYUS

The 73 islands in the Ryukyu chain compose a gentle southwesterly arc 684 km/425 miles south of Kyushu and the main part of the Japanese archipelago. These southerly islands have a semitropical climate, and remain lush and green the year around.

Temperatures are generally mild, though they can climb into the low 90s in summer and drop to the low 50s in winter. Rain-laden storms frequently sweep across the archipelago, keeping humidity high; some of these storms reach typhoon proportions. The coolest, driest period—and best time to visit—is from October through March.

Okinawa, the hub

Largest and most developed of Japan's islands is Okinawa, about 1,600 km/1,000 miles southwest of Tokyo. Sunny skies, sandy beaches, and warm, clear waters make this island a popular vacation destination for Japanese tourists. Nearly 113 km/70 miles long and varying from 27 km/17 miles to 43 km/27 miles wide, Okinawa supports a population of more than a million.

During Okinawa's early history, the island had closer trade and cultural ties with China than with Japan. But in 1609 a force of 3,000 Satsuma invaders defeated the weak, almost defenseless Okinawan army, and the island came under Japanese administration.

Official involvement between Okinawa and the United States began in 1853 when Commodore Perry landed, signing a pact of friendship with the Okinawan government. Nearly a century later—early in 1945—the U.S. and Japan fought the last major battle of World War II on the island. Okinawa was administered by the U.S. from the end of the war until May 15, 1972, when it was returned to Japanese jurisdiction.

Exploring Naha

Naha, Okinawa's capital, is the island's transportation hub and a good starting point for tours of Okinawa and other Ryukyu islands. Airline flights link Naha Airport with Tokyo (2¹/₂ hours) and other Japanese cities, as well as with Taiwan, Hong Kong, Guam, and the Philippines. Island transportation includes taxis, buses, and local tours. For information on accommodations, see page 41.

Situated on the island's west coast, Naha was almost leveled during World War II, but has since been completely rebuilt. The city's population exceeds 300,000. On Kokusai-dori, Naha's most fashionable shopping street, you can browse through shops and department stores for jewelry, watches, and typical handicraft items. Okinawan artists make lacquerware, *Tsuboya* ware (pottery), *bingata* (vivid batik-type fabrics), and *bashofu* (a handwoven cloth made of banana tree fibers and unique to Okinawa). Local traditions and history are reflected in the articles' designs.

Before setting out to explore the island, take a look at Naha's main sights.

Naminoue Shrine. Thousands of Okinawan Shintoists, clad in bright holiday kimonos, come here to worship every New Year. From the shrine's garden, enjoy the superb view over the East China Sea.

Tomari (International) Cemetery. Many foreigners who died on Okinawa—including a number of Commodore Perry's men—are buried here. The oldest graves are those of Chinese immigrants from the 1750s. A nearby monument marks the place where Perry and his crewmen first landed on the island.

University of the Ryukyus. The site of Shuri Castle, seat of the Okinawan government for many centuries, is now a university campus. Originally constructed in 1188, the castle was destroyed during the 1945 battle for Okinawa. The gate at the entrance to the university is a reconstruction of the castle's original gate.

Beyond Naha

Elsewhere on the island you'll see sugar cane fields and, near the fishing village of Itoman, interesting old tortoise-shaped tombs. At the southern end of the island are memorials to World War II dead. North of Naha, the island is principally known for its pineapple fields, beaches, and marine attractions.

Okinawa Marine Park. About halfway up the island, near Nago, the Okinawa Marine Park offers an underwater observatory, aquarium, beach areas for water sports, glass-bottom boats, and a fine restaurant.

Motobu Peninsula. Several of the attractions constructed for the Expo '75 International Ocean Exposition remain as permanent installations on the western end of Motobu Peninsula.

Among these is the Oceanic Culture Museum, a multihalled complex whose exhibits portray the traditions and cultural patterns of peoples of the Pacific.

Another is the Aquapolis, a unique floating city designed to show the practicality of habitation on a seaborne vessel. The two-story structure contains a submersible deck, underwater observatory, moving walkway, café-terrace, and life capsule to provide working and living quarters for residents.

Visitors can view coral reefs and underwater life at Expo Memorial Park.

Other island attractions. Elsewhere on the island you can visit the ruins of Nago, Nakijin, and Nakagusuku castles; the Yudori tombs and the Futenma Shrine in the Futenma area; the bullfighting arena at Gushikawa (bullfights are generally held on Sundays); and the seashell museum, stalactite grotto, and Buddhist temple near Kin.

Trips to other islands

From Naha you can travel by plane or boat to other islands in the Ryukyu group. Principal islands are Miyako, Ishigaki, and Iriomote. Iriomote National Park's marine areas are known for their large-scale coral reefs.

KNOW BEFORE YOU GO

Here are some important facts and details to help you in planning your trip to Japan:

Entry/exit procedures. Tourists entering Japan need only a passport and a tourist visa. Free to U.S. citizens, the visas are valid for 5 years; you can get one at a Japanese consulate (in New York, Boston, Chicago, Kansas City, Atlanta, New Orleans, Houston, Seattle, Portland, San Francisco, Los Angeles, Honolulu, or Anchorage) or at the Japanese Embassy in Washington, D.C.

Steamship passengers without visas may obtain a special in-transit landing permit good for 15 days, provided they travel by a designated route and depart by the same vessel they arrived on. Air and sea passengers with a stopover of 72 hours or less may be granted a permit for landing without a visa if they limit their travel to areas near the airport or port.

If coming from an area where a cholera breakout has occurred, you'll need an international health certificate showing inoculation against the disease. Check with the U.S. Public Health Service for other recommended inoculations.

Departing passengers (except those in transit or under 2 years old) pay an airport departure tax when flying out of Tokyo's Narita Airport: adults ¥2000, children 2 to 12 years ¥1000.

Customs. Visitors to Japan may take in 400 cigarettes, 500 grams of tobacco or 100 cigars, three bottles of liquor, and a reasonable amount of film.

Currency. Japan's *yen* is the official currency. You can take yen into Japan or convert your dollars at authorized foreign exchange banks or authorized money changers (located at airports and seaports). When converting money, you will be issued a *Record of Purchase of Foreign Means of Payment*. Upon departure you may be asked to show this paper.

Health conditions. Hospital and medical services are good; many English-speaking doctors are available. Medicines and toiletries can be purchased in all large cities. In the cities, drinking water is excellent.

Time. The time difference between the U.S. west coast and Japan is 17 hours. When it's noon Sunday in Tokyo, it's 7 P.M. Saturday in San Francisco.

Tipping. A service charge, varying from 10 to 15 percent, will usually be levied by hotels and restaurants. Tipping is unnecessary for taxi drivers, sightseeing bus drivers, bellboys, and guides; but a 10 percent tip is customary for drivers of hired cars.

Language. In the main cities, you'll find English spoken by travel industry personnel and some store sales people. The Japan National Tourist Organization's Japan Travel-Phone service provides English-language assistance and travel information throughout Japan. It also publishes a useful *Tourist's Handbook*.

Climate. Though Japan's climate is temperate, the country does have decided seasonal changes. Since Japan stretches some 2,993 km/1,860 miles from north to south, you'll find considerable temperature differences between Hokkaido, the northernmost island, and Okinawa, the southernmost.

The climate of Honshu, the main island, is frequently compared to that of America's Midwest, although Honshu rarely experiences such extreme temperatures. The best months for visiting are March, April and May (blossom time), and October and November (brilliant foliage and chrysanthemum time). From mid-June to early July, rain falls nearly every day. July, August, and early September are hot (low 70s to high 90s) and humid.

Hokkaido and northern Honshu get considerable snowfall, but the southern half of Honshu and the large island of Kyushu have very mild winters (40s to 60s). Tokyo may get a few light snowfalls in February or March. Okinawa enjoys a semitropical climate.

As a general rule, pack lightweight clothing for spring and summer visits, and lightweight woolens, sweaters, and jackets for autumn visits. A warm topcoat or extra warm sweaters are essential for winter.

Local customs. Try to match the courtesy of the Japanese. As you enter temple buildings, remove any head covering and your shoes. In entering Japanese houses or inns), remove shoes and slippers as custom indicates (see page 36).

For more information. Your best source of information is the Japan National Tourist Organization. Its headquarters is on the 10th Floor, Tokyo Kotsu Kaikan Bldg., 10-1, 2-chome, Yuraku-cho, Chiyoda-ku, Tokyo. U.S. branch offices are in New York, Chicago, Dallas, San Francisco, and Los Angeles.

The Japan National Tourist Organization has Tourist Information Centers in Tokyo and at New Tokyo International Airport (Narita) (see "The Essentials/Tokyo," page 25) and in Kyoto (1st floor, Kyoto Tower Bldg., Higashi-Shiokojicho, Shimogyoku).

KOREA

A unique travel destination encompassing bustling
cities, jagged mountains, ancient royal tombs,
pine-dotted islands, ornate palaces, shimmering blue
waterways, sandy beaches, spicy cuisine

P oetically called "The Land of the Morning Calm," Korea has more than one country's share of breathtaking scenery. Just a day's trip east of the modern capital of Seoul takes you into the rugged glory of Mount Sorak National Park, where jagged peaks soar above pine forests and cascading waterfalls. Along the country's southern coast, tiny tree-clad islands, sleepy fishing villages, and a vast expanse of calm, blue water greet you along the Hallyo Waterway. Near the southern tip of the peninsula, the volcanic island of Cheju juts majestically out of the ocean, an enchanting, windswept spot famed for its scenic beauty.

The Korean peninsula has for centuries served as a passageway for foreign invaders—Asians en route to Japan, or Japanese (before and during their 36-year-occupation) bound for Asia. World War II and the Korean War split the nation physically and politically, creating two separate countries—North Korea and South Korea. The northern portion is now the Democratic People's Republic of Korea. The southern segment, though officially named the Republic of Korea, is known as South Korea or, simply, Korea, and it is with this country that this chapter deals.

Despite its strife-ridden past, Korea has survived—with style. Seoul resembles large cities everywhere. Buildings and modern hotels tower over busy expressways. But, never far away, tucked into the contemporary cityscape, are ancient palaces and relic-filled museums, reminders of the country's long history of dynastic rule.

Beyond Seoul, rural life is little changed from bygone days. Country people live in cottages of mud and stone, enclosed by walls; farmers still work their fields entirely by hand; occasional harvest dances and regional festivals reflect age-old traditions. Just 322 km/200 miles southeast of the capital stands the ancient royal city of Kyongju, once the center of the Silla Dynasty. At the peninsula's southern tip, the modern port city of Pusan offers a pleasing mixture of sandy beaches and Buddhist temples and monasteries.

A GEOGRAPHICAL SKETCH

The Korean peninsula pushes out to sea some 960 km/600 miles southward beyond the Asian mainland. South Korea is in the lower half, bordered by the Democratic People's Republic of Korea (North Korea) in the upper arm of the peninsula. North Korea, in turn, is bordered by China and the Soviet Union. Japan lies 112 km/70 miles east of South Korea's southern tip. The Yellow Sea washes the western shores of the Korean peninsula; on the east, the land meets the East Sea, beyond which is the Sea of Japan.

A rugged landscape

South Korea stretches about 483 km/300 miles south from the Demilitarized Zone that separates North and South Korea. The country's total area is 99,135 square km/ 38,276 square miles.

Forested mountains ripple the landscape of northern and eastern South Korea. Along the east coast, these craggy pinnacles drop abruptly to the sea in a shoreline

Fanciful figures, abstract patterns, brilliant paintings add artistic touches to Kyongju's Pulguksa Temple.

of sheer cliffs. Toward the west and south, the country's mountainous backbone diminishes into smoother plains and basins. Myriad bays and inlets bite into the gently sloping western coast. South Korea includes some 3,000 islands, sprinkled mostly beyond its western and southern peninsular shores.

Wildlife and crops

Between the northern plant forms of Manchuria and Siberia, and the subtropical vegetation of southern Japan, Korea forms a sort of transitional zone. Coniferous forests grace its higher altitudes, and broad-leafed evergreens grow in the south. Few virgin forests remain; most existing forest consists of secondary growth and reforested areas.

Groves of pine and broad-leafed trees cluster sporadically on the undulating hills, especially near Buddhist temples and historical sites. Barley, wheat, soybeans, and millet grow on the upper fields, and rice is cultivated in the lowlands.

Despite recent conservation efforts, tigers, leopards, wild boar, and lynxes that once roamed both forests and cultivated lands have now disappeared. Bears and wolves can still be found in mountainous areas. Protected species include the woodpecker, Chindo dog, and several species of migratory birds.

A LENGTHY HISTORY

Archeological finds indicate that paleolithic man lived in Korea at least 30,000 years ago, having migrated south from Manchuria. According to Korean legend, a mythical being called *Tangun* descended from heaven and became chief of the primitive clans and tribes living on the rugged peninsula. Either way, this is a land of history.

Kingdoms, then dynasties

From the various tribal groups living in Korea, three kingdoms developed between the 2nd and 4th centuries: They were Koguryo in the north, Paekche in the central southwest, and Silla in the southeast, and they waged war for hundreds of years. Finally, in 668, Silla conquered the other two, uniting the population for the first time under one sovereignty.

By 918, corruption, strife, and decentralization had weakened the empire born of Silla's victory. A new dynasty, Koryo (from which Korea derived its name), came into power.

In the 11th century, Tartar and Mongol armies invaded Korea, and Kublai Khan swept down from China in 1213. Eventually the Mongols began a 130-year occupation of the country, exploiting and humiliating the Koreans. When the Ming Dynasty replaced the Mongols in China, a simultaneous palace coup in Korea launched the Choson (also known as Yi) Dynasty in 1392.

During the long Choson Dynasty (1392–1910), Korea achieved its greatest cultural triumphs. Most important was the development of a phonetic alphabet called *hangul*, considered one of the most precise writing systems ever devised. Great advances were made in science, philosophy, music, and technology as well.

Foreign invaders

From 1592 to 1598, Japan invaded the peninsula, intending to go on to conquer China. Though the Japanese were successful on land, the Koreans' iron-clad ships wreaked havoc on the Japanese navy.

Thirty years later Korea again suffered invasion, this time from the north, by Manchurian warriors. Korea's response to this intrusion and other skirmishes with foreigners was to withdraw from contact with the outside world for the next 250 years. Reluctantly, it finally opened its ports to Japan in 1876, and during the 1880s signed treaties of friendship and commerce with the United States and several European countries.

The turn of the century saw an Asian power struggle among Japan, China, and Russia that resulted in a Japanese takeover of Korea in 1910. Japan's rule lasted through the end of World War II.

After Japan's defeat in that war, Korea was divided at the 38th parallel and occupied by Russian troops to the north and American troops to the south. On August 15, 1948, Syngman Rhee, first president of the Republic of Korea, took control of South Korea from the U.S. Military government; by the end of 1948, the Democratic People's Republic of Korea was established in the north.

War breaks out

Stability was short-lived. North Korean troops swarmed across the 38th parallel on June 25, 1950, capturing the South Korean capital city of Seoul in 3 days. By August they had pushed down the peninsula to Pusan. Under the United Nations banner, 16 countries responded to the defense of South Korea.

Within 3 months the U.N. and Republic of Korea forces pushed the North Koreans back up the peninsula to the Yalu River on the Chinese border. The fighting flowed back and forth when Chinese soldiers entered the war. Finally the situation stabilized once again near the 38th parallel.

The Korean War technically ended on July 27, 1953, when an armistice agreement was signed. Since then, the Armistice Commission has held many meetings at Panmunjom in the Demilitarized Zone between North and South Korea, in an attempt to settle alleged violations of the truce terms and create a peace treaty.

Elections and martial law

President Syngman Rhee won reelection in 1952, 1956, and 1960. He resigned shortly after the 1960 election

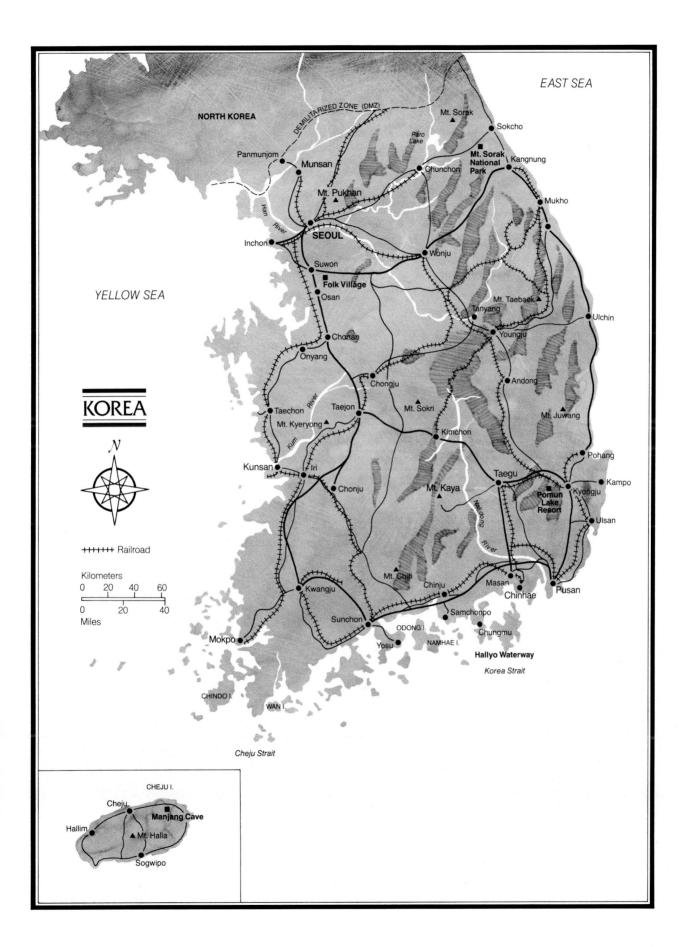

EAST SEA

NORTH KOREA

DEMILITARIZED ZONE (DMZ)

Mt. Sorak ▲

Paro Lake

Sokcho

Panmunjom ● ● Munsan

Chunchon ●

Mt. Sorak National Park ■

Kangnung

Mt. Pukhan ▲

Mukho ●

Han River

SEOUL

Inchon ●

Wonju ●

Suwon ●

Folk Village ■

Osan ●

Mt. Taebaek ▲

YELLOW SEA

Tanyang ●

Ulchin ●

Chonan ●

Youngju ●

Onyang ●

Chongju ●

Andong ●

Kum River

Taechon ●

Taejon ●

Mt. Sokri ▲

Mt. Kyeryong ▲

Mt. Juwang ▲

KOREA

N

Kimchon ●

Pohang ●

Kunsan ●

Iri ●

Taegu ●

Kampo ●

Chonju ●

Mt. Kaya ▲

Pomun Lake Resort ■

Kyongju ●

Railroad

Ulsan ●

Kilometers

0 20 40 60

Nakdong River

Masan ●

0 20 40

Miles

Mt. Chiri ▲

Chinju ●

Chinhae ●

Pusan ●

Kwangju ●

Sunchon ●

Samchonpo ●

ODONG I.

Chungmu ●

Mokpo ●

Yosu ●

NAMHAE I.

Hallyo Waterway

Korea Strait

CHINDO I.

WAN I.

Cheju Strait

CHEJU I.

Cheju ●

Manjang Cave ■

Hallim ●

▲ Mt. Halla

Sogwipo ●

Village elders *soak up spring sun near ancient burial mounds and royal tomb sites that protrude from Kyongju plain.*

Radiant fabrics *line walls, crowd counters in Korean Folk Village's costume shop. Short side trip from Seoul offers capsule look at re-created way of life.*

following numerous student demonstrations.

Major General Park Chung Hee staged a military coup, became acting president, and rewrote the constitution under martial law. He formed the Democratic Republican Party. As its presidential candidate, he won election in 1963, 1967, and 1971.

On October 17, 1972, President Park again declared martial law, and under a new constitution approved in a public referendum, the president's powers were expanded. But in October 1979, he was assassinated.

Korea's current president is Roh Tae Woo.

A PROUD AND ANCIENT PEOPLE

Koreans are descended from a melting pot of Mongol tribes that migrated south from Central Asia. Eventually the people interbred, becoming a homogeneous group with a culture all its own. Despite Korea's proximity to China and its 36 years of domination by Japan, its people have maintained a distinct cultural identity. They have preserved their own unique customs, dress, cuisine, arts, and language.

Today's Koreans

Prior to 1930 most Koreans lived on farms, but today about 60 percent of Korea's 40 million people live in cities, towns, and large villages. In Seoul, the population exceeds 10 million.

Though most city dwellers wear western clothing, you'll still see people—especially in the countryside—in the national dress. For men, this includes the *paji* (baggy trousers gathered at the ankles), a *chogori* (loose jacket), and a *turumagi* (long flowing overcoat). The upper-class male's traditional headgear—called a *kat* and woven of coarse horsehair that is heavily varnished—resembles a tall stovepipe hat.

Traditionally garbed Korean women appear fragile and feminine in the *chogori-chima,* a short flared jacket or blouse tied with ribbons and worn over a high-waisted skirt. Favorite colors are white and light blue.

Religious beliefs

Korea's main religion is Buddhism, which has played an important historical role in Korea's cultural development. Christianity, followed by about 20 percent of the populace, has been practiced since the 19th century.

TRIP PLANNING AIDS

A number of international airlines, including Korean Air, fly into Korea from cities around the world. (Korea is 8,000 air miles from the U.S. west coast.) Besides Seoul's Kimpo International Airport, the country's main entry point, there are international airports at Pusan and Cheju Island as well.

Certain cruise and cargo/passenger shipping companies include the Korean ports of Pusan or Inchon on their Orient itineraries. Ferries transport both passengers and vehicles between Pusan and Shimonoseki, Japan, daily except Saturdays and between Pusan and Osaka, Japan, twice weekly.

Hotel choices

Throughout Korea, comfortable tourist hotels await you in large towns and at popular resorts and sightseeing spots. Many of these are air-conditioned western-style high-rise buildings—but very few have a fourth floor, because in Korea four is an unlucky number. Hotels usually feature both Korean and western restaurant fare, coffee shops, cocktail lounges, nightclubs, and barber and beauty shops; several hotels offer swimming pools, shopping arcades, and health clubs.

In small towns and villages, *yokwan* (Korean-style inns) may be the only available accommodation. Less expensive and similar to Japanese *ryokan* (see page 36), these inns offer a chance to experience the Korean way of life.

Local transportation

Within Korea, a traveler can choose from all the usual modes of transport: air, rail, bus, rental car, and taxi.

Traveling around the country. Korean Air schedules frequent connections between major cities, and Korean National Railway, an excellent system, allows access to most corners of the country. Among several types of service, the speediest is the *Saemaul* (super express), Korea's equivalent of Japan's bullet train. A less expensive choice would be the air-conditioned buses that link major cities with efficient service. Local buses (without air conditioning) connect towns and villages.

Both chauffeur-driven and self-drive cars are available for hire. Most road signs are in both Korean and English. However, since traffic careens at a frantic pace (supposedly only on the right), it could be hazardous to take the wheel.

City transport. For greatest freedom and ease in getting around cities inexpensively, use metered taxis. Seoul has three types of taxis. Yellow and green taxis are inexpensive, and beige "call" taxis are moderately priced. Drivers may not speak English; have your hotel clerk write out your destination in Korean.

Tours. Korea's tour operators offer a wide variety of excursions to show the city sights of Seoul and such nearby attractions as Kyongju, Pusan, Mount Sorak, the East Coast, Cheju Island, and Chungmu.

Dining out

Korea's distinctive national cuisine features spicy food, some dishes zestier than others. Prevalent are such flavor enhancers as garlic, red peppers, sesame oil, and soy sauce.

Local food and drink. Be sure to try these popular Korean specialties: *pulgogi* (strips of beef marinated in a blend of soy sauce, sesame oil, garlic, onion, and spices, then broiled over a charcoal brazier); *shinsollo* (meat, fish, eggs, vegetables, and nuts cooked at your table in a charcoal-heated, chimneyed "hot pot"); and *kalbi* (steamed or broiled ribs).

A typical Korean meal includes a meat or fish soup, rice, and several meat and vegetable dishes. No menu is complete without *kimchi*, a peppery combination of

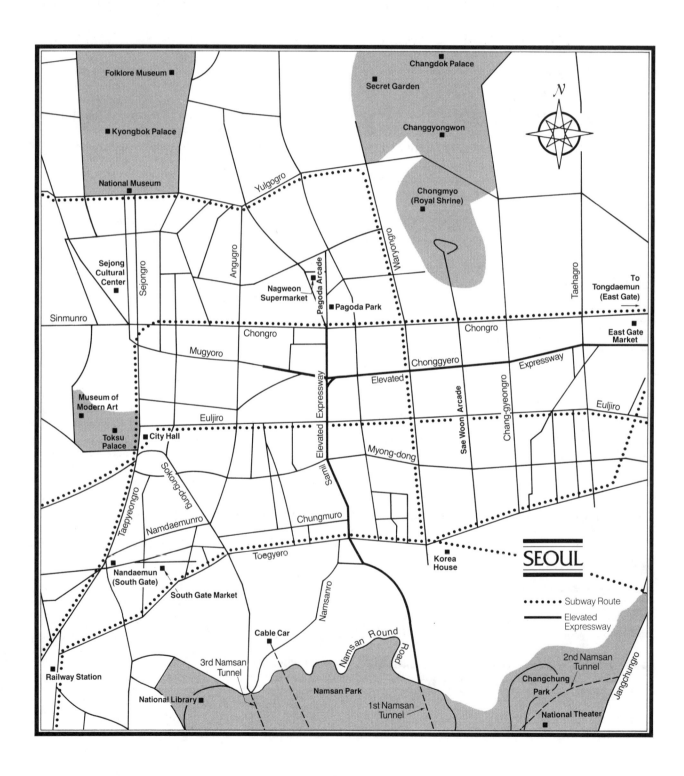

pickled cabbage, turnips, radishes, and other vegetables, fermented together in large earthenware jars.

Local beers are OB and Crown. You have a choice of three traditional wines: *takchu*, *yakchu*, and *soju*, the latter being the strongest.

Dining establishments. Most major hotels have several restaurants, offering you a choice of western, Chinese, Japanese, and Korean cuisine. Outside the hotels, major cities have a variety of restaurants worth trying, and prices are generally reasonable.

The entertainment scene

Korea's nightclubs are found mainly in hotels; elsewhere in major cities, the after-dark entertainment scene includes theater, restaurants, discotheques, cocktail lounges, and dance halls, as well as the casinos of Seoul, Inchon, Pusan, Kyongju, and Cheju Island.

Shopping discoveries

Browsing through department stores, arcades, city markets, and roadside stores can be rewarding. Prices are

THE ESSENTIALS/**SEOUL**

Korea's capital city of Seoul offers all the conveniences and comforts a traveler could wish.

Getting there

Most people fly to Seoul, but you can also arrive by sea. Trains and buses, as well as domestic flights, connect the capital with other points on the peninsula.

Air. Korean and many foreign carriers provide international service to and from Seoul. Korean Air also links Seoul with major Korean cities. To reach your hotel from Kimpo International Airport—about a 40-minute ride—you can catch either an airport express bus or a taxi.

Sea. If you travel by ship, you'll probably dock at either Inchon or Pusan.

Rail and bus. Express train and bus services connect Seoul with numerous domestic destinations.

Hotel choices

Accommodations range from modest to luxurious. Better hotels offer most modern amenities, including air conditioning.

Seoul has many fine hotels, including the centrally located King Sejong, Koreana, Lotte, Pacific, Plaza, President, Royal, Seoulin, and Westin Chosun. Namsan area hotels include the Ambassador, Hilton International, Hyatt Regency, Shilla, and Tower. Others include the Hotel Seoul Olympic, in the northern hills; the Riverside and Seoul Palace, south of the Han River; and the Sheraton Walker Hill, a resort-gambling complex 16 km/10 miles southeast of the city.

Getting around

Local transportation includes bus, subway, and taxi services. Rental cars with drivers are also available, and express buses travel to outlying areas.

Tours

Beyond the sights of Seoul, day tours may taken in Suwon (see page 79), Panmunjom (page 79), and the Korean Folk Village (page 77). An overnight excursion will show you Mount Sorak National Park (page 79).

Dining out

Major hotels in Seoul have excellent restaurants and coffee shops serving western and Japanese fare, as well as Korean dishes.

The city abounds with small, family-run Korean restaurants where you can sample the country's traditional cuisine (see page 72) at reasonable prices. There are even restaurants specializing in a particular dish like *samgye-t'ang* (ginseng chicken soup) or *naengmyon* (cold buckwheat noodles).

There are also fast food places selling hamburgers and pizzas.

Entertainment

Traditional Korean dancers perform regularly at Korea House (see page 77) and during hotel theater-restaurant and nightclub floor-shows. For other traditional entertainment, try the National Theater or the Sejong Cultural Center.

Each major hotel has its nightclub, with a band for dancing. Bars, beer halls, cabarets, and nightclubs brighten the after-dark hours throughout Seoul. Korea's most famous nightspot is the Pacific Nightclub at Walker Hill, where a gambling casino also operates 24 hours a day, 7 days a week.

For more information. The Korea National Tourism Corporation maintains information centers at its head office in Seoul, located at 10 Ta-dong, Chung-gu, and at all airports in Korea.

fixed in department stores, but bargaining remains a way of life in other places. Department stores are open from 10 A.M. to 7 P.M. daily (except 1 day every other week); smaller stores are open from 8 A.M. to 10 P.M.

What to buy. Handicrafts and souvenirs include lacquerware (some inlaid with mother-of-pearl), brassware, bamboo items, ceramics, gold and silver jewelry, amethyst and smoky topaz gems, silks and silk brocades, hand-tailored clothing, factory-made garments, embroidery, costumed dolls, and celadon ware.

What not to buy. The United States restricts the import of products made from animals and plants it has officially listed as endangered or threatened. The fact that these items are sold abroad doesn't mean they'll be allowed into the United States (see page 9).

Recreation

Sports fans, whether spectators or participants, will find Korea eventful—with both the new and the familiar.

Traditional athletics include *taekwondo* (Korea's national form of martial arts), *ssirum* (wrestling), *yudo* (judo), and *kung-do* (archery). Soccer stands out as the most popular modern spectator sport—followed by track and field events, baseball, volleyball, Ping-Pong, football, boxing, weight lifting, and horse racing.

With eight national parks, Korea offers hikers and mountain climbers plenty to explore. In addition there are golf, tennis, horseback riding, fishing, swimming, water-skiing, and snow skiing at five ski resorts from December through February.

SEOUL, A MODERN CAPITAL

Strolling Seoul's broad boulevards today, it's difficult to believe that as recently as 1953, much of the city lay in rubble. But extensive restorations have erased most of the war-inflicted scars, and modern Seoul stands as a stunning showcase of Korean enterprise. It received additional attention as host city for the 1986 Asian Games and the 1988 Summer Olympic Games. The country's political capital also serves as the cultural, commercial, and industrial center of South Korea.

Lining the main streets are high-rise buildings of steel and glass. In the shadows of these modern edifices stand traditional tile-roofed houses, stately old palaces, tranquil gardens, and treasure-filled museums, reminding you of Korea's heritage. Beyond the rush of the busy thoroughfares, narrow alleys connect hodgepodge rows of tiny houses, each squeezed against its neighbor and shielded from the street by a high wall.

Seoul's history as a political center dates back to 18 B.C. when it was the capital of the Paekche Kingdom. This site again became the capital in 1394, when King Taejo, founder of the Choson Dynasty, chose the land on the north side of the great bend in the Han River for his principal city. He enclosed it by building miles of fortified walls and massive gates. Segments of the wall and five of the city's nine original gates survive. Namdaemun, the Great South Gate, marks the city center. Originally constructed in 1398 and considered Korea's foremost national treasure, the gate has been dismantled and rebuilt several times.

Getting your bearings

For a bird's-eye view of Seoul, take a cable car to the top of Namsan (South Mountain). Rising 275 meters/901 feet from the city's center, the peak can also be reached by car. Atop the wooded mountain stands the 479-meter/1,571-foot Seoul Tower, its observation deck commanding a spectacular view of the city and the mountain-rimmed bowl in which it sits.

Far below, elevated expressways snake their way around glass high-rise buildings. At the northern end of the city, bordering the foot of the mountains, you can glimpse royal palaces built by King Taejo in Seoul's earliest days; nearby stand the Blue House (presidential residence), executive offices, the National Museum, and other government structures. Spreading south of the palaces are major office buildings, stores, and markets.

Palaces and parks

The flavor of Seoul's royal past lingers on in beautifully preserved palace compounds. Sheltered from the noise of modern city life, you can stroll through exquisite grounds among examples of intricate early Korean architecture.

Kyongbok Palace. Set behind the National Museum at the north end of Sejongro, this palace was originally built in 1395 by King Taejo. It was burned during the Japanese invasion of 1592, and not rebuilt until 1867.

Within its 16-hectare/40-acre compound stands a 10-story, intricately decorated pagoda. But chief among the wonders here is the Kyonghoeru banquet hall, which seems to float on its surrounding pond strewn with lotus blossoms. It is a hall without walls, its tile roof supported by 48 stone pillars.

Changdok Palace and Secret Garden. About a mile east of Kyongbok Palace, a massive wooden gate dating from the late 14th century marks the main entrance to Changdok Palace, one of Seoul's oldest buildings. Originally constructed by the Choson Dynasty in 1405 as a separate eastern palace for Kyongbok, Changdok Palace was destroyed during the Japanese invasion of 1592 and rebuilt in 1611.

Though the palace buildings aren't as grand as those of Kyongbok, this more extensive complex remains the most beautifully preserved of Seoul's royal

Cheju market stalls *offer shoppers array of vegetables, fruits, clothing, hats. City is gateway to island's popular scenic vacation attractions.*

Hallyo Waterway *stretches west from port of Pusan along southern coastline to Yosu. Hydrofoils ply island-studded waters, pass through national maritime park.*

residences. Deep inside the grounds is the large, beautifully landscaped Piwon (Secret Garden). Here, inviting paths lead to pavilions, ponds, springs, wooded areas, and a replica of an upper-class country house.

Changgyongwon. A gateway on the eastern side of Changdok's Secret Garden leads to a beautiful park surrounding a few remaining buildings of yet another Choson Dynasty palace called Changgyong.

Toksu Palace. Across from the Seoul City Plaza on Taepyeongro, Toksu Palace was originally built in the 1500s as a royal villa. Among its impressive attractions are the Throne Hall and the Museum of Modern Art, the latter located in one of several Renaissance-style buildings added to the grounds near the start of this century.

Other attractions

In addition to palaces and parks, Seoul offers a bounty of historical landmarks and museums.

Historical collections. Don't miss the National Museum, housed in the former five-story capitol building on the grounds of Kyongbok Palace. Some 23 well-lighted exhibition rooms display 7,500 art and historic objects featuring the history and culture of Korea, with emphasis on the Choson Dynasty (1392–1910). Japanese and Chinese culture are represented as well.

Treasures include royal jewels, Buddhist-oriented works from the Silla era, famed celadon ceramics from the Koryo Dynasty, and *punchong* ware and paintings from the Choson Dynasty. There are also 1,000-year-old Buddha images, ancient coins, weapons, central Asian relics, and Chinese and Japanese artifacts.

Also on the palace grounds is the National Folk Museum. Some 5,000 exhibits ranging from cooking utensils to costumes and folk art depict Korean life during the dynastic periods.

The museums are open from 9 A.M. to 5 P.M. The National Museum is closed on Mondays, and the National Folk Museum on Tuesdays.

FESTIVAL TIME IN KOREA

Korean holidays—whether religious, political, or simply traditional—celebrate the country's rich heritage. Some events occur by the lunar calendar, falling on a different day each year. When you arrive, check with the Korea National Tourism Corporation (see page 73) or read one of Seoul's English-language newspapers for currently scheduled celebrations.

New Year's Day. The first three days of the new year are highlighted with family celebrations. People wear their best clothes, and children bow to parents and grandparents to reaffirm family ties.

Independence Movement Day. Celebrated on March 1, this holiday recalls the Korean uprising against the Japanese in 1919. There's a ceremonial reading of the Korean Proclamation of Independence.

Buddha's Birthday. Religious ceremonies in May at Buddhist temples throughout the country commemorate Buddha's birth. Lanterns decorate temple courtyards and are carried in evening parades.

Memorial Day. On June 6, the country honors its war dead with memorial services at national cemeteries throughout the country.

Constitution Day. The country celebrates the 1948 proclamation of the constitution of the Republic of Korea each year on July 17.

Liberation Day. Parades highlight August 15, the anniversary of Korea's 1945 liberation from the Japanese. The date also marks the formal proclamation of the Republic of Korea.

Moon Festival (Chusok). This harvest celebration—Korea's Thanksgiving—occurs in late September or early October. Many people visit their ancestors' tombs and make food offerings.

National Foundation Day. On October 3, the country celebrates the legendary founding of Korea by Tangun, who established the kingdom of Ancient Choson in 2333 B.C.

Hangul Day. On October 9, the country celebrates the 15th century creation of *hangul,* the Korean alphabet.

Christmas. This holiday is celebrated in Korea, as it is in western countries, on December 25.

KOREAN FOLK VILLAGE

Nestled in forested hills just 32 km/20 miles south of Seoul, this hamlet recreates the Korean world of yesteryear. After stepping through its entrance gate—guarded by male and female devil posts—you journey back in time to the long span (1392–1910) of the Choson Dynasty.

In the Korean Folk Village, a community of people follows the customs of ancient rural Korea. Sandy paths are edged by walls, fences, and village houses such as might have been occupied by Choson Dynasty merchants, craftspeople, or farmers. Be sure to tour the *yangban*'s (aristocrat's) home, a separate compound of 10 buildings that displays the wealth of Korean rural squires.

Wearing traditional dress, residents of the village do everyday tasks and crafts in the manner of several centuries ago. Scholars in tiny shops pen Chinese calligraphy, artisans produce pottery, blacksmiths forge farm tools, and weavers create beautiful silken cloth. Nearby, farmers thresh barley and grind grain by hand.

Soothe your hunger at a traditional restaurant near the village's entrance or at one of the many food stalls, where you can watch chefs prepare regional specialties. Twice daily, villagers entertain with music, folk dancing, and acrobatic stunts. On Sundays and national holidays, people of the village demonstrate the pomp and costuming of a traditional Korean wedding or funeral. The village operates its own inn, as well as a recreational area that features a swimming pool, archery field, and children's playground.

Open daily from 10 A.M. to 5 P.M., the Korean Folk Village is included in some organized tours from Seoul. On your own, you can reach it by taxi, rental car, or express bus.

Korea House. At Namsan Hill's northeast base you can enjoy an encapsulated version of Korean culture at Korea House. The traditionally-designed building—constructed without nails, bolts, or metal fasteners—has Korean-style rooms and a handicraft gallery. Dressed in bright, flowing costumes, Korean women present a free folk dance and musical program at 8:30 nightly, except holidays.

Seoul Grand Park. Located on the southern outskirts of Seoul at the foot of Mount Ch'onggyesan, the park features Seoul's zoo, containing more than 4,000 animals, and a botanical garden. It is open daily from 9 A.M. to 7 P.M. March through November, from 9 to 6 in winter.

Sports facilities. Olympic Park and Seoul Sports Complex, the major venues for the 1988 Olympic Games, are both located just south of the Han River, about a 30-minute drive southeast of downtown Seoul. The two facilities are 4 km/2 miles apart.

Shopping tips

You'll find a wealth of goods in Seoul's department stores, underground arcades, and city markets.

Where to shop. Though Seoul's department stores are well stocked with general merchandise, the basement food sections may turn out to be your favorite stops. They'll perk up your senses with Korean culinary delights, giving you a chance to try an array of local foods.

The Itaewon shopping district, a short distance from downtown on the south side of Mount Namsan, is noted for its shopping bargains, with stores selling everything from tailor-made garments to leather goods and suitcases.

ORIENTAL REFLECTIONS

From the heart of Asia came the people of the Orient. In ancient times, migrants made the long journey southward from Asia to the Korean peninsula and the islands of Japan, then settled and developed individual cultures and traditions.

Meanwhile, within the heart of Asia, the rich Chinese culture evolved, and in time the heritage and people of China spread beyond its borders. Today, Chinese influences are prevalent in Hong Kong, Macau, and Taiwan. Adding to this Oriental racial mix are the aboriginal tribespeople of Taiwan and Japan, and the latecomers—the westerners.

At right, a bearded Chinese gentleman's ancient eyes gaze out on a world much changed with the passage of time. Clad in colorful kimonos, Japanese girls (bottom left) smile shyly as they prepare to attend the Shichigosan festival. A costumed Ami tribeswoman from Taiwan (bottom right) dances to a rhythmic native melody.

Markets. Of the many, the East Gate Market is the largest, best known, and easiest to find. It's located just southwest of the gate, between Chongro and Chonggyero streets. Within this huge arcade is everything from foodstuffs and household utensils to clothing. On the second floor of the interconnected buildings, traditionally clad vendors almost blend into the thousands of yards of colorful silks and brocades spread along the crowded aisles.

A smaller market near the South Gate, diagonally across from the Seoul Tokyu Hotel, runs parallel (a block south) of Nandaemunro. Like the East Gate Market, the South Gate Market features hundreds of stalls crammed with merchandise.

Seoul side trips

Several sites within a day's distance from Seoul reveal more of Korea's fascinating history. Organized tours include most of the following attractions; if you prefer venturing on your own, you can ride local buses.

A walled city. Best preserved of Korean walled cities is Suwon, located 48 km/30 miles south of Seoul. King Chongro built Suwon in 1795; it was rebuilt in the 1970s, having been severely damaged 20 years before. The city abounds in pavilions, gates, watchtowers, and colorful markets. For the best view, stroll atop the stone walls encircling the city.

Panmunjom. The once obscure farming village of Panmunjom, 56 km/35 miles north of Seoul, gained international recognition when it was selected in 1951 as the site for armistice talks. For more than three decades, Panmunjom has remained the site of continuous talks on alleged peace violations and negotiations for an eventual peace treaty. A major visitor attraction today, Panmunjom stands in the center of the Demilitarized Zone that separates North and South Korea.

You need to make reservations to visit Panmunjom. The Korea Travel Bureau operates guided coach tours Monday through Friday from Seoul. Allow 8 hours for the tour.

Mount Sorak National Park. On an overnight—or longer—excursion you can visit the Mount Sorak area, near Sokcho on the east coast. Noted for its natural beauty, the park lies just below the Demilitarized Zone, 161 km/100 miles northeast of Seoul. Sokcho is an hour's flight or a 4-hour express bus ride from Seoul, and there are local buses to mountain lodges.

The pine-forested mountains, dominated by 1,708-meter/5,603-foot Daechong-Bong peak, provide a year-round vacationland. In winter, snow-capped peaks attract skiers; spring carpets the slopes with wildflowers; summer lures hikers to explore cool forests; and autumn throws a scarlet and gold mantle over the mountainsides. Just beyond the park lies the East Sea, bordered by miles of beaches.

KYONGJU, CITY OF KINGS

In its glorious past—57 B.C. to A.D. 935—the city of Kyongju reigned as capital of the rich Silla kingdom and, with a population of 300,000, was one of the world's largest cities. Today it is a museum without walls, home to 130,000 residents.

From Seoul, you can reach Kyongju (322 km/200 miles southeast) by express train or bus, or you can fly as far as Taegu or Ulsan and transfer to a Kyongju bus. Two-day sightseeing tours operate from Seoul. For accommodation choices, see page 80.

Pomun Lake Resort, an extensive tourist development 8 km/5 miles northeast of Kyongju, includes several deluxe hotels, convention facilities, a marina, a golf course, and a large shopping center.

Royal relics

Over 200 Silla Dynasty tombs in the Kyongju area have yielded ancient treasures. These are on display in the city's National Museum.

The Sillas built almost thiefproof tombs, capping the subterranean chambers with great heaps of river boulders covered, in turn, by mounds of earth.

In the heart of the city, you can stroll the tree-shaded paths of Ancient Tombs Park. Its 20 tombs include the 5th century Chonmachong (Heavenly Horse Tomb), containing replicas of the riches excavated from it.

On the outskirts of town, the Kyongju branch of the National Museum displays such artifacts as gold crowns, jewelry, belts, weapons, decorative tiles, statuary, and pottery. Especially spectacular is the huge Emille Buddhist Temple Bell, cast in bronze in A.D. 777.

Temple touring

Savor the mysterious and ancient beauty of two temples that nestle against Mount Toham, not far from Kyongju.

Pulguksa Temple. On the lower slopes of Mount Toham, 16 km/10 miles southeast of Kyongju, one of Korea's largest and most impressive temples stands among surrounding pine trees. Restored to its original beauty in 1972, Pulguksa Temple dates back 1,500 years. Colorful painted flowers, goddesses, demons, fanciful animals, and abstract patterns parade along roof beams, eaves, and ceilings. An 8-meter/25-foot Buddha has graced the temple since the 8th century.

Sokkuram Cave Temple. Located at the crest of Mount Toham, 8 km/5 miles from Pulguksa Temple, manmade Sokkuram Cave Temple was built in a style similar to the cave temples of India. Overlooking the East Sea, the grotto was positioned so the first rays of the rising sun would strike the larger-than-life-size granite Buddha inside the domed, circular cave.

PUSAN, SOUTHERN PORT CITY

Partially encircled by mountains, Pusan nestles in a valley, facing the sea. Home to some 3 million people, it is Korea's second largest city and busiest port. Along its wide, tree-lined streets, planter boxes brim with flowers. Within the Pusan area lie hot springs, beach resorts, mountainside temples, and parks.

From Seoul (402 km/250 miles to the north), you can reach Pusan by plane, express train, or express bus. Seoul tour operators include Pusan in their far-reaching itineraries. From Cheju Island, both car ferry and plane service are available. You can also fly to Pusan from major Japanese cities, or take a vehicular/passenger ferry from Shimonoseki or Osaka, Japan, to Pusan.

Get around the city by taxi, rental car, or local bus. City tours with English-speaking guides are not a regular event, but you can arrange one through Pusan sightseeing operators. For information on local accommodations, see "Hotel tips," below.

HOTEL TIPS/KOREA

Look through the following list for major hotels located in popular destinations throughout Korea.

Mount Sorak. Area accommodations include the New Sorak Hotel, Mt. Sorak Tourist Hotel, and the Sorak Park Hotel.

Kyongju. At Pomun Lake, a resort area just east of the city, hotels include the Kolon, the Kyongju Chosun, and the Kyongju Tokyu.

Pusan. Hotels in the Pusan area include the Commodore, Crown, Ferry, Haeundae, Kukje, Moonhwa, Paradise Beach, Phoenix, Pusan Plaza, Pusan Royal, Pusan Tourist, Sorabol, Tong Nae Tourist, and Westin Chosun Beach.

Chungmu and Yosu. Accommodations include the Chungmu Tourist Hotel and, in Yosu, the Yeosu Tourist Hotel.

Cheju. Island hotels include the Cheju Free Port, Cheju Grand, Cheju KAL, Cheju Prince, Cheju Royal, Hyatt Regency Cheju, and Seogwipo KAL.

Sights to see

Here are some highlights you should try to include in your schedule while you're in Pusan.

Pusan Fish Market. Early risers can enjoy the activity and pungent odors of the country's largest fish market. Each morning before sunrise (about 5 o'clock), fishing boats begin unloading their catch, and women sort and clean the fish in preparation for the daily auction.

Pomosa. About 24 km/15 miles north of Pusan, on the slopes of Mount Kumjeong, stands this tranquil temple. Since its founding in about 678, this complex has been a center of Korean Buddhism. On a 10-minute walk from the parking lot, you cross a stone bridge and pass through several gates to reach a complex of about 30 buildings half hidden by trees.

Tongdosa. This elaborate monastery complex is scattered over a wide, forested valley 40 km/25 miles north of Pusan. The site contains some 45 hermitages and nunneries, an 8th century stone pagoda, and a large tower. Yongchwisan (Holy Eagle Mountain) rises above the compound.

Outdoor pleasures

Beautiful beaches, bubbling hot springs, and verdant parklands attract outdoor enthusiasts to the Pusan area.

Beaches and spas. About 16 km/10 miles northeast of the downtown area, the white-sand expanse of Haeundae Beach curves along the shore, its boardwalk lined with hotels, restaurants, and casinos. Women and children sell shell necklaces, and photographers snap souvenir photos for tourists. You can rent beach equipment and bicycles. On the western side of town you'll find Songdo Beach, another popular stretch of sand.

Haeundae offers hot springs, too; another spa—Tongae Hot Springs Resort, famed for its medicinal waters—bubbles inland (14km/9 miles) at the foot of Mount Kumjeong.

Kumgangwon. Also at the foot of Mount Kumjeong, you can saunter through the botanical gardens, zoo, and playground of Kumgangwon (Kumgang Park). Its prime attraction is a cable-car ride to the top of the mountain, where there's an ancient castle.

Along Hallyo Waterway

The shimmering blue of the Hallyo Waterway, Korea's inland sea and national park, stretches westward from Pusan to Yosu. Within its reaches are nearly 400 islands ranging from rocky crags to gently sloping carpets of greenery.

Hydrofoils ply the Hallyo Waterway, connecting Pusan and Yosu several times daily and stopping en route at Chungmu and other coastal villages. You can also make the journey between Pusan and Yosu by bus or taxi along the South Coast Expressway.

Sightseeing operators in both Seoul and Pusan offer package tours to Chungmu (usually combined with a stop at Cheju Island). For information on accommodations in Chungmu and Yosu, see page 80.

CHEJU ISLAND

Southwest of the beaten track, 97 km/60 miles from the mainland, Cheju Island borders the southern edge of the Cheju Strait. A favorite vacation spot and honeymoon retreat, the island has a unique charm, a balmy climate, and scenic surroundings conducive to leisurely pleasure. Towering Mount Hall (1,950 meters/6,398 feet) rises dramatically from the island's center. At its base lie lush farmlands and pastures fenced in by rock walls.

Cheju City, the island's gateway and largest town, is on the north coast. There's plane service from Seoul or Pusan, or you can ride a ferry from Mokpo or Pusan or take a hydrofoil from Yosu. Some international flights from Japan stop here, and tours from Seoul and Pusan may include the island.

To get around locally, hire a taxi or rent a car or bicycle. For accommodation information, see page 80.

KNOW BEFORE YOU GO

As you plan a trip to Korea, you'll need to take into account these important details.

Entry/exit procedures. To enter Korea, you must have a valid passport and proof of onward passage. U.S. citizens do not need a visa for stays of 15 days or less. Tourist visas are valid for 60 days and are issued by the Korean consulates. Consular offices are located in Anchorage, Chicago, Honolulu, Houston, Los Angeles, New York, and San Francisco. The embassy is located in Washington, D.C.

You must show an international health certificate, verifying inoculation against cholera, if you're arriving from an infected area. For further information on what inoculations are recommended, contact the U.S. Public Health Service prior to leaving home.

You pay an airport departure tax of W5,000 when you fly out of Korea.

Customs. Without paying duty, you're allowed to bring in 400 cigarettes, 50 cigars, or 250 grams of pipe tobacco, as well as two bottles of liquor and a reasonable number of personal items.

Currency. The *won* is Korea's unit of currency.

Health conditions. Hospital and medical services are good, and English-speaking doctors are occasionally available. In large city hotels, tap water is usually safe to drink; when in doubt, ask for boiled water or bottled drinks.

Tipping. It is not customary to tip in Korea. Hotels and restaurants add a 10 percent service charge to the bill; a small additional tip is not necessary. Taxi drivers and others who serve travelers are usually not tipped.

Time. When it's Monday noon in Seoul, it's 8 o'clock Sunday evening in San Francisco—a difference of 16 hours.

Language. The written Korean language is called *hangul*, a phonetic system. English, required in schools, is spoken by many people in the tourist industry.

Weather and what to wear. Korea is a four-season country in the northern temperate zone, its climate similar to that of New England. The best months to visit are April, May, June, September, and October. July and August are generally hot and humid. Monsoon rains occur during the summer months. From December to February, Korea can be cold; temperatures often drop below freezing in Seoul, and snow falls in the higher elevations.

Take a heavy coat and woolens for late fall and winter visits, lighter-weight clothing for spring and summer, and rainwear at any time of year—it's a must. Conservative dress is customary at some restaurants and hotels—ties for men, dresses for women.

For more information. Your best source of travel information is the Korea National Tourism Corporation, C.P.O. Box 903, Seoul; or any of its offices in the United States: 510 W. Sixth Street, Suite 323, Los Angeles, CA 90014; 1188 Bishop Street, Century Square PH 1, Honolulu, HI 96813; 4th & Vine Building, Seattle, WA 98121; 230 N. Michigan Avenue, Suite 1500, Chicago IL 60601; and 460 Park Avenue, Suite 400, New York, NY 10022.

TAIWAN

A country rich in scenery and Chinese tradition, with
majestic mountains, ornate temples, priceless art
treasures, noisy cities, a dramatic river gorge,
tranquil lakes, lively festivals

L ying about 160 km/100 miles off the coast of
mainland China, Taiwan is an important
link in the Pacific chain of islands that extends south from Japan to the Philippines
and Indonesia. Rich in Chinese culture,
Taiwan (also known as the Republic of
China or R.O.C.) preserves many of the ancient traditions and priceless art treasures of early China.

Sixteenth century Portuguese sailors named it Ilha
Formosa (Beautiful Island). Outside the industrialized
cities, you see landscapes reminiscent of those which
have inspired generations of Chinese artists—green
mountains climbing into wispy clouds, lush rice fields
tended by conical-hatted laborers, and ornate temples
and pagodas marking homage to Buddhist and Taoist
gods and goddesses.

In prosperous Taipei, island capital and industrial
hub, the culture of ancient China mingles with that of a
modern urban community. In shadows cast by high-rise
office buildings and department stores nestle ornate
temples and open-air markets.

A favorite excursion from Taipei is the thrilling
drive through the narrow Taroko Gorge—river-hewn
through marble—and over the rugged East-West Cross-
Island Highway. It's a region of spectacular mountain
scenery. Along the fertile coastal plains, you'll pass historic cities and see farmers tending their rice fields and
vegetable plots. Scenic resorts, including Sun Moon
Lake, dot the mountains ranging down the center of the
island. To the south is the tropical beauty of Kenting,
Taiwan's first national park.

A GLANCE AT GEOGRAPHY

Taiwan is really an island province of the Republic of
China, which includes roughly 80 islands strewn east of
mainland China like a scattered jigsaw puzzle. Washed
by the Pacific Ocean on their eastern shores, the islands
are set apart from the mainland by the Taiwan Strait.

The main island of Taiwan (meaning "terraced bay")
averages 137 km/85 miles in width, and stretches 386
km/240 miles from north to south, covering an area of
35,962 square km/13,885 square miles. Other important
island constellations are the Penghu (Pescadores) archipelago of 64 islands, and the groups of Quemoy and
Matsu, just a few miles off China's Fukien province.

Mountains—almost everywhere

Volcanic mountains—now dormant—on Taiwan's
northern coast, between the Tamsui River and the
eastern port of Keelung, have given birth to numerous
hot springs and fumaroles. Evergreen-covered mountains and terraced hills march down the middle of the
island, forming the Central Mountain Range, which
boasts 62 peaks over 3,048 meters/10,000 feet high. The
range's highest peak is Yushan (Jade Mountain, also
known as Mount Morrison), at 3,950 meters/12,960 feet.

On its western slope, the Central Range gives way
to foothills and fertile alluvial plains. These western lowlands account for 75 percent of Taiwan's arable land and
support its major cities and a majority of its people.

Multiroofed *Wen-Wu Temple overlooks serene Sun Moon Lake, popular vacation site in central Taiwan. Temples, hotels, and aboriginal villages rim lake shore.*

Local flora

Taiwan's mountain slopes are heavily forested. Among the island's 200 species of trees, the most common are spruce, fir, yellow and red cypress, hemlock, and camphor. Hollow-stemmed bamboo, often growing to a height of more than 30 meters/100 feet, is also plentiful and is used extensively for utensils, furniture, baskets, beds, and houses.

Farms on Taiwan's rich western alluvial plain produce much of the island's food.

A HISTORY OF MIGRATORY WAVES

Earliest inhabitants of the island were aboriginal tribes, of proto-Malayan origins, who settled along the coastal plains to live by fishing and farming.

By the 12th century, clusters of Chinese had migrated to the island from the mainland. In 1206, the same year that Kublai Khan founded the Yuan dynasty, Taiwan became a protectorate of the Chinese empire.

The Europeans arrive

Late in the 16th century, Portuguese sailors discovered, and apparently fell in love with, the main island. Their charts and tales of Ilha Formosa soon attracted other Europeans.

In 1624, ships representing the Dutch East India Company arrived off the island's southwest shore, near present-day Tainan. The Dutch merchants opened trading posts, introduced Protestantism to the area, and built two forts—Fort Zeelandia and Fort Providentia (Chihkan Tower)—which still stand today.

Two years later the Spanish landed at Keelung on the island's northeast coast. They constructed Fort San Salvador here and Fort San Domingo at Tamsui; they also built the island's first Catholic churches. In 1641, the Dutch drove the Spanish off the island.

Chinese migration

During Taiwan's 17th century period of European occupation, political events took place in China that presaged a major change in Taiwan's future population. Ming rule had for some time been weakened by internal revolts, primarily protests against heavy taxation. Manchu warriors swarmed down from Manchuria, capturing Beijing (Peking) in 1644.

Among the armed resisters of Manchu rule was Cheng Ch'eng-kung (also known as Koxinga), who in 1661 fled with his followers to Taiwan. He drove out the Dutch and turned the island into a Ming stronghold. But in 1682, Manchus wrested the island away, incorporating it into their empire; two years later it became a prefecture of the nearby mainland province, Fukien.

It was during this period that the first immigration wave to Taiwan from China took place. Thousands of farmers traveled across the Taiwan Strait aboard Chinese traders' junks; these immigrants and their descendants settled into farming the island's rugged but rich terrain. In 1887, Taiwan acquired status as a province.

Japanese take over

In 1895, after the defeat of China in the First Sino-Japanese War, Taiwan was ceded to Japan. The Taiwanese revolted, declaring the first republic known in Asia. But the new republic faltered and, despite 100 or more uprisings, the Japanese remained in charge for 50 years.

During the 1930s, Taiwan served as Japan's forward base for invasion of Southeast Asia. After Japan's defeat in 1945, the islands reverted to their status as a province of China.

Emergence of the Republic of China

The Republic of China was founded in 1911 on the China mainland. Chiang Kai-shek organized the mainland government on nationalistic and democratic precepts set down by Dr. Sun Yat-sen. But China's struggle against the Japanese from 1937 until 1945 and the internal conflict between the nationalists and communists weakened the nation.

After taking Beijing in January 1949, the communists pressed southward, capturing Guangzhou (Canton) in October. Generalissimo Chiang Kai-shek resigned his post as president of the Republic of China and, with his followers, moved to Taiwan where he reassumed the presidency of the Republic of China in Taipei on March 1, 1950. He died in Taipei on April 5, 1975, about halfway through his fifth term as president.

Taiwan today

In an astonishingly brief time, Taiwan has seen a boom in industrial growth and economic expansion. Today, when compared with its Asian neighbors, the country enjoys a per capita income second only to Japan's.

The government of Taiwan takes its shape from a constitution established in 1947, when the nationalist government still existed on the mainland. The president and vice-president are chosen by the National Assembly which is, in turn, popularly elected. The president oversees the Five Yuans (branches), which perform executive, legislative, judicial, examination, and control functions.

When President Chiang Kai-shek died, Vice President Yen Chia-kan succeeded him for the remainder of the Generalissimo's 6-year term. The National Assembly elected the Generalissimo's elder son, Chiang Ching-kuo, as President in 1978 and 1984. Upon his death in 1988, Vice President Lee Teng-hui succeeded him for the remainder of the 6-year term which ends in 1990.

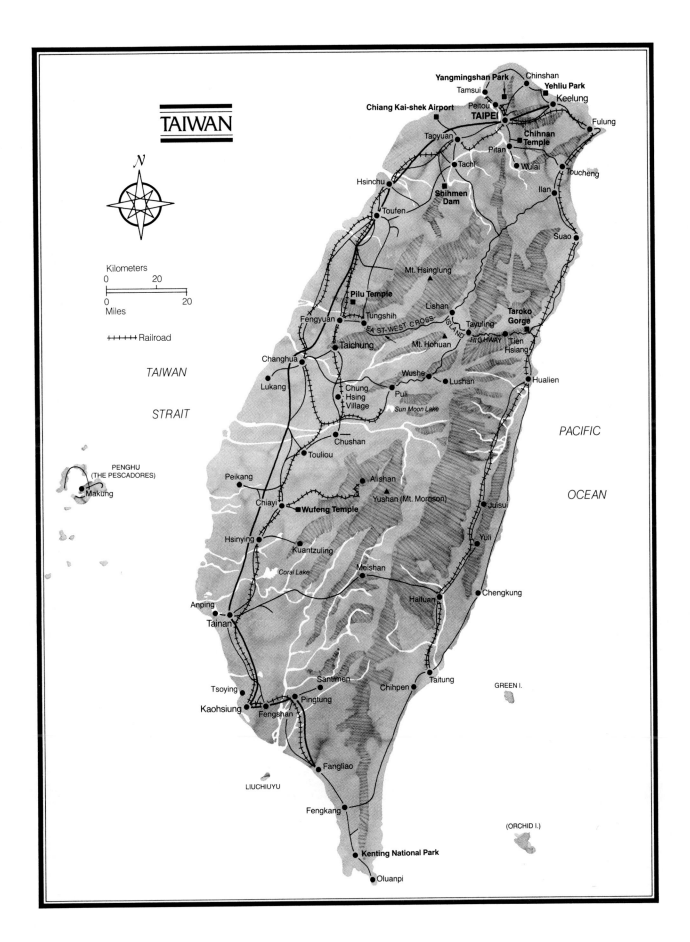

TAIWAN

N

Kilometers
0   20
0   20
Miles

+++++ Railroad

TAIWAN

STRAIT

PACIFIC

OCEAN

Yangmingshan Park   Chinshan
Tamsui   Yehliu Park
Chiang Kai-shek Airport   Peitou   Keelung
TAIPEI   Fulung
Taoyuan   Chihnan
Pitan   Temple
Tachi   Wulai
Hsinchu
Toufen   Shihmen   Toucheng
Dam
Ilan
Suao
Mt. Hsinglung
Pilu Temple
Lishan   Taroko
Tungshih   Tayuling   Gorge
Fengyuan   EA ST-WEST CROSS- ISLAND   Tien
Taichung   Mt. Hohuan HIGHWAY Hsiang
Changhua   Wushe
Lukang   Chung   Lushan   Hualien
Hsing
Village   Puli
Sun Moon Lake
Chushan
Touliou
PENGHU
(THE PESCADORES)   Peikang   Alishan
Makung   Chiayi   Yushan (Mt. Morrison) Juisui
Wufeng Temple
Hsinying   Yuli
Kuantzuling
Coral Lake   Meishan
Anping   Chengkung
Haituan
Tainan
GREEN I.
Tsoying   Santimen   Chihpen Taitung
Pingtung
Kaohsiung Fengshan
LIUCHIUYU   Fangliao
(ORCHID I.)
Fengkang
Kenting National Park
Oluanpi

Fluttering flags *line the approach to Chung Cheng Memorial Hall in Taipei. Building honors Taiwan's late president Chiang Kai-shek.*

National Palace Museum *near Taipei ranks among world's greatest galleries. Only a portion of priceless art can be exhibited at one time.*

TAIWAN'S PEOPLE

Most of Taiwan's 19.5 million people are Chinese. Many descend from mainland Chinese families that have lived on the island for centuries. Others are newcomers who fled from mainland China in 1949, after the communist takeover.

Taiwan's 323,000 aborigines are believed to be descendants of peoples from southern China and Southeast Asia. Most tribal groups live in the Central Mountain Range and along the eastern coast.

Mostly urbanites

Adapting to the modern pace of Taiwan's industrial success, many rural citizens have moved from the countryside to such heavily populated cities as Taipei, Kaohsiung, or Taichung. Like urbanites everywhere, Taiwan's city dwellers occupy high-rise apartment buildings. A cosmopolitan people, they generally prefer western-style dress—although on special occasions women still appear in the traditional *chi pao* (high-necked, full-length dress with slit skirt).

Beyond the bustling cities, rural areas offer the traveler an entirely different look at Taiwan. Ancient villages, walled with adobe and brick, doze placidly amid shimmering rice fields.

Honor for cultural roots

Despite the enthusiasm with which Taiwan has embraced western technology, the country has not allowed western culture to undermine its reverence for Chinese traditions. The richness of a cultural heritage reaching back to antiquity is evident in festivals, artwork, religious practices, and architecture.

TRIP PLANNING BASICS

Numerous airlines fly to Taiwan from points scattered across the globe. From the west coast of the United States, the distance is about 7,500 air miles. More than a dozen international carriers, including Taiwan's China Airlines, serve Taipei's Chiang Kai-shek International Airport. International flights also land at Kaohsiung on the island's southwest coast.

Several steamship companies stop at Keelung (29 km/18 miles northeast of Taipei) and Kaohsiung.

Hotel choices

Taipei offers a good choice of international-standard hotels. Elsewhere on the island, you'll find first-class accommodations only in major cities and resort areas. The special features on pages 89 and 96 list hotels.

Local transport tips

Within Taiwan, China Airlines and Far Eastern Air Transport provide regular air service between Taipei and other major cities and towns.

Taking the train. Over 1,000 km/621 miles of railroad track links towns in Taiwan. From Taipei, you can travel south along the west coast as far as Fangliao (beyond Kaohsiung)—or go north to Keelung and then head south along Taiwan's eastern coast to Taitung. Either way, electric, air-conditioned express trains assure cool, quick transport.

Traveling by bus. Air-conditioned express buses travel at frequent intervals between Taiwan's major towns and cities. Bus service also connects villages in the mountainous interior.

Car plus chauffeur. Through local travel agencies, you can hire chauffeur-driven cars for either a one-day city tour or longer trips. Obviously, it's wise to make sure that your driver speaks some English.

Renting a car to drive yourself means higher risk than you may realize. Traffic careens along at a frantic pace, and Chinese road signs add to the confusion.

Taxis. Low-cost taxis provide the easiest city transportation. Few drivers speak English, so have your hotel desk clerk write down your destination and other instructions in Chinese characters. Also be sure to have the name of your hotel written down in Chinese, to prevent trouble finding your way back.

Tours. Visitors can select trips from a wide array of organized tours covering most of Taiwan's major attractions. Excursions last from a half day to 6 days.

Feasting on regional cuisines

Taiwan enjoys well-deserved culinary fame for its many delicious regional Chinese dishes. Popular among Eastern epicures are Taiwan's specialties from Sichuan, Beijing, Hunan, Guangzhou, and Shanghai. For appetizing details, see "A Chinese Cuisine Primer," page 124.

When you crave a change of pace from Chinese cuisine, you can sample the menu at restaurants that serve foods from other Asian countries—or western cuisine, if you're hungry for it. Steak houses are particularly popular.

The entertainment scene

In Taipei and other big cities, after-dark entertainment ranges from quiet piano bars and hotel supper clubs to huge dance pavilions and theater-restaurants. Besides serving dinner, the latter offer music and shows performed by singers, gymnasts, acrobats, magicians, and dancers, both Chinese classical and aboriginal.

Chinese opera. For many westerners, Taiwan's most fascinating attraction will be a night at the opera. Chinese-style opera music may sound harsh to the western ear. Songs and dialogues are delivered in strange, falsetto tones. But you'll enjoy the colorful and elaborate costumes and the actors' graceful movements.

Unlike a performance of *Aida*, a Chinese opera like *The White Snake* or *The Flying Dragon* may include rousing, circuslike acrobatics, mime, staging without props, and masklike make-up in every color from gold to green revealing whether a character is good or evil.

Other cultural entertainment. With luck, in the countryside you may catch a traveling troupe presenting *pu tai hsi*—a puppet show sometimes set to music. Look for performances on village street corners or near temples; plots are based on Chinese legends.

Handicraft treasures

In recent years, a Chinese arts renaissance has rewarded Taiwan shoppers with locally made goods of prime quality. In department stores, government-sponsored

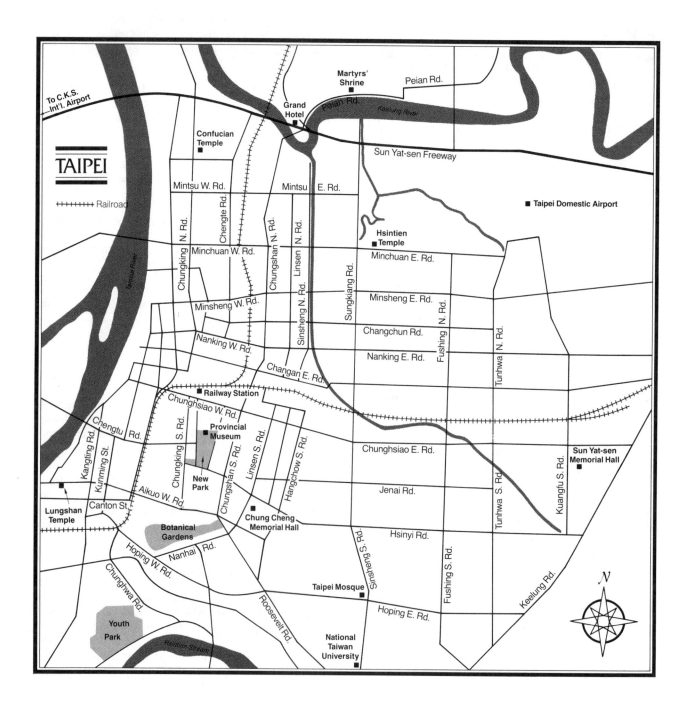

handicraft centers, and better shops, prices are fixed. Elsewhere, you'll need to bargain.

What to buy. Local factories and cottage industries produce furniture and woodcarvings, handmade carpets, silk and other textiles, clothing, coral and jade jewelry, porcelain and pottery, marble items, opera masks, dolls, toys, beaded and brocaded handbags, and handpainted vases and screens. Other good buys include bronze, brass, lacquerware, and weavings.

A gift idea. For more than 2,000 years, the Chinese have been stamping documents with a signature seal called a *chop*. Still made today from jade, soapstone, ivory, or wood, personalized chops—their handles elaborately carved—make delightful and exotic gifts.

What not to buy. The United States restricts the import of products made from animals and plants it has officially listed as endangered or threatened. The fact that these items are sold abroad doesn't mean they'll be allowed into the United States. For more information on restrictions, see page 9.

For the sports enthusiast

Taiwan offers visitors ample opportunity to enjoy sports—both Chinese and western.

THE ESSENTIALS/TAIPEI

Here's a brief information sheet to help you plan a smooth and pleasant stay in Taiwan's capital city of Taipei.

Getting there

Air. China Airlines and foreign flag carriers provide international service to Taipei. Connecting Chiang Kai-shek International Airport with Taipei, 40 km/25 miles southwest, are hotel limos, taxis, and buses. All take about 40 minutes.

From the domestic airport near downtown Taipei, China Airlines and Far Eastern Air Transport offer daily flights to other major Taiwan cities.

Sea. Cruise and cargo/passenger ships call at Keelung, 29 km/18 miles northeast of Taipei.

Rail. Train routes link Taipei with cities on Taiwan's east and west coasts.

Bus. Air-conditioned express buses travel between Taipei and major cities in central and southern Taiwan.

Where to stay

Taipei caters to visitors with a variety of good downtown hotels. Major hotels are air-conditioned and offer all expected services.

Leading centrally-located international class hotels in Taipei include the Ambassador, Asia World Plaza, Brother, Hilton International Taipei, Howard Plaza, Imperial, President, Ritz, and Lai-Lai Sheraton. The impressive Grand Hotel crowns a hill outside the main business district.

Moderately priced hotels are located near Chiang Kai-shek International Airport.

Getting around town

In hectic Taipei, taxis are the simplest mode of city transport. Have your hotel clerk write out your destination in Chinese characters, since most drivers don't speak English.

Tours

Half-day tours show off city sights, the Wulai-Pitan area (see page 96), and the north coast (see page 95). You can also join an exciting full-day tour to Taroko Gorge (see page 97).

Dining out

City restaurants serve a wide range of dishes—from the regional cuisines of China to specialties of Japan, Korea, Southeast Asia, and the western world. Most hotels have Chinese and western restaurants.

The entertainment scene

Night life choices abound, from theater restaurants to discos, dance halls, and bars. Don't miss your chance to see an unforgettable Chinese opera. Floor shows, both international and Chinese versions, are performed at many major hotels.

For more information

Contact the Tourism Bureau, 280 Chunghsiao East Road, 9th Floor, Sec. 4, Taipei, or the Taiwan Visitors Association, 111 Mingchuan Road, 5th Floor, Taipei.

Sports for spectators. Popular local spectator sports include football (soccer), basketball, and baseball.

If you awake at dawn, you can also watch—and even join—Taiwan's numerous fitness buffs. Residents firmly believe in exercise; early each morning, parks and other open spaces come alive with the exertions of the energetic. Some people engage in vigorous movements to a disco beat, others prefer *t'ai-chi ch'uan*.

Recreational pursuits. Just as in the west, visitors to Taiwan can enjoy golf, tennis, and water sports. The Taiwan Golf and Country Club at Tamsui, near Taipei, is the country's best golf course. Two dozen other clubs offer golfing throughout the rest of Taiwan. Prefer tennis? Several Taipei hotels have courts.

TAIPEI, THE COUNTRY'S CAPITAL

Taipei, the island's largest city, is the cultural, economic, transportation, and political center of the country. Located in the northern part of Taiwan, the provisional capital sits in a basin bounded by three rivers: the broad, meandering Tamsui to the west; the Keelung to the north; and the Hsintien to the south. Mountains surround the city.

A brief history

Originally built by the Manchus in 1709, the early settlement of Taipei was encircled by a 5-meter/18-foot wall with five massive stone gates. The tiny enclave protected the Manchus and other local peoples from marauding pirates and foreign brigands.

During Japan's 50-year occupation of Taiwan, Taipei served as territorial headquarters. As the city grew, the walls were demolished. Four of the original gates remain. You can recognize these by their rounded archways and Chinese roofs.

A look around town

At first glance, the Taipei skyline is uninspiring. Although decorative dragons march along an occasional rooftop, most of Taipei's architecture is undistinguished—blockish buildings lining straight, traffic-clogged streets.

Anything exotically "Chinese" in Taipei requires seeking out—join a city tour to catch major sights. Further exploration by taxi or on foot is also worthwhile.

Some important sights

Of all Taipei's attractions, art treasures displayed at the National Palace Museum (see page 92) draw the most visitors. Other monuments of note include the Chung Cheng Memorial Hall, Presidential Square, the Grand Hotel, and National Revolutionary Martyrs' Shrine.

Chung Cheng Memorial Hall. In the heart of downtown Taipei, off Aikuo E. Road, this Chinese classical-style building honors Taiwan's late president, Chiang Kai-shek. An exquisite building, its lower level exhibits a display detailing the late president's achievements. A giant bronze statue of Chiang Kai-shek dominates a massive hall upstairs. During the hall's open hours, from 9 A.M. to 5 P.M. daily, you can watch hourly changing of the guard ceremonies.

Presidential Square. Marking the center of Taipei, Presidential Square flanks Chungking South Road, northwest of Chung Cheng Memorial Hall. Fronting its massive expanse sits the austere and imposing Presidential Building; here are housed the offices of the president of the Republic and the Ministry of National Defense.

Grand Hotel. Heading north from Presidential Square along Chungshan North Road, you'll cross the Keelung River, arriving soon afterwards at the Grand Hotel.

Even if you aren't staying here, you'll find this is an unusual hotel to see—one living up to its name. Situated atop a hill north of the Keelung River, the Grand Hotel combines lavish Chinese palace-style architecture with a luxurious atmosphere.

National Revolutionary Martyrs' Shrine. This great shrine honoring war heroes stretches along Peian Road northeast of the red and gilded Grand Hotel. Uniformed soldiers stand watch at the entrance, and fierce marble lions guard the main building, designed to resemble Peking's Hall of Supreme Harmony.

Commemorating those who died in the 1911 revolution on the mainland and during ensuing wars, the shrine is open daily from 9 A.M. to 5 P.M.

Touring temples

Among some 145 temples sprinkled throughout Taipei, you'll come across many fine examples of Chinese architecture. Fanciful dragons, unicorns, and phoenixes guard colorful curved-eave rooftops. Of special interest are Lungshan, Confucian, and Pao An temples.

Lungshan Temple. Originally built in 1740, this is the oldest, best-known, and most colorful of Taipei's Buddhist temples. It rises above a maze of shops and houses in the old port area of Wanhua on Kwangchow Street, west of the Botanical Gardens.

Confucian Temple. Honoring China's most revered philosopher and teacher, this classical temple compound stands behind wooden gates on Chiuchuan Street, west of Chunshan North Road. Except on September 28, Confucius's birthday, the yellow tile-roofed temple and its compound remain quiet and serene.

Richly embellished *National Revolutionary Martyrs' Shrine in Taipei honors Chinese war heroes. Pageantry marks memorial services in March and September.*

Suspension bridge dangles *across Taroko Gorge, spectacular 12-mile-long ravine carved through marble mountains by Liwu River. Gorge features plummeting waterfalls and pagodas.*

Pao An Temple. Dragonlike serpents crowning its roof ridge attract attention to this 230-year-old Taoist temple, located directly across the street from the Confucian Temple. Monks in red robes move quietly past writhing dragons decorating the temple's columns and interior.

Museum enrichment

Along with visiting Taipei's temples, be sure to enrich your trip by exploring the city's museums. You'll glimpse fascinating details of Taiwan's history.

National Museum of History. Located at the southern end of the Botanical Gardens, this museum houses a number of China's cultural treasures. The building reflects classical Chinese style.

The museum's collection contains Chinese art objects dating from 2,000 B.C.—oracle bones and ritual vessels from the Shang and Chou dynasties, earthenware from the Sui and Tang dynasties, stone engravings from the Han Dynasty, and jade articles from the Chou Dynasty. East of the museum are the National Art Hall and National Science Hall.

Taiwan Provincial Museum. Housing eclectic displays of zoology, anthropology, sea life, Chinese calligraphy, and tomb rubbings, this museum flanks the north side of New Park.

TAIWAN'S ART TREASURES

One of Taiwan's main attractions, Taipei's splendid National Palace Museum stays open daily from 9 to 5. Its stunning collection spans more than 30 centuries (1766 B.C. to 1911 A.D.) of Chinese art. You don't have to be an art expert to appreciate the glorious colors of a cloisonné enamel vase, the elegant simplicity of a porcelain bowl, or the intricate detail in a handpainted scroll.

The palace-style museum buildings, blending classical and modern Chinese design, rise against a wooded hillside in the suburb of Waishuanghsi, located about 20 minutes north of central Taipei. Beneath the glazed green tile roof are three floors of exhibits containing a fraction of the museum's 600,000 items. Since this is far too vast a collection to display at one time, the museum rotates selected exhibits every 3 to 6 months. Between displays, pieces wait in protective caves tunneled deep into a mountainside behind the museum.

Exhibits on display offer a selection of the finest and most representative pieces in each of the main categories: bronze, jade, porcelain, paintings and scrolls, calligraphy, tapestries and embroideries, lacquerware, enamelware, ivory, rare books, and historical documents. Most items are labeled in both Chinese and English.

Assembled over the centuries by China's rulers, the vast array of treasures includes the former Imperial Collection, once housed in Beijing's Forbidden City. For centuries it was accessible only to the emperor and members of the royal household. Each dynasty added new works of art, often taking them from

private citizens under their domain. The collection became a national treasure when the Qing (Ch'ing) Dynasty fell in 1911.

During the past 40 years, the art objects have been moved several times when China has been threatened by invasion and war. In 1948 the major part of the collection was shifted from China to Taiwan. The present museum opened in 1965.

FESTIVAL TIME IN TAIWAN

A glance through the list below shows how much the Chinese enjoy a chance to celebrate. They pay homage, as their ancestors have for centuries, to an amazing assortment of deities. Major historical events and heroes receive fanfare, too, as does the world-famous Chinese New Year.

Check locally for current event scheduling; many traditional festivals follow the lunar calendar, which changes from year to year.

Republic of China's Founding. On January 1 and 2, Taiwan comes alive with holiday activity as parades and dragon and lion dancers commemorate the inauguration of Dr. Sun Yat-sen. In 1912, he became the first Provisional President of the Republic of China.

Chinese Lunar New Year. With family feasts and more lion and dragon dances, Taiwan observes the most important date of the Chinese calendar. The Lunar New Year occurs in January or February, depending on the year.

Lantern Festival. Held 15 days after the Chinese New Year celebration, this event marks the end of the New Year period. Plazas and temples, decorated with lanterns, are packed with children carrying their own favorite lantern creations.

Kuan Yin's Birthday. In the last part of March, Taipei celebrates the birthday of the goddess of mercy with elaborate observances at the 250-year-old Lungshan Temple in Taipei.

Buddha Bathing Festival. During May, Buddha's images are paraded through the streets and sprinkled with water as part of Buddha's birthday celebration.

Birthday of Ma-Tsu. In April or May, Taiwan's popular and powerful goddess of the sea is honored with lavish celebrations at her temples.

Koxinga's landing. At the end of April, ceremonies commemorate Koxinga's landing in Taiwan and the ouster of Dutch colonists. Main celebrations are held in Tainan.

Dragon Boat Festival. In late May or June, dragon boat races commemorate the death of poet-statesman Ch'u Yuen. Best observation sites are Taipei's Tamsui River and Kaohsiung's Love River.

Birthday of Taipei's city god. During June, Taipei honors its local deity, Cheng Huang, with dragon and lion dances, actors on stilts, and firecrackers.

Ghost Festival. Buddhists believe the souls of the dead are released from the underworld on this day in late July or early August for a month's "vacation" on earth. Families offer special sacrifices to placate and honor ancestral spirits.

Mid-autumn Festival. (Moon Cake Festival). People gather at such scenic spots as Wulai, Pitan, and Shihmen Dam near Taipei to celebrate the harvest and to observe the bright autumn moon.

Confucius's Birthday. On September 28, Taiwan honors this famous teacher and philosopher born in 551 B.C. At all Confucius temples in Taiwan, ancient dances are performed to ritual music.

National Day. On October 10—Double Ten Day—a massive parade in front of Taipei's Presidential Building celebrates the founding of the Republic of China in 1911.

Retrocession Day. On October 25, with athletic events and lion and dragon dances, Taiwan celebrates its 1945 retrocession from Japan and return to Chinese rule.

Birthday of President Chiang Kai-shek. The birthday of the deceased president is remembered on October 31.

Birthday of Dr. Sun Yat-sen. On November 12, the Republic of China observes the 1866 birth of Dr. Sun, leader of the 1911 revolution and founder of the Republic.

Constitution Day. This national holiday on December 25 commemorates the constitution adopted in 1946 by the National Assembly.

Vendor casts critical eye *at his food display in readiness for housewives who shop daily for fresh produce. Conical hats remain part of rural dress.*

Inviting beach *near Taiwan's tropical southern tip is part of Kenting National Park, scenic region noted for swimming, diving, bird watching, and colorful flowers.*

Shopping finds

If you enjoy shopping, Taipei can be an adventure. Here you can browse for hours, strolling from shop to shop, in quest of a rare jade object, a Chinese musical instrument, or a handpainted scroll.

Where to shop. Taipei's main shopping district spreads along Chunghua Road, Chengtu Road, and neighboring side streets. In this bustling locale, you can choose from the varied wares of large government-approved department stores, small shops, markets, and street vendors.

The Chunghua Bazaar, on Chunghua Road, opulently fills eight adjoining buildings, three stories high, with at least a block's worth of shops. Like major hotels everywhere, many in Taipei include shopping arcades.

In search of craft items. Handicraft hunters can find everything on their lists, plus extra surprises, at the Taiwan Handicraft Promotion Center, 1 Hsuchow Road, near the city's East Gate. Here, at fixed prices, you'll find objects made of jade, brass, marble, and bamboo, as well as lacquerware, pottery, and furniture. Also known as the Chinese Handicraft Mart, the center stays open daily from 9 A.M. to 5:30 P.M. Poke around Chungshan North Road for still more handicraft shops.

For further pottery choices, stop at the China Pottery Arts Company showroom on Nanking East Road, or visit the company's Peitou factory.

Outdoor fun

Tucked away amidst the bustle of Taipei, scattered islands of green tranquility offer you a chance to observe the highly developed art of Oriental landscaping. Ingenious design often makes a handkerchief-sized plot seem spacious.

Botanical Gardens. Southwest of the traffic circle at the end of Chungshan South Road, you can enjoy a leisurely stroll through the inviting Botanical Gardens on Nanhai Road. In the walled-in garden area, you'll find some 700 species of native subtropical and temperate-zone shrubs, trees, and other plants.

New Park. One block northeast of the Presidential Square, you can wander through this oasis of lawns edged with flower beds and shade trees. Aesthetic extras are lotus-filled pools, pavilions, and a three-tiered pagoda.

Shuang Hsi Park. Within sight of the green hills of northern Taipei, you can visit a Chinese park landscaped along ancient guidelines. Covering a little more than 1 hectare/3 acres, the park contains pavilions, fountains, arched bridges, grottoes, and pleasant, tree-shaded walks. It is located in a fork of the road leading to Yangmingshan and the National Palace Museum.

A TRIP TO THE NORTH

Just a short distance from Taipei, the road north leads to beautiful parks, hot springs, historic towns, and beaches. Easily reached on an organized coach tour, these attractions are also accessible by chauffeured car or local bus.

Nearby sights

Rewarding side trips from Taipei, through the northeastern hills, are lush Yangmingshan Park and Taiwan's famous hot springs resort, Peitou.

Yangmingshan Park. In springtime, you'll find a profusion of cherry and azalea color throughout this park. Adding complexity to the palette of pinks and reds are blossoming Camellia, plum, and apricot trees. Shaded walkways wind past waterfalls, rock gardens, fish pools, and pavilions. During the blossom season, the park—only 16 km/10 miles from Taipei—often draws crowds from the city.

Peitou. Along the scenic return trip from mountainous Yangmingshan, visit Peitou, famous for both hot springs and pottery.

As you descend into Peitou's valley surroundings, the lush landscape gradually turns rocky and barren. Clouds of steam rising from odoriferous sulfur pools indicate hot springs that feed the therapeutic baths of Peitou's tiny hotels and inns.

Looming beyond the sulfurous mists, the town itself clusters around a main shopping street. Among the varied goods for sale, you'll find much pottery made in nearby factories. The China Pottery Arts factory offers tours of its workshop, where you can observe successive stages of production, including the meticulous handpainting of each exquisite piece. Finished pieces are available for sale; you can also have pottery customcrafted to order.

Round the loop

From Peitou you can make a loop drive north to historic Tamsui and around the island's northern headlands to the port of Keelung. The route offers views of fishing craft, mariners repairing nets, and farmers working on terraced hillsides. Follow the loop in reverse, if you prefer, visiting Keelung first (from Taipei), then driving back to Peitou.

Historic Tamsui. Eight km/5 miles north of Peitou, you'll reach the coastal village of Tamsui near the mouth of its namesake river. Surrounded by terraced rice fields and mountain slopes covered with bamboo and orange groves, this old fishing village was once Taiwan's most important trading center.

Yehliu Park. From Tamsui, the highway swings north then turns to skirt the East China Sea. Soon it approaches one of Taiwan's natural wonders—Yehliu Park, fronting the ocean about 11 km/7 miles northwest of Keelung. Over the centuries, winds and waves have sculpted rock formations into fantastic shapes—a sphinxlike Egyptian queen, a forest of huge mushrooms, a griffin, a turtle, and a giant sandal.

Port of Keelung. The island's chief northern port lies along the northeast coast 29 km/18 miles from Taipei.

Enclosed on three sides by steep cliffs, Keelung is an interesting fishing port, highlighted by a busy harbor and the remains of the old Spanish bastion, Fort Salvador. The town's architecture reflects the influence of foreign occupation by the Spanish, Dutch, French, Manchus, and Japanese.

High on a hill, overlooking the city and harbor, looms a 23-meter/74-foot statue of Kuan Yin, goddess of mercy. Her hollow interior houses a staircase leading to a panoramic view of the city below.

HOTEL TIPS/TAIWAN

The following is a list of hotels for major tourist areas in central and southern Taiwan. For Taipei hotel listings, see page 89.

Eastern Taiwan

Hualien. CITC Hualien and Marshal hotels.

Central Taiwan

Taichung. National, Park, and Taichung hotels.

Sun Moon Lake. Evergreen and Sun Moon Lake hotels (both overlook the lake).

Southern Taiwan

Tainan. Tainan and Red Hill hotels.

Kaohsuing. Ambassador, Grand, Holiday Garden, Kingdom, King Wang, and Summit hotels.

Kenting. Cesar Park Hotel.

SHORT JOURNEYS SOUTH

Enticements not far south of Taipei include another temple, a resort area, and an aboriginal village. Travel by organized tour from the city—or hire a chauffeured car.

Lin Family Gardens. Situated at Panchiao, a town adjoining Taipei, is this beautiful 300-year-old family compound and garden. Recently restored to its original condition, it offers visitors a glimpse into the highly refined lifestyle of Taiwan's early Chinese well-to-do.

Chihnan Temple. A drive into the hilly countryside southeast of Taipei delivers you to one of Taiwan's earliest and largest Taoist temple complexes. Centuries-old Chihnan Temple stands halfway up the slope of Monkey Hill, near the village of Mucha, about 8 km/5 miles from Taipei. From the wooded site, known as the Temple of Eight Immortals, you have a panoramic view of Taipei.

Pitan resort. The lure of nature draws hikers and picnickers 11 km/7 miles south of Taipei to Pitan (Green) Lake. Enjoy mountainous scenery along its tree-lined shore, swim in its tiny inlet, or hire a boat.

Wulai aboriginal village. If you want to see tribal dances performed by tattooed and costumed aborigines, the most accessible place from Taipei is Wulai, located some 23 km/14 miles south of the city in a rocky ravine of the Hsintien River. The area is heavily commercialized, and the tribespeople expect tips for dance performances, as well as payment when posing for photographers. In Wulai's shops you can browse among items made from fabric handwoven by the aborigines (see page 100).

In a narrow-gauge rail car, you can take a diesel-powered ride from the village up its nearby hillside to view an 18-meter/60-foot waterfall. For spectacular mid-air sightseeing, switch to an aerial cable car and visit Dreamland Forest Recreation Park.

Window on China. Miniature reproductions of historic and cultural sites in Taiwan and mainland China draw visitors to this 74-acre park in Lungtan, 53 km/33 miles southwest of Taipei. Tiny electric ships, trains, and cars move along small waterways, tracks, and roads; miniature figures, also animated electrically, populate the exhibits. The complex is open daily from 8:30 A.M. to 5:30 P.M. in summer, with shorter hours in winter.

Shihmen Reservoir. About 56 km/35 miles southwest of Taipei, in the foothills of the Central Mountain Range, Shihmen Reservoir has become a favorite recreation area for fishing and picnicking.

Lion's Head Mountain (Shih Tou Shan). Temple enthusiasts and hikers will enjoy visiting this Buddhist temple complex, located on a mountain about 113 km/70 miles southwest of Taipei. It's about a 3-hour drive from the capital through Hsinchu and Toufen.

Ten temples and a seven-story pagoda stretch along a steep footpath from the sacred mountain's base to the top—457 meters/1,500 feet above sea level. All the temples open into natural caves.

TAIWAN'S DRAMATIC INTERIOR

Lofty mountain peaks rise between deep river valleys and fertile plains in the varied and lovely landscape of central Taiwan. Should you have time to explore this part of the island, the journey from Taipei south is an exciting excursion, well worth an extra few days. The trip will take you to Hualien, then through awesome Taroko Gorge. If you have time, travel the length of the East-West Cross-Island Highway, explore the city of Taichung, slip out to Sun Moon Lake, or venture a ride on a narrow-gauge train from Chiayi to the Alishan Forest Recreation Area. At the very least, you'll need 4 days to explore all these central Taiwan sights.

First stop, Hualien

Best known to visitors as the take-off point for tours into the Taroko Gorge via the East-West Cross-Island Highway, the coastal town of Hualien lies southeast of Taipei. You can travel there by air, bus, or rail from Taipei. Hualien, a shipping port, has shops and markets that are fun to explore. They are typical of small cities everywhere in Taiwan.

Visit to a marble factory. Hidden within Hualien's neighboring mountains lie rich deposits of marble. The transformation of marble blocks into decorative articles is an important Hualien industry. Visitors can stop at a marble factory to watch the process. The largest plant, operated by the Retired Servicemen's Engineering Agency, is located not far from the airport.

Aboriginal dances. During your stay in Hualien, try to catch an Ami cultural show at the Ami Culture Village. Musicians and dancers belong to the largest of the country's aboriginal tribes, the Ami. The lively dances, often based on autumn harvest themes, blaze with the performers' traditional bright red Ami garb.

Taroko Gorge—carved through marble

The most popular destination outside of Taipei is the Taroko Gorge, a spectacular 19 km/12-mile-long slice cut by the Liwu River through the marble of Taiwan's Central Mountains. The Taroko Gorge marks the eastern end of the 120-mile-long East-West Cross-Island Highway (see right). Many Taipei tour operators offer day or overnight excursions.

The gorge looks most glorious in April and October, though mist and fog sometimes obscure the high peaks. Don't take this trip from June to September—during this time typhoons are a threat, and the heavy rainfall often causes landslides, making the road impassable.

Winding your way through the gorge. A red-columned archway, 23 km/14 miles north of Hualien Airport, marks the entrance of your breathtaking journey into the gorge. Shortly beyond rise steep cliffs, washed by plummeting waterfalls; the Liwu River rages below. In many places the sun's rays penetrate the narrow chasm only at midday.

Hewn from marble cliffs, the highway winds high above the river's roar, passing through 38 tunnels along its way. Giant windows have been cut into the Tunnel of Nine Turns—one of the most lengthy. Here you can peer through to the narrow marble canyon and winding river.

Temples and pagodas. An occasional pagoda or pavilion tucked among the rocks adds fairy tale beauty to your journey through the gorge.

At the far end of the gorge, a pair of marble Chinese lions guard the approaches to the Bridge of Motherly Devotion. Eventually, you'll arrive at Tien Hsiang Lodge, a popular luncheon stop and turn-around point for most Taroko Gorge excursions. From Hualien, the trip to Tien Hsiang and back takes about 4 hours.

East-West Cross-Island Highway

From Tien Hsiang, at the western end of the Taroko Gorge, you may opt to continue across the remainder of the East-West Cross-Island Highway. Completed in 1960, the 193-km/120-mile-long road opened up the island's mountainous interior as it provided an overland route between Taiwan's east and west coasts.

An engineering marvel, the narrow highway precariously hugs the sides of steep mountains for most of its serpentine route, and passes through tunnels beyond counting. Ten thousand workers spent 46 months building the impressive thoroughfare.

Travel particulars. Marking the midway point on a journey to the west coast is Lishan, about 4 hours' drive from Hualien. Allow another 4 hours to reach Taichung. Most travelers stop overnight at Lishan Guest House, 1,945 meters/6,381 feet above sea level. If you choose to stop overnight after visiting Taroko Gorge, you can stay at Tien Hsiang, making the full journey through the mountains the next day.

Rewards and pitfalls. Cloud-filled gorges, soaring mountain peaks reminiscent of traditional Chinese paintings, dense forests of pine and cypress—you'll enjoy all these beautiful sights when you journey across the East-West Cross-Island Highway. Near Lishan, apple, pear, and plum orchards cover steep hillsides.

However majestic the scenery, the trip may become hazardous in wet or misty weather. Don't try to traverse the highway during heavy rains. Landslides—common in wet weather—can close portions of the road for days, forcing you to turn back or even leaving you stranded. Sporadic spells of heavy fog may obscure your view—a frightening experience on such a narrow, winding road.

Taichung, provincial capital

Encircled by mountains rising from a western plain, Taichung ranks as Taiwan's third largest city. Though it offers nearby attractions of its own, the city is better known as the departure point for trips to Sun Moon Lake and Alishan in the island's mountainous interior. From Taipei, you can reach Taichung by plane, train, or bus. While in the vicinity, set aside a few hours to peruse the Handicraft Exhibition Hall at Tsaotun, 19 km/12 miles south of Taichung. Here you can collect locally made bamboo items, furniture, jewelry, cloisonné, lacquerware, and toys.

Sun Moon Lake—cool and serene

Nestled in the mountains 80 km/50 miles southeast of Taichung, serene Sun Moon Lake attracts vacationers from all over Taiwan.

From Taipei, you can join organized tours to Sun Moon Lake only, or take ones that combine the East-West Cross-Island Highway (including Taroko Gorge) with a visit to Sun Moon Lake, or the lake with Alishan. Another option is to take a round-the-island tour from Taipei, which will include the lake among its stops.

The 2-hour drive from Taichung takes visitors through rice and sugar cane country, uninterrupted except for an occasional tile-roofed farmhouse or country town. In its final miles the road climbs to the lake, which lies 762 meters/2,500 feet high, on the western boundary of the Central Range.

Completely encircled by forested peaks, Sun Moon Lake offers a cool and serene setting. Local attractions include the Formosan Aboriginal Culture Village, with artifacts and primitive dwellings representing Taiwan's nine surviving aboriginal tribes.

By rail up Mount Ali

One of Taiwan's most pleasant overnight trips consists of a ride up Mount Ali to the tiny village of Alishan, located at an elevation of 2,275 meters/7,465 feet. Departing from the small west coast town of Chiayi, about 80 km/50 miles south of Taichung, a narrow-gauge, alpine express train chugs and puffs along its 72-km/45-mile ascent. During the 3-hour trip, you'll climb from flat farmlands dotted with peaked grain stacks through stands of brilliant calla lilies. Spring-blooming azaleas crowd the forested lower mountains before the landscape gives way to deep valleys and misted peaks. The rail line goes through 50 tunnels and crosses 80 bridges.

THE TROPICAL SOUTH

In the south, Taiwan's landscape offers tropical enchantment. Here you'll find both balmy, beautiful beaches and historically important cities. From Chiayi, travel south to explore historic Tainan, the large seaport of Kaohsiung, and—near the tip of the island—Kenting National Park and Oluanpi (land's end).

Trains, airplanes, and special air-conditioned tourist buses travel southward to Kaohsiung from Taipei several times a day. Round-the-island tours, ranging from 3 to 6 days, include several stops in southern Taiwan. Other tour operators offer excursions of 1 to 3 days that travel exclusively to the south.

Historic Tainan

Cradle of Taiwan's history and culture, the ancient city of Tainan lies 11 km/7 miles inland from the Taiwan Strait. First settled by wandering Hakka people, the city served as a foothold for the Dutch until Cheng Ch'eng-kung (Koxinga) drove them off the island in 1661.

Located about 362 km/225 miles south of Taipei, this city of some 600,000 people fascinates visitors with remnants of its early history.

Fort Providentia (Chihkan Tower). The Dutch named it Fort Providentia in 1650; after 300 years and an earthquake, the Chinese rebuilt the fort, changing its name to Chihkan Tower. In the days when the Dutch tricolor flew over the fort, ships sailed up to its front gate. Land reclamation has pushed back the sea, leaving the fort on Mintsu Road on the city's northern side. The only elements now remaining are an ancient well and two buildings housing historical documents.

Fort Zeelandia. Eleven km/seven miles west of Tainan at Anping, you can visit the second Dutch fort (built here in the 1630s). As in the case of Fort Providentia, land reclamation and alluvial fill have changed this fort's surroundings from waterfront to inland. The flags of six nations flew over its ramparts before the Chinese rebuilt the structure, renaming it Anping Castle.

Confucian Temple. Standing at the southern side of the city's great traffic circle, southwest of the Tainan Railroad Station, you'll see the red gateway to the Confucian Temple on Nanmen Road. Set in a tree-shaded garden, the burnt red central temple reflects an ancient, classical Chinese architectural style. Built in 1665, the temple is one of Taiwan's oldest.

Koxinga Shrine. South of the traffic circle on Kaishan Road stands a memorial to Taiwan's beloved warrior-liberator Koxinga. Inside the bright red shrine, you'll see an imposing image of the hero who died in 1662, a year after driving the Dutch out of Taiwan.

THE WORLD OF ENTERTAINMENT

Fabulous costumes, elaborate make-up, ancient legends, tumbling acrobats, nearly life-size puppets, masked performers, folk dancers, energetic drummers—all these are part of the wonderful world of traditional Oriental entertainment. Whether it be Japanese kabuki or Beijing opera, Korean folk dancing or Chinese acrobatics, all express art forms passed down through the ages.

At right, costumed Korean performers, known for their graceful choreography, leap to the beat of their music. With a swirl of pastel colors, a silk-clad Chinese woman (bottom left) skillfully executes a ribbon dance during a Hong Kong cultural show. Elaborate attire and make-up adorn a Beijing opera actor (bottom right); make-up and costuming reveal whether a character is good or evil.

TAIWAN'S ABORIGINAL WEAVERS

With hands skilled from years of experience, an Atayal tribeswoman deftly weaves coarse ramie fiber into a length of colorful cloth. Back and forth the shuttle slides, creating dazzling stripes of red, black, and blue in a design passed down from tribal ancestors.

Atayal women collect wild, shrubby ramie plants from neighboring hillsides in central Taiwan. Using their teeth, they strip off the bark to expose the plants' inner stem fibers. Following time-honored techniques they separate the fibers into strands, twisting and spinning them onto a weighted spindle to form a single thread. The entire ball of thread is then immersed in a vat of brilliant colorfast dye (made from native roots). When the thread ball dries, the women stretch the threads, looping them around a warping board, separated at top and bottom by bamboo poles.

To begin weaving, women sit on a mat with legs outstretched, their feet touching the weaving "logs" in front of them. The logs stand about 1 meter/3 feet high, tapering at the top, where a trough holds the material. Bound to the logs by a backstrap, the women hold the remainder of the loom in their laps. By leaning back and forth, they can increase or decrease thread tension.

If you venture through Taiwan's Central Mountains, be sure to stop at Wushe (1 hour's drive north-

east of Sun Moon Lake) to watch Atayal tribeswomen at their work.

Lengths of fabric are sewn into tablecloths, handbags, placemats, vests, ponchos, skirts, and even rugs. Look for these unique pieces at native handicraft stores (on Taipei's Chungshan North Road), or shop directly at a weaver's doorstep.

On to bustling Kaohsiung

From Tainan, you might explore the west coast for further hallmarks of history, then dip down to the southernmost tip of Taiwan. South of Tainan, the road to Kaohsiung (53 km/33 miles away) winds through hills, plots of sugar cane, banana plantations, and rice paddies. Situated at the edge of an important deep-water harbor, Kaohsiung ranks as Taiwan's second largest city, and is one of the Orient's busiest ports.

City attractions. Visitors and residents alike enjoy swimming at Hsitze Bay, strolling through Kaohsiung's public park along the banks of the Love River, viewing the city and harbor from atop Shoushan Park, and visiting the Ming Dynasty tomb of Prince Ning Ching.

Cheng Ching Lake. Set in parklike grounds about 8 km/5 miles northeast of Kaohsiung, this 103-hectare/255-acre artificial lake claims distinction for its Bridge of Nine Bends, built to foil evil spirits.

You enter the park through a tile-roofed gateway. Inside are waterfalls, flower gardens, a clock constructed from flowers, and willow-lined paths. Meander on to see classical-style pavilions and pagodas, an avenue of orchids, and an aquarium stocked with fresh and saltwater tropical fish.

Lotus Lake. About 11 km/7 miles north of Kaohsiung, photographers enjoy stopping to capture the serene beauty of Lotus Lake at Tsoying. The famous Spring and Autumn Pavilions, twin pagodalike structures, rise from a quiet lagoon; nearby stands a lakeside Confucian Temple. Lotus blossoms carpet the lake in summer.

Kenting National Park

South of Kaohsiung, at Taiwan's tropical tip, the countryside becomes wild, its mountains crowding closer to the sea. Designated as Taiwan's first national park, the site is a 326-square-km/126-square-mile tract that includes Kenting Botanical Gardens and Oluanpi Lighthouse (at land's end).

Kenting Botanical Gardens. Garden lovers will take home fragrant memories of this 170-hectare/420-acre garden, a $1^1/_2$-hour bus or taxi trip from Kaohsiung. Stroll among hundreds of varieties of tropical trees and plants (many labeled in English, Latin, and Chinese). Kenting Gardens also includes one of the largest experimental forests in the Orient. Walkways lead among the plants to rock caves and a tall observation tower overlooking the sea.

Oluanpi Lighthouse. From Kenting, it's only a bit further to land's end—Oluanpi—where a lighthouse, built in 1883, marks the island's southern tip. Famous for its multicolored butterflies, Oluanpi also offers fresh seafood and swimming beaches strewn with seashells.

KNOW BEFORE YOU GO

Documents, shots, what to pack—all are covered in this brief list of details to consider before you depart for Taiwan.

Entry/exit procedures. A visa, passport, and proof of onward passage are needed to visit Taiwan. Along with your application form, you will need 3 photos when applying for the multiple-entry visa valid for 5 years for stays of up to 60 days.

Apply for your visa at the nearest Coordination Council for North America Affairs (CCNAA). Offices are located in Los Angeles, Honolulu, San Francisco, Seattle, Houston, Kansas City, Chicago, Atlanta, New York, and Washington, D.C.

If arriving from an infected area, you'll need a cholera inoculation. Check with the U.S. Public Health Service for other recommended inoculations.

You pay a passenger service tax of NT$300 on departure from Taiwan.

Customs. In addition to personal items, visitors may bring in duty-free 25 cigars, 200 cigarettes, one pound of tobacco, a one-liter bottle of liquor, one still camera, one movie camera, and a reasonable amount of film. Prohibited items include firearms, narcotics, and pornography.

It's advisable to declare any silver or gold jewelry you bring into Taiwan; customs limits you to a maximum of 62.5 grams of each upon departure. Stereo systems, televisions, and video recorders must be declared.

Currency. The New Taiwan dollar (NT$) is the official currency. Upon entry and departure, you must declare all your foreign currency. Unlimited foreign currency may be brought in and, if declared on arrival, may be taken out. Without a declaration, not more than U.S. $5,000 in cash or the equivalent in any other foreign currency may be taken out. You're also restricted from importing or exporting more than NT$8,000 in cash. When converting money, always get an official exchange receipt; you'll need one for reconversion. Most major credit cards are accepted in Taiwan.

Health conditions. Medical facilities are very good in Taipei and the major cities. Most hotels and drug stores carry everyday medicines and toiletries.

Tipping. Light tipping is the rule in Taiwan. Most hotels and restaurants add a 10 percent service charge.

Time. The time difference between the U.S. West Coast and Taiwan is 16 hours. When it's noon Sunday in Taipei, it's 8 P.M. Saturday in San Francisco.

Language. Mandarin is the official language, but many people speak Taiwanese (a variant of a southern Chinese dialect) and Japanese. The younger generation and those engaged in the tourist trade speak some English.

Climate. Mostly subtropical, Taiwan's weather warms to tropical temperatures on the southern half of the island. Balmiest months are October through April, when the temperature averages 21°C/70°F in Taipei to 24°C/75°F in the south. From late May to September, the country turns hot and humid. Rainfall averages about 100 inches annually, with light showers misting 200 days out of the year.

Take lightweight clothing for most certain comfort during warmer spring, summer, and autumn months. At any time of the year, a lightweight raincoat and umbrella come in handy.

For more information. Contact the Tourism Bureau, Republic of China, P.O. Box 1490, Taipei, Taiwan. In the United States, you can write to the Taiwan Visitors Association offices at 166 Geary Street, Suite 1605, San Francisco, CA 94108; 1 World Trade Center, Suite 8855, New York, NY 10048; or 333 North Michigan Avenue, Suite 2329, Chicago, IL 60601.

HONG KONG

A thriving metropolis packed into a tiny space, its flashy
facade of high-rises and neon colliding with a
Chinese world of colorful street markets, wizened
calligraphers, timeworn temples, romantic junks

n world maps, Hong Kong looks like a tiny decimal point at the southern tip of China's Guangdong Province. Yet despite its minuscule size, Hong Kong is one of the great travel destinations of the world today.

Part of Hong Kong's allure is its exceptional setting: a spacious, crescent-shaped harbor bordered by the Kowloon Peninsula and the jagged, mountainous bulk of Hong Kong Island. Hong Kong ranks with Sydney, Rio de Janeiro, Capetown, San Francisco, and Pago Pago as one of the world's truly breathtaking harbors. Constantly alive, Victoria Harbour presents a changing scene of freighters and cruise ships, cross-harbor ferries and teakwood junks, naval vessels and hydrofoils, sampans and yachts.

Rising from its shores is a striking array of high-rise buildings ranging from hotels and offices to apartment-house blocks. They crawl up the steep mountain slopes of Hong Kong Island and crowd to the water's edge on some of the world's highest-priced real estate. With each passing year, more and more land is reclaimed from the harbor, providing growing room for the ever-burgeoning city. After dark, the ranks of tall buildings become a dazzling band of lights shimmering in the black night waters.

Another part of Hong Kong's magnetism lies in its foreignness. At first glance, Hong Kong appears to be just one more skyscraper-strewn modern city. But on closer examination, you quickly uncover distinctions. You wander through narrow streets signed with bright calligraphy, crowded with vendors dispensing food from

bubbling pots and sizzling pans, and edged by shops stocked with everything from brightly colored cotton cloth to woks to dried fish and pressed duck. You pass fortune tellers and letter writers tucked into tiny street-side crannies, and temples wreathed in smoke from smoldering incense.

Suddenly you realize the massive office buildings, fancy hotels, elegant shops, nightclubs, and dazzling lights are all a western facade. Hong Kong's population is primarily Chinese. Both Chinese and English are the official languages.

Hong Kong thrives on commerce; bargains from around the world are displayed in shops and stores. Its hotels rank among the finest in the world, and the city's cuisine is renowned.

Beyond the city centers of Hong Kong Island and Kowloon, you will still find a peaceful countryside of small farms and villages, isolated islands trimmed with sandy beaches, and quiet waterways.

AT CHINA'S DOORSTEP

Hong Kong occupies 1,070 square km/413 square miles bordering China's southeastern coast. Located on the east side of the Pearl River Estuary, Hong Kong lies only 145 km/90 miles southeast of China's Guangzhou (Canton). Across the estuary, 64 km/40 miles to the west, is Macau, a 400-year-old Portuguese outpost.

Geographically, Hong Kong is divided into three main areas; Hong Kong Island; the Kowloon Peninsula; and the New Territories, stretching from Kowloon to the

Hong Kong Island's *skyscrapers tower above bustling harbor. Kowloon and New Territories lie across water.*

China border. Curving between the mainland and Hong Kong Island is Victoria Harbour, a broad natural deep-water port.

Enclosing the harbor on the south is Hong Kong Island, marked by a rugged backbone of rocky hills. The island's highest peak, Victoria, rises 551 meters/1,809 feet above the water. Major business, commercial, residential areas, and hotels lie along the island's northern shore, with additional residential areas on the southwest side of the island.

Across the harbor to the north is Kowloon Peninsula, a flat piece of land edged by steep hills. Its southern tip is home to shopping and entertainment areas, and hotels. Many of Hong Kong's chief manufacturing districts are also located on the peninsula. Hong Kong International Airport (Kai Tak) juts into the harbor from the peninsula's northern edge.

Farther north, the territory's third geographic region, the New Territories, stretches some 38 km/24 miles from Kowloon to the China border. In recent years, this rural area has seen new development. In addition to farmlands and older towns and villages, there are also new large industrial centers and resettlement housing estates. Also included in the New Territories are 235 islands, many of them small and uninhabited. Only Lantau, Peng Chau, Cheung Chau, and Lamma are of any size and importance.

Nature's beauty

Even with a large population (5.5 million), a thriving business and manufacturing community, and limited land area, Hong Kong still offers peaceful countryside for both its residents and visitors. Hikers and nature lovers can enjoy countryside walks across wooded hillsides, around reservoirs, up mountain peaks, and along island beaches. Nature trails wind through 21 officially-designated country parks.

Over the centuries, much of Hong Kong's subtropical vegetation has been cut and cleared. Yet a surprising number of flowering shrubs, low-growing trees, ferns, and fragrant flowers remain. Colorful flowers and beautiful gardens are part of the Chinese tradition, and there are small parks scattered through the city.

Local wildlife

More than 360 species of birds inhabit the territory, along with some 200 species of butterflies.

Large mammals native to the area include Chinese pangolins (scaly anteaters) and rhesus monkeys. Less abundant are barking deer (heard only in the spring), badgers, otters, and an occasional Chinese leopard. Snakes (some poisonous), lizards, and frogs are well represented.

The underwater world contains numerous species of fish, terrapins, turtles, toads, and the Hong Kong newts or salamanders.

A HISTORY OF COMMERCE

Archeological evidence reveals that Chinese lived in Kowloon 5,000 years ago, but Hong Kong's modern history doesn't really begin until much later—around the 15th century—with the growth of trade between Europe and the East.

Foreign traders arrive

Marco Polo traveled overland from Europe in the 13th century, opening the west's first trade route with China. Between the 15th and 18th centuries, Portugal, Britain, and other European nations established trade relations with Guangzhou (Canton). Britain soon dominated all European Trade with China.

Working relations between Guangzhou and foreign traders were not the best. The Chinese considered all foreigners barbarians and restricted their movements in Guangzhou. Traders were confined to Guangzhou's factory area along the Pearl River and were allowed to reside there only during the September-through-March trading season. Their families remained in the Portuguese colony of Macau throughout the year.

Opium's influence. For many years China prospered, trading its tea and silk for silver. Trouble started, though, when the foreign powers began to import opium from India, thereby shifting the balance of trade. The Chinese emperor grew more and more alarmed as opium addiction among the Chinese increased while the country's silver stockpile decreased (as a result of its being used as payment for the drug). To counteract the problem, he appointed a special commissioner to stop the opium trade. Hostilities began when some 20,000 chests of British opium were seized at Guangzhou and destroyed.

The beginnings of a free port. From 1840 to 1860, a continuous state of aggression existed between the Chinese and the British. Britain wanted to expand trade with China and have its own offshore trading post free of Chinese interference. The Chinese wanted to stop the flow of opium into their country and to restrict further foreign trade in Asia.

In 1842 the Chinese were forced to open several Chinese ports to trade, and to cede Hong Kong Island to Britain. Though the island was proclaimed a free port, the British doubted it would ever become a world trading center. When the British took possession, Hong Kong Island was nothing more than a sparsely settled, rocky piece of ground. Its 2,000 inhabitants, living in a cluster of Chinese villages on the island's south coast, made their living by fishing, cultivating the scanty soil, and engaging in occasional piracy.

Hong Kong grows. In 1860 China ceded more land to the British: the lower portion of Kowloon Peninsula, up to

Boundary Street; and Stonecutters Island, just west of Kowloon. In 1899 the British obtained a 99-year lease on the New Territories, thus greatly increasing Hong Kong's geographical size. It now extended some 38 km/24 miles north of Kowloon and included 235 additional islands.

By the turn of the century, Hong Kong had become a great shipping port and a center for trade with China. Its population swelled to 300,000 people, most of them Chinese.

War years and beyond

During World War II, Japan invaded Hong Kong and deported to China almost a million people—about two-thirds of Hong Kong's Chinese residents. By the end of the war, Hong Kong's population had plummeted to 600,000. Suffering from a serious food shortage and a severe decline in trade, its future was highly uncertain.

In the years following the war, some 750,000 Chinese refugees flooded into Hong Kong; more arrived after Shanghai fell to the Communists in 1949. Thousands of Chinese—from illiterate farmers to educated businessmen—sought refuge in the colony. Many came empty-handed; others brought the means to found great banks, trading companies, and shipping houses. Hong Kong again thrived as one of the world's great free ports.

Hong Kong today. Hong Kong continues to be a great free port. It champions free enterprise with minimal taxes and government regulations and is one of Asia's leading manufacturing and commercial centers. Hong Kong's locally produced goods for export include textiles, clothing, plasticware such as toys and dolls, electrical machinery and appliances, and photographic and optical goods.

Currently, Hong Kong is still a British colony. Under authority emanating from the British crown, the territory's government includes a Governor, an Executive Council, and a Legislative Council.

In 1997, when Britain's lease over most of Hong Kong expires, it will be transferred back to the People's Republic of China. According to an agreement between Britain and China, Hong Kong will keep its present economic and social system until 2047. It will retain the name Hong Kong and its status as a capitalist, free-port enclave within the communist country. Its chief executive will be appointed by Beijing, but its government will be composed of elected local inhabitants, and it will have its own currency and flag.

HONG KONG'S PEOPLE

Nearly 98 percent of Hong Kong's 5.5 million people are Chinese. The remaining 2 percent of the population consists of long- and short-term residents from Great Britain, the U.S., Australia, Canada, Japan, Portugal, India, and Southeast Asia.

The Chinese

Hong Kong's Chinese inhabitants are predominantly of Cantonese (Punti) stock. The next largest ethnic groups are Sze Yap and Chiu Chow. Cantonese is the principal Chinese dialect spoken.

It is said that the Punti migrated south from China in the 10th century and were known as the "land people." The rural Hakka, referred to as "guests" of the Punti, arrived later. Many Hakka are still farmers in the New Territories. Hakka women are easily recognized by their black *sam foo* (tunic and trousers) and wide-brimmed straw hats.

The nomadic Tanka and Hoklo from Fukien province were known as the "water people" and were fisher folk. They lived their entire lives aboard junks in floating villages, sheltered from occasional typhoons at Yau Ma Tei, Causeway Bay, Aberdeen, and Sha Kei Wan. Today, many of these people have come ashore to live, abandoning their hard life at sea to work in factories.

Lifestyle based on tradition

Because of a predominantly Chinese population, Chinese cultural traditions are evident in Hong Kong's festivals, foods, crafts, drama, and music. Even in the colony's modern urban areas, ancient Chinese values often shape the day-to-day existence of its people.

Dress. Many Chinese, including those engaged in western business, have adopted western-style clothes. However, you'll still find older people, fisher folk, and agricultural workers wearing the loose-fitting sam foo.

Religion and superstition. Many Chinese follow the Buddhist religion, combined with adaptations of Taoist beliefs, devotion to ancestor worship, and animism (ascribing a soul to certain natural objects). Confucianism is also popular. The water people worship Tin Hau, goddess of heaven and protectress of mariners and fisher folk, honoring her with temples and a yearly festival.

Hong Kong also has synagogues, mosques, and Christian churches of many denominations, some offering services in English.

DISCOVERING KOWLOON

The Kowloon Peninsula's soaring rows of massive skyscrapers nestle between the rugged hills of the New Territories and the shimmering, boat-dotted waters of Victoria Harbour. The streets of this tiny (10.5-square-km/4-square-mile) peninsula teem with humanity; some 2.5 million people call Hong Kong's "Kowloon side" home.

One of Kowloon's most fascinating aspects is its many Chinese temples, markets, and cultural influences. As you stroll around the older part of Kowloon, you'll become entranced by its narrow shop-lined streets shaded by a jumble of signs covered with Chinese calligraphy.

In striking contrast to old Kowloon is the fast-paced pulse of modern Kowloon, which boasts plush, high-rise hotels and office buildings. New skyscrapers are continually being added to the skyline. Everywhere you turn you'll see construction projects encased in webs of bamboo scaffolding. Below these growing edifices, city thoroughfares appear jammed with trucks, taxis, cars, and buses all vying for road space both day and night.

Getting your bearings

For an idea of Kowloon's layout, imagine the peninsula bisected by an inverted T. The head of the T, Salisbury Road, crosses the peninsula's southern tip. Nathan Road heads north, perpendicular to Salisbury Road, leading straight and wide up the peninsula 3 km/2 miles to Boundary Street, the border between Kowloon and the New Territories. Beyond Boundary Street is New Kowloon, an area of high-rise housing estates and factories.

From Hong Kong Island, you can reach Kowloon by ferry, by highway through the Cross-Harbour Tunnel, or by Mass Transit Railway. One of the best ways to explore the traffic-congested peninsula is on foot, using public transportation for outlying destinations. You'll find taxis and buses lining traffic islands in front of the Star Ferry Pier. Mass Transit Railway trains also travel up the peninsula, and local tour operators offer tours which include Kowloon.

Along the waterfront

A good place to begin your Kowloon exploration is along the waterfront at the peninsula's southern tip. At the western end of the waterfront is the Star Ferry Pier, docking point for the popular commuter ferry running between Hong Kong Island and Kowloon.

Harbour City. West of the Star Ferry Pier, this massive complex stretches north along the waterfront and boasts some 600 stores, 3 hotels, and 50 restaurants. Built in stages, Harbour City includes Ocean Terminal with three floors of shops; Ocean Centre famed for its high-tech products and trendy boutiques; and Ocean Galleries where shoppers are transported by moving walkways. All arcades are interconnected.

Space Museum. On Salisbury Road east of the Star Ferry Pier, a white-domed building houses one of the world's largest and best-equipped planetariums. The Hong Kong Space Museum includes a Space Theatre featuring sky shows and a Hall of Solar Sciences with a solar telescope. The Exhibition Hall focuses on both astronomy and man's exploration of space.

Adjacent to the Space Museum is the Hong Kong Cultural Centre. Still under construction, it will house two theaters, a concert hall, meeting facilities, restaurants, and a Museum of Art.

East Tsim Sha Tsui. A waterfront promenade, offering an unobstructed view of Victoria Harbour, stretches from neighboring New World Centre eastward into East Tsim Sha Tsui. This area has major hotels and more shops.

Up Nathan Road

Major hotels and shops are also concentrated near the southern end of the peninsula along Nathan Road and its intersecting streets, in the area known as Tsim Sha Tsui.

The southern end of broad Nathan Road, often called the "Golden Mile," presents numerous opportunities for shopping, dining, and nightclubbing. In the evening, the whole area is aglow with hundreds of bright neon signs advertising shops and services. Day and night, the streets are packed with shoppers.

Kowloon Park, on the west side of Nathan Road between Haiphong and Austin roads, includes a Chinese garden with lotus pond, rose garden, and aviary. The Hong Kong Museum of History is also located here.

Strolling through Yau Ma Tei

Though Nathan Road has always been a focal point for shoppers seeking quality, don't overlook the colorful Jordan Road area, a maze of busy, cluttered streets near the peninsula's western shoreline north of Tsim Sha Tsui. About a 10-minute taxi ride (or 2-minute Mass Transit Railway trip) north from the Star Ferry Pier, Jordan Road marks Yau Ma Tei's southern boundary. Sandwiched between Tsim Sha Tsui and Mong Kok, it is believed to be one of the first Kowloon districts developed by the British in the 1860s.

Off the area's western shore is Yau Ma Tei's typhoon shelter, with a breakwater shielding hundreds of junks and small boats from the open sea. Harbor cruises provide a closer look at life in this floating village.

Some interesting streets. Strolling Yau Ma Tei's streets, you'll discover a little of old Hong Kong. Narrow lanes lead to stores displaying a fascinating array of goods. You'll see rattan shops brimming with baskets of every size and shape; and porcelain shops with everything from flower pots to complete sets of Chinese dishes, including spoons, soy sauce containers, and chopstick holders.

On Canton Road, for example, there are shops selling mah-jongg sets and a shop devoted totally to bamboo steamers. Brides-to-be shop on Shanghai Street for Chinese wedding gowns. There are also a number of stores selling gold and jade, embroidered goods, and electrical items.

On Shanghai Street, at the Soy Street intersection, is Wan Loy teahouse, the early-morning gathering place for bird lovers and their pet birds. Hong Lok Street's morning bird market sells Asian songbirds and cages.

Temple of 10,000 Buddhas *features more than 12,000 images. Steep flight of stairs leads to hillside complex overlooking Shatin in New Territories.*

Blazing neon signs *turn Hong Kong night into day, lighting the way for bargain-seeking shoppers in city that never seems to sleep.*

Begin your stroll at the Jordan Road Ferry Pier and walk east along Jordan Road. Then let your feet and your curiosity take charge. The Hong Kong Tourist Association has a fact sheet detailing Yau Ma Tei attractions.

Several markets. Most famed of the area's shopping destinations is perhaps the Jade Market at the junction of Kansu and Battery streets. Between 10 A.M. and 4 P.M. daily, jade of every description is sold at some 400 stalls. Rings, pendants, beads, bracelets, and loose stones form a sea of green, spreading out over tables and overflowing onto ground-level display areas.

Haggling is a must, as is careful examination of the merchandise. The quality, color, and price of jade can vary widely. Look for pure color with translucency. Authentic jade is very hard and can't be easily scratched.

During the daytime, Temple Street (1 block east of Shanghai Street) is quiet, but in the evening between 8 and 11 P.M., it turns into a mammoth outdoor bazaar some 6 blocks long. Shop owners compete for attention with blaring music and a motley array of merchandise. Tables and stalls, illuminated by bare lights, overflow with everything from sweaters and shirts to pop records and cure-all medicines. Street singers add to the din created by the hawkers and hagglers. Fortunetellers peer into patrons' futures with the aid of bamboo slips, palm readings, and cards.

Tin Hau Temple. Within this complex, west of Nathan Road between Public Square and Market streets, are four temples. The main one is dedicated to Tin Hau, goddess of heaven and patroness of seafarers. It attracts numerous residents from the nearby Yau Ma Tei typhoon shelter. There's also Fook Tak Temple, home of To Tei, the earth god; a temple devoted to Shing Wong, the city god; and Shea Tan Temple, dedicated to the local community.

HONG KONG ISLAND

Hong Kong Island rises steeply from Victoria Harbour's ship-filled waters. Its northern shore, facing Kowloon Peninsula, is jammed with office skyscrapers; beyond the business center, residences and smart apartment buildings climb the island's steep slopes; a mantle of lush vegetation crowns the hills. The island's highest mountain, Victoria Peak, looms some 551 meters/1,809 feet above the harbor. On the other side of this peak lies yet another Hong Kong: sheltered coves, sandy beaches, and outdoor recreation areas.

When the island was first settled in the late 1800s, it was a way station for European trading ships on the China route. Today, it ranks as the territory's major administrative, financial, and cultural center. Many of the territory's banks, insurance companies, and multinational corporations have offices on Hong Kong Island. Interspersed with blocks of offices are hotels.

The island's varied districts

Curving along the harbor, Central District (officially Victoria City) forms the island's cosmopolitan main commercial center. Walking westward, you can explore the narrow lanes and crowded streets of Western District, with shops selling everything from herbal medicine to antiques. Immediately east of Central District is Wanchai, made famous by the film *The World of Suzie Wong*.

Farther east, near the Cross-Harbour Tunnel to Kowloon, Causeway Bay presents highly diverse images—a junk-filled typhoon shelter and high-rise hotels, Chinese shops and the World Trade Center.

Strung along the island's southwest side is Aberdeen, famed for its floating restaurants and junk-crowded harbor. A drive along the island's southern beachfront road offers vistas of rambling homes and tall apartment buildings, and long expanses of beach.

From Kowloon, Hong Kong Island can be reached by ferry, by highway through the Cross-Harbour Tunnel, or by Mass Transit Railway.

Districts along Hong Kong Island's northern shore can be explored by bus, taxi, tram, and Mass Transit Railway (with a western terminus of Sheung Wan and an eastern terminus of Chai Wan). Double-decker trams journey the width of the north shore from Kennedy Town to Shau Kei Wan, with an additional route to Happy Valley.

Beyond its urban areas, you can visit Hong Kong Island by car, taxi, or local bus. Tour operators feature Hong Kong Island on half- and full-day tours.

The Hong Kong Tourist Association publishes walking guides and fact sheets featuring walks in Central and Western districts, Causeway Bay, and other attractions.

The cosmopolitan Central District

Each day thousands of commuters disembark from the Star Ferry from Kowloon into Hong Kong Island's Central District. The ferry terminal stands along the waterfront near the 57-story Connaught Centre.

Underpasses and overpasses funnel pedestrian traffic directly into the district's business and commercial center. Paralleling Connaught Road along the island's north shore are the district's other main streets: Des Voeux Road Central and Queen's Road Central.

Start from Statue Square. Emerging from the Star Ferry underpass next to the Mandarin Hotel, you look out on an impressive scene. East of the hotel stands the raised promenade of Statue Square, with its neat green lawns, ornamental kiosks, and reflecting pools. South of the square, looking toward Des Voeux Road Central, an appealing garden dominated by a bronze statue of Sir Thomas Jackson Bart (an early chief manager of the Hongkong and Shanghai Bank) will catch your eye.

East of the square, the Cenotaph commemorates Hong Kong's war dead. The City Hall complex overlooks the square's harbor side. A concert hall, theater, libraries, and Hong Kong Museum of Art are housed here.

Transportation hub. Jutting into the harbor northwest of Connaught Centre is Blake Pier, departure point for many water tours. Farther west is the Outlying Districts Services Pier, with ferry service to outlying islands. The ultramodern twin-towered Shun Tak Centre complex west of this pier includes the Hong Kong/Macau Ferry Terminal plus a hotel, shopping arcade, and offices. An overhead pedestrian promenade stretches from the Star Ferry Pier to the Hong Kong/Macau Ferry Terminal.

Shopping diversity. The Landmark shopping arcade, on Des Voeux Road Central near Pedder Street, features splashing fountains, an airy five-story central atrium, and shops selling designer-brand goods. Other Central District shopping arcades include the Princes Building, adjacent to Statue Square, and Swire House on Connaught Road Central near Pedder Street.

Boutiques also line Des Voeux Road Central, and there are a number of factory outlets in Central District.

Exploring the Western District

The Western District may be undergoing a physical face-lift, but the fundamental character of life remains intrinsically Chinese. For an in-depth look at this character, stroll the streets of the district and watch its rich panorama unfold around you.

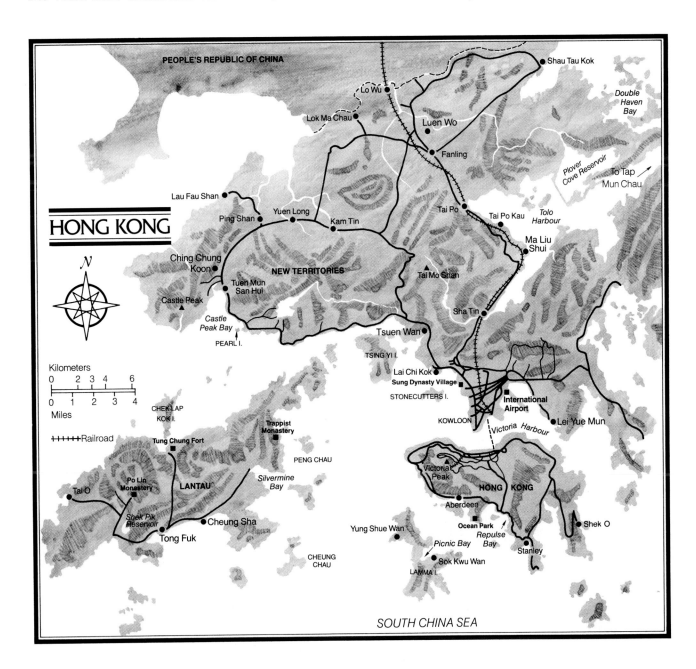

Peak Tram *transports passengers to top of Hong Kong Island's Victoria Peak for spectacular panoramic views. Lower terminus is on Garden Road.*

Aberdeen Harbour's *water dwellers receive all supplies—even soft drinks— by sampan. Older residents may never have set foot on shore.*

Central Market. On Des Voeux Road Central is Hong Kong's largest public market. Within its high-domed rooms, passageways are lined with stalls selling seafood, poultry, meat, and produce. It's open daily from 6 A.M. to 1 P.M. and from 4:30 to 7 P.M.

Colorful alleys. Near Central Market, between Des Voeux Road Central and Queen's Road Central, are several interesting side alleys.

To the east are Li Yuen Street East and West. Both alleys are noted for bargains in clothing and handbags.

To the west is Wing On Street or "cloth alley", offering a kaleidoscope of fabrics for sale at reasonable prices. Nearby Wing Sing Street, known as "egg street," has shops selling everything from fresh duck and quail eggs to salted eggs and "100-year-old" eggs.

Street specialties. Throughout Western District, you'll find streets whose shopkeepers specialize in a particular product. For example, Man Wa Lane has been the home of Chinese chop (signature stamp) makers for 60 years. In winter, Chinese go to Bonham Strand East to buy snakes for snake soup. Bonham Strand West is the center of the wholesale ginseng and medicinal herb trade.

Still other streets you'll want to explore include Des Voeux Road West, famed for its preserved-food shops selling shrimp paste, dried mushrooms, and shark's fin; and Queen's Road West, with its Chinese wedding attire.

Curio and antique shops line Hollywood Road. Steep Ladder Street, running north and south of Hollywood Road, is really a series of short, well-worn granite stairs broken only by the flat landings of cross streets and alleys. Still another stair-step path, Pottinger Street (east of Ladder Street), runs from the central waterfront area all the way to Hollywood Road.

Man Mo Temple. Built in 1847, this temple stands at 124 Hollywood Road off Ladder Street. "Man" is the god of literature and "Mo" is the god of war.

Changing Wanchai

East of the Central District, Hennessy Road marks the beginning of Wanchai. At one time, this area was a jumble of neon signs advertising hundreds of tawdry bars, popular haunts of military personnel on shore leave. Today, Wanchai is changing. Many bars have been converted to restaurants. Old buildings are being torn down, and new buildings erected.

Important new additions include the Hong Kong Arts Centre off Gloucester Road near the waterfront, and the neighboring Academy for Performing Arts. Also nearby is the Hong Kong Convention and Exhibition Centre, currently under construction.

The Museum of Chinese Historical Relics, in Causeway Centre on Harbour Road, displays artifacts and cultural treasures from China.

Causeway Bay—A contrast in old and new

Farther east along the harbor, you'll find old and new side by side. Causeway Bay, the site of the Cross-Harbour Tunnel, has added new hotels, department stores, shopping arcades, restaurants (including a whole street devoted to food, see page 120), and the World Trade Centre.

In contrast, Old Causeway Bay retains dozens of Chinese streets with small stores, street markets, and tea houses. Out in the harbor, junks and sampans float side by side in Causeway Bay's typhoon shelter.

Walking the mid-levels

Many narrow, tree-lined roads and lanes climb the slopes of Victoria Peak behind the Central District, winding past stately colonial houses and modern apartment buildings. You can explore on a self-guided stroll.

Start at the corner of Queen's Road Central and Ice House Street, where you'll find Battery Path (a pedestrian walkway) leading to St. John's Cathedral, Government House, and the Zoological and Botanical Garden.

St. John's Cathedral. Built in 1847 in early Victorian Gothic style, Hong Kong's first permanent church is marked by twin spires. Many of its memorial tablets were destroyed during World War II, but a record book records the colony's early history. It recounts deaths at the hands of pirates, in typhoons, in the fire of 1851, and on ships lost in the South China Sea. Garden Road flanks the church's east side.

Government House. West of Garden Road on Upper Albert Road, you'll find the residence of His Excellency the Governor of Hong Kong. Built by the British in the late 1850s, the house was embellished with an Oriental tower by the Japanese in the 1940s. It is closed to visitors. The surrounding mid-levels area was once the main European residential quarter.

Zoological and Botanical Gardens. Across from Government House you can walk the shaded paths of gardens spreading over several acres of sloping and terraced land. The zoological collection includes a large aviary of tropical birds.

Flagstaff House Museum of Tea Ware. Located off Cotton Tree Drive west of St. John's, this museum features historic Chinese tea ware. It's housed in Hong Kong's oldest western-style building, built in 1844 as the home of the Commander of the British Forces.

Atop Victoria Peak

Stern and inhospitable, the granite face of Victoria Peak forms a dramatic backdrop for one of the world's most beautiful harbors. Rising 551 meters/1,809 feet on the island's western end, Victoria Peak has viewpoints offering spectacular panoramas of Hong Kong Island, Victoria Harbour, Kowloon Peninsula, the South China Sea, and Hong Kong's scattered islands.

Since westerners first began trading in the Orient in the mid-19th century, Victoria Peak has occupied a special place in the hearts of Hong Kong residents and visitors. Wealthy colonial merchants built mansions on its rugged green slopes, a cooler site than the lowland streets.

Both buses and minibuses provide service to and from the summit, but it's more fun and scenic to take the Peak Tram (a funicular railway).

Riding the Peak Tram. Built in 1888, the Peak Tram transports commuters and visitors from Central District up to Victoria Peak Station, located 137 meters/450 feet below the summit. Propelled along by a moving steel cable, 72-passenger tram cars counterbalance each other during ascent and descent. The tram stops at five stations each way along the steep grade. Passengers sit on wooden slat benches facing uphill.

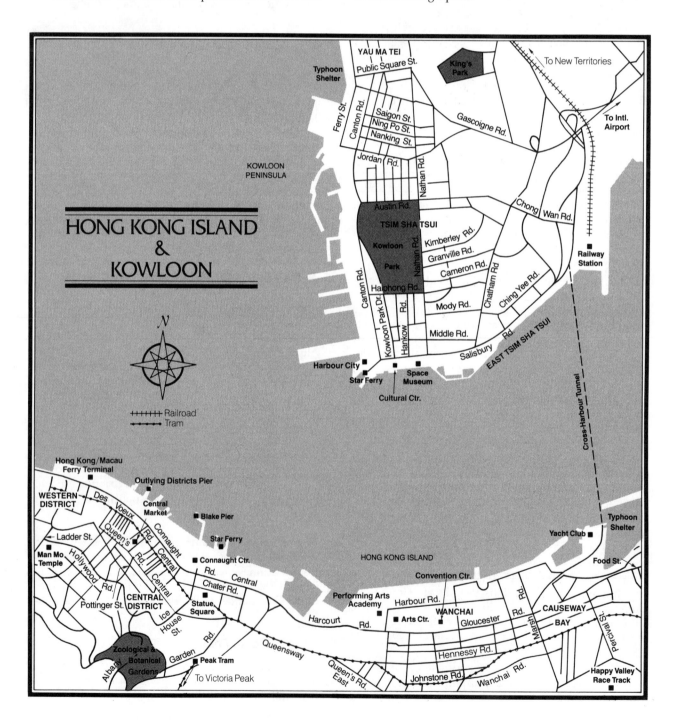

THE ESSENTIALS/**HONG KONG**

Here are a few basics to help you in planning a trip to Hong Kong.

Getting there

Hong Kong is served by air and sea transportation.

By air. Some 32 international airlines, including Hong Kong-based Cathay Pacific, serve Hong Kong International Airport (Kai Tak). Located on Kowloon Peninsula, the airport is about 6 km/4 miles from Kowloon hotels and 13 km/8 miles from Hong Kong Island hotels. Transportation to and from the airport includes hotel cars, taxis, and airport buses.

By sea. Many steamship companies include Hong Kong on itineraries of their cruise ships and cargo/passenger liners. Ships dock at Ocean Terminal on Kowloon or offshore in the harbor.

Where to stay

Most of Hong Kong's major hotels are located on Kowloon's southern tip and in the Central, Wanchai, and Causeway Bay districts of Hong Kong Island. All major hotels are air-conditioned, and offer restaurants, shopping arcades, health clubs, and other services. Most hotels add a 10 percent service charge and 5 percent government tax.

On Kowloon, major hotels include the Grand Tower, Holiday Inn Golden Mile, Holiday Inn Harbour View, Hongkong, Hyatt Regency, Kowloon, Marco Polo, Miramar, New World, Park, Peninsula, Prince, Regal Meridien Hong Kong, Regent, Royal Garden, Shangri-La, and Sheraton. Smaller downtown Kowloon hotels include the Ambassador, Empress, Fortuna, Grand, Guangdong, Imperial, International, Nathan, New Astor, Ritz, and Shamrock.

There's a Regal Meridien at the airport.

On Hong Kong Island, Central District hotels include the Furama Inter-Continental, Hong Kong Hilton, Mandarin, and Victoria. Wanchai–Causeway Bay hotels include the Caravelle, Excelsior, Harbour, Harbour View International House, Lee Gardens, New Harbour, Park Lane, and Ramada. In the Western District is the Emerald. On Cheung Chau Island, visitors stay at the Warwick Hotel.

The YMCA and YWCA offer inexpensive lodging in Kowloon.

Getting around Hong Kong

It's easy to move around compact Hong Kong. Public transportation includes buses that follow regular routes on both sides of the harbor and in the New Territories. Mini-buses follow irregular routes. Trams run along the northern shore of Hong Kong Island. The Mass Transit Railway (rapid transit system) connects Hong Kong Island with the Kowloon Peninsula. The track extends as far as Kwun Tong in eastern Kowloon and Tsuen Wan in the western part of the New Territories. On Hong Kong Island, the north shore route runs from Sheung Wan in the western part of the island to Chai Wan in the eastern part.

The Kowloon-Canton Railway runs from Kowloon's Hung Hom Station through the New Territories to Lo Wu on the Chinese border. Visitors without visas for China must alight at Sheung Shui, one stop before the border.

Taxis operate day and night on both sides of the harbor and in the New Territories. Rickshaws (two-wheeled vehicles pulled by the driver) are disappearing in Hong Kong, but you can still find them near the Hong Kong Island Star Ferry terminal. Negotiate the fare

with the driver before starting out. Rental cars are available with or without a driver. You'll need either a state or international driver's license. Traffic keeps to the left.

Water transportation focuses on the numerous ferries, *walla wallas* (motorized small boats), Chinese junks, and sampans. For more on exploring by water, see page 117.

Tours

Half- and full-day tours cover points of interest on Hong Kong Island, in Kowloon, and in the New Territories. Special tours are offered to Sung Dynasty Village, Ocean Park, Aberdeen and Stanley Village, Lantau, Cheung Chau, Macau, and China. You can also take special tours of the waterways and local nightlife.

Dining out and entertainment

Hong Kong's specialty is Chinese cuisine, particularly Cantonese dishes.

The territory's entertainment scene ranges from plush supper clubs with bands for dancing, to Chinese opera performances and discos. For more information, see page 120.

For more information

Hong Kong Tourist Association information and gift centers are located in the Star Ferry Concourse, Kowloon; Buffer Hall, Hong Kong International Airport; G8 Empire Centre, 68 Mody Road, East Tsim Sha Tsui, Kowloon; and 35th floor, Connaught Centre, Central District, Hong Kong Island. For telephone information service, call 3-7225555.

The Hong Kong Tourist Association's handy fact sheets and brochures are available in its information and gift centers.

The tram's lower terminus is on Garden Road in Central District, a short distance uphill from the Hong Kong Hilton Hotel. The upper station is housed in the Peak Tower, a distinctive structure resembling a flying saucer on stilts. It contains restaurants, shops, and viewing areas with panoramic vistas of Hong Kong.

Tram cars leave both stations every 18 minutes from 7 A.M. to midnight. City scenery unfolds during the 8-minute steep uphill trip. There's shuttle bus service from the Star Ferry Pier to the lower terminus.

Mountaintop strolling. From the upper terminus, you can venture forth on a stroll around the mountain along Lugard and Harlech roads. On your walk you may hear the wind whispering through pine trees and bamboo, and perhaps glimpse wild mountain camellias and brilliant butterflies. Below you stretches the beauty of Hong Kong. From the mountain's south side there are great views of Hong Kong's outlying islands of Cheung Chau, Lamma, and Lantau.

Mt. Austin Road, across from the terminus, leads to the summit of Victoria Peak. It takes about 30 minutes to climb the steep 1-km/¾-mile route to the top, where you'll find beautiful gardens.

Hong Kong Island's other side

The southern side of Hong Kong Island differs greatly from the urban north shore. Coastal roads along the island's heavily indented southern shore wind beside the South China Sea. Here visitors find sheltered coves, beaches, and fishing communities.

You can reach the island's southern coast by heading east or west out of the Central District by bus or taxi. It's even possible to cut across the center of the island on the Wong Nei Chung Gap Road or through the Aberdeen Tunnel. Destinations along the southern coast are also included in Hong Kong Island tours.

Aberdeen. In the early morning, junks and fishing boats trailing whitewater wakes leave the sheltered confines of Aberdeen Harbour. For more than 100 years, this fishing community on the island's southwestern shore has provided the territory with fresh fish.

However, in recent years Aberdeen Harbour's floating city of junks, home to those whose major livelihood is fishing, has dwindled. Now only about 5,000 water people live here. The rest have resettled ashore in high-rise housing estates overlooking the harbor.

Organized sampan tours take you on a 20-minute, narrated cruise around Aberdeen Harbour. Day and evening harbor cruises also include Aberdeen.

On your water journey through Aberdeen Harbour, you'll see boats maneuvering narrow waterways, fishermen mending nets or tinkering with diesel engines, produce vendors guiding vegetable-laden sampans toward waterbourne families, and children and small animals clambering over the decks of anchored

junks. Aberdeen's three ornate floating restaurants are a beehive of activity with sampans and hawker boats sailing to and from them.

Once back on land, stroll past shops and souvenir stalls lining Aberdeen's Main Road. Once famous as a pirate haunt, Aberdeen was one of Hong Kong's earliest settlements. Many older buildings line narrow streets, clothes-laden bamboo poles (Hong Kong's answer to the clothesline) jutting from their windows.

Ocean Park. On a promontory overlooking the South China Sea midway between Aberdeen and Deep Water Bay, a 73-hectare/180-acre entertainment/oceanarium complex provides a unique blend of marine-life exhibits and outdoor recreational activities.

The park is divided into two levels. The 16-hectare/40-acre lowland area includes a waterfall garden, a greenhouse complex of tropical plants, a butterfly house, a multipurpose theater, and a children's playground, farm, and zoo. Also on this level is Water World, with a variety of aquatic rides.

The 57-hectare/140-acre headland site includes Ocean Theatre, where high-divers, dolphins, sea lions, and a killer whale perform. There's also a huge aquarium and Wave Cove, where sea lions, penguins, and dolphins frolic in machine-generated waves. Sharing the hilltop with the oceanarium is an amusement area with thrill rides.

The bilevel park is connected by an aerial cable car that, during a 7-minute ride, offers a panoramic view. The world's longest escalator connects the upper level with the lower-level parking lot at the Tai Shue Wan entrance. En route, you can stop for a walk through a giant aviary.

Reclaimed land at Tai Shue Wan will be the site of The Middle Kingdom, a cultural village that will tell the story of Chinese civilization from 2205 B.C. to A.D. 1911.

Miles of sandy beaches. The main road skirting Hong Kong Island's southern shoreline leads east from Aberdeen to a dozen beaches and numerous sheltered coves. Most of the beaches have changing rooms, beach umbrella rentals, and refreshment stands available for day visitors.

Within 15 minutes of Aberdeen, the road curves around the western end of Deep Water Bay. Enclosed by green hills, on weekends its shallow, offshore waters attract thousands of people. Across from the beach are the 9-hole golfing greens of the Royal Hong Kong Golf Club. (Visitors can golf here weekdays only.)

The narrow and winding paved coast road continues southeast past the beaches of Repulse Bay, Middle Bay, and South Bay toward the village of Stanley. Smaller beaches and sandy coves interrupt the island's steep, rocky coastline, providing underwater adventure for the skin diver and tranquility for the swimmer who wants to get away from crowds. Access to these areas requires negotiating steep paths or a flight of steps.

Priests in bright regalia *perform service at Ching Chung Koon, Taoist monastery at Castle Peak.*

FESTIVAL TIME IN HONG KONG

Exuberant festivals and colorful events enliven Hong Kong's yearly calendar. The Chinese population lives by its own lunar calendar, celebrating traditional holidays and religious occasions in the time-honored manner of their ancestors. Many festivals reflect ancient Chinese superstitions and mythological beliefs dating back millennia. Since the Chinese calendar is based on phases of the moon, festivals and other special events occur on different dates each year. Check with the Hong Kong Tourist Association for current dates. The following list covers some of Hong Kong's major celebrations.

Chinese New Year. In late January or early February, the streets resound with greetings of *"Gung hay fat choy"* ("May you be blessed with prosperity in the New Year"). Most businesses remain closed for 3 to 4 days while the Chinese settle debts, exchange gifts, and celebrate with dragon dances and parades. Bright red signs hang from buildings and Hong Kong's waters abound with junks, walla wallas, and other small craft gaily decorated for the occasion.

Yuen Siu (Lantern) Festival. Marking the traditional end of the 15-day Chinese New Year season, Chinese families celebrate at home while thousands of lanterns illuminate streets, houses, temples, and ancestral halls.

Hong Kong Arts Festival. Held annually in January or February, this month-long festival brings together some of the world's top artists and performers in a programmed series of concerts, recitals, and displays.

Birthday of Tin Hau. Brightly decorated junks herald the birthday of this goddess of the sea, an important fisher-folk deity. A big celebration at the Tin Hau Temple on Joss House Bay and in Yeun Long highlights the day. Special ceremonies are also held at other Tin Hau temples throughout Hong Kong.

Cheung Chau Bun Festival. This week-long event in May features religious observances, Chinese opera, and a fiestalike atmosphere that can be felt over the whole island. On the third day there's a colorful float procession and special "good-luck" buns are distributed.

Birthday of Lord Buddha. In mid-May, statues in Buddhist temples and monasteries are cleaned in honor of Siddhartha's birth.

Dragon Boat Festival. Commemorating the death of national hero Ch'u Yuen, Hong Kong's Annual Dragon Boat Races are held in June. Amid a festive atmosphere, boat crews race their "dragon boats" at Sai Kung, Tai Po, Aberdeen, Yau Ma Tei, Shau Kei Wan, and Stanley.

In addition to races between local teams, there are the Hong Kong Dragon Boat Festival–International Races with overseas participants.

Yue Lan Festival. The Festival of the Hungry Ghosts occurs in August or September with offerings to spirits of the dead temporarily released from the underworld.

Hong Kong Food Festival. This month-long festival in August–September includes special restaurant menus and food presentations and events.

Birthday of Confucius. In remembrance of Confucius, ceremonies are held at Causeway Bay's Confucius Temple in October.

Mid-Autumn Festival. This event, held in September or October, is also called the Moon Cake Festival. It celebrates the uprising against Mongol war lords by Chinese who hid secret messages in moon cakes. Today's cakes contain ground lotus and sesame seeds or dates, and sometimes a duck egg.

Asian Arts Festival. Asian artists perform biennially in October or November during this cultural festival.

Chung Yeung Festival. During this festival in early October (also called the Festival of Ascending Heights), it's the Chinese belief that if one climbs to high places he will avoid disaster. The Victoria Peak Tram is extremely crowded at this time.

Christmas. Many Hong Kong residents celebrate this Christian day of worship. Christmas lights twinkle brightly in the downtown areas.

CRUISING HONG KONG'S WATERWAYS

Hong Kong's vast harbor bustles with maritime activity both day and night—passenger and vehicle ferries plowing their businesslike way between Hong Kong Island and Kowloon, anchored freighters loading and unloading cargoes, bobbing sampans and fishing junks maneuvering among the larger ships, heavily ladened barges chugging steadily toward their various destinations, and sleek hydrofoils skimming across the water to and from Macau (see page 125). The best way to observe this colorful harbor scene is to take a water excursion, either on your own or on a tour.

The popular green-and-white vessels of the Star Ferry transport passengers daily across the busy waters of Victoria Harbour, journeying between Hong Kong Island's Central District and the tip of Kowloon Peninsula. Ferries leave both piers every 5 minutes between 6:30 A.M. and 11:30 P.M. The 7- to 10-minute trip costs a meager HK $0.70 for first-class passage. There's also ferry service between Central District and Hung Hom (within walking distance of the Kowloon–Canton Railway Terminal). Black-and-white Yau Ma Tei ferries transport cars and trucks, as well as passengers, between Kowloon's Jordan Road and Central District from 6 A.M. to midnight.

Additional cross-harbor transportation is provided by *walla wallas*, small motorized boats. With 24-hour service between Kowloon Public Pier and Queen's Pier in Hong Kong Island's Central District, these boats are particularly convenient for late revelers who miss the last ferry.

For longer rides, combined with some outer-island exploring, you can board a ferry on Hong Kong Island for Lantau, Peng Chau, Cheung Chau, and Lamma is-

lands. Trips take 45 minutes to an hour. There's also ferry service to islands in Tolo Harbour from the New Territories.

Hong Kong's tours provide several more good opportunities for you to spend time afloat. Sailing craft differ widely: classic, high-sterned junks, air-conditioned cruisers, and a replica of a 19th century brigantine are a few of the types of vessels you may choose from. Local tours ply the waters of Victoria Harbour, Yau Ma Tei typhoon shelter, Aberdeen, and visit Lantau and Cheung Chau islands. You can enjoy the harbor's beauty by day, relax on a sunset cruise, or behold the glistening lights of the city by night on an evening excursion or dinner cruise.

Additional details on ferry routes, schedules, and tours may be obtained from information and gift centers of the Hong Kong Tourist Association (see page 113).

Stanley. The village of Stanley is fast becoming a fashionable residential area with plush, high-rise apartments dotting hillsides overlooking Stanley Bay.

Bargain hunters flock to Stanley Market, a collection of stalls and shops lining narrow lanes. Goods include designer sportswear, jeans, silk blouses and dresses, leather jackets, bed linen, sweaters, porcelain, and rattan furniture.

SHOPPING OPPORTUNITIES GALORE

Shoppers find that Hong Kong offers an almost overwhelming array of imported goods. The territory leads most of Southeast Asia and rivals other international shopping centers in its variety of quality imported goods. Knowledgeable shoppers can still obtain good buys on watches, perfumes, luggage, leather products, fabrics, optical goods, clothing, quality jewelry, furs, electronic equipment, and to a lesser extent, camera equipment.

When buying electrical goods, check to make sure they will work with your home electrical current. When the product includes a guarantee, try to get a worldwide or international one. The local sole agent (manufacturer's representative) will be able to tell you what guarantees are available.

If you plan to purchase major items, be sure to check the prices at home first. Once you're in Hong Kong, it's advisable to compare prices before buying.

Bridal procession passes *along Sung Dynasty Village street. Visitors to replica of centuries-past Chinese community explore craft shops, inspect manor house, take tea in handsome pavilion.*

Once haven *for South China Sea pirates, peaceful Cheung Chau (accessible by Hong Kong Island ferry) offers a look at typical Chinese lifestyle.*

Check with the local sole agent to find out the recommended retail price and authorized dealers. Many of the territory's most reliable stores and shops are members of the Hong Kong Tourist Association and display its symbol, a red junk, in their windows.

The Hong Kong Tourist Association's *Official Guide to Shopping, Eating Out, and Services in Hong Kong* includes shopping tips and a list of sole agents and HKTA member stores.

Bargaining is a way of life in Hong Kong. The only places you don't bargain are larger department stores, stores carrying products made in China, nicer boutiques, and anywhere else where prices are clearly marked in Hong Kong dollars. In many shops and at local markets, you'll find no marked prices. By bargaining, you can usually reduce the price 10 to 20 percent.

Where to shop

Half the fun of shopping in Hong Kong is exploring its variety of shopping locales—narrow, neon-lit streets and massive, multistory arcades, smart hotel boutiques and open-air market stalls, large department stores and small factory outlets.

In Kowloon many tailors, jewelry merchants, and other shops are clustered at the lower end of Nathan Road and its side streets. Farther up Nathan Road in Yau Ma Tei lies another group of shops. Harbour City's series of shopping arcades, near the Star Ferry Pier, makes one-stop shopping easy. There are also numerous shopping arcades in East Tsim Sha Tsui.

Across the harbor on Hong Kong Island, you'll find the major department stores and shops along Queen's Road Central, Des Voeux Road Central, and in the Causeway Bay area. These stores include Sincere, Wing On, Lane Crawford, and Chinese Merchandise Emporium. Causeway Bay's Japanese department stores include Daimaru, Mitsukoshi, Matsuzakaya, and Sogo.

Chinese merchandise. For goods from China, visit Chinese Arts and Crafts Emporium in Star House, Kowloon; Chung Kiu Chinese Products Emporium, 532 Nathan Road, Kowloon; Yue Hwa Chinese Products Emporium, 300–306 Nathan Road, Kowloon; or Chinese Merchandise Emporium, 92–104 Queen's Road Central, Hong Kong Island. All carry a wide range of goods produced in China, including painting and calligraphy scrolls, jade, antiques, porcelain, lacquerware, tea ware, embroidery, textiles, clothing, and jewelry.

Gift ideas. For small gifts and souvenirs, stop at one of the Welfare Handicraft Stores in Kowloon or on Hong Kong Island. They are located in Kowloon in Ocean Terminal, on Salisbury Road near the Star Ferry Pier, and on the island in the Connaught Centre basement. You'll come across a variety of low-priced goods produced by Hong Kong's handicapped people: pewter, embroidered items, ivory, painted scrolls, ties, and brocade boxes.

Store hours. Hong Kong's stores and shops generally have no set hours. Most of Hong Kong Island's Central and Western District shops are open from 10 A.M. to 6 P.M. Causeway Bay and Wanchai stores stay open until 9:30 P.M. Kowloon and East Tsim Sha Tsui hours vary. Some are open from 10 A.M. to 7:30 P.M., and others stay open until 9 P.M. Some small shops located on side streets and alleys on both sides of the harbor may stay open as late as midnight. Except for large department stores and Central District shops, most stores are open 7 days a week. Many stores close for several days during Chinese New Year.

Some buying particulars

With such an extraordinary array of goods and stores to choose from, you may find it hard to decide which "treasures" to purchase and from where. The following helpful hints may aid you in making those decisions.

From the jeweler. Hong Kong claims to have more jewelry stores per square mile than any other city in the world, and each one of them offers a large selection of gems and settings. Hong Kong is also noted for its jewelry craftspeople capable of producing beautiful custom-made pieces. Competition thrives between stores, so you'll have a fair chance of getting a favorable price. There are also jewelry factory outlets.

Heading the list of possible gem purchases are diamonds. Hong Kong prices are said to be 10 percent below world market prices. For more information on diamonds and a list of reputable dealers, stop by the Diamond Information Centre, 1707 Lane Crawford House, Queen's Road Central, Hong Kong Island.

Chinese believe that jade provides protection from disease and accidents and brings happiness and good fortune to those who wear it. The amount of jade for sale in Hong Kong is impressive. Though green is the most common color, jade also comes in brown, white, yellow, purple, and orange. But beware; some pieces being sold as jade aren't really jade at all. To be sure of quality, it's best to shop at reputable stores who are members of the Hong Kong Tourist Association.

Besides diamonds and jade, you'll also find gold, sapphires, rubies, opals, topaz, amethysts, red coral, pearls, and tiger's-eye at good prices. When purchasing jewelry, get a receipt detailing the item's price, gold content, and so forth—needed for U.S. Customs.

Tailoring to taste. Hong Kong abounds in tailoring establishments. In the "Yellow Pages" of the phone directory, you'll find 11 pages of listings for tailors.

At one time you could get a suit in 24 hours for an astonishingly low price. But that time has long since passed. Hong Kong tailors have become world-renowned for quality in craftsmanship, and that quality takes both time and money to produce. When having a suit made, allow time for at least three fittings. If you insist on a rush job, you may be unhappy with the results. Tailors are willing to bargain to some extent. However, if the price is too low, you may get poor quality fabric and inferior thread. Reliable tailors can be found in hotel shopping arcades and nearby shopping centers.

Some shops specialize in custom-made women's apparel including coats, suits, and dress/coat combinations. Hong Kong shoemakers can custom-make shoes for you, too.

Still other buys. "Designer label" clothing seconds and overruns are often for sale at vast reductions in prices in Hong Kong markets like Stanley (see page 117) and in factory outlets in Hung Hom industrial area on the east side of Kowloon, Tsim Sha Tsui, and Central District, Hong Kong Island. Here you'll find sports and casual knitwear, silk clothes, suits, accessories, lingerie, furs, and leather garments. The Hong Kong Tourist Association publishes the helpful pamphlet *Factory Outlets in Hong Kong (Ready-to-Wear & Jewelry)*.

What not to buy. The United States restricts the import of products made from animals and plants it has officially listed as endangered or threatened. The fact that these items are sold abroad doesn't mean they'll be allowed into the United States. For more information on restrictions, see page 9.

Arts and crafts

Throughout Hong Kong you can observe craftspeople plying ancient trades, skillfully producing artistic and useful goods. If you wish to seek out local craftspeople, ask for a copy of the Hong Kong Tourist Association's pamphlet *Museums & Arts & Crafts*. It lists locations where you can watch craftspeople at work and, in some cases, purchase handmade products. You'll need to call ahead for appointments.

PLEASURABLE PASTIMES

After enjoying Kowloon's and Hong Kong Island's sightseeing and shopping opportunities, you'll find you still have plenty of other recreational options to choose from. The colony has a multitude of restaurants featuring an extraordinary selection of cuisines. Nightlife varies from Chinese opera to discos. For the somnolent, there are beaches to bask on; for the energetic, hiking, golf, or tennis sites are readily accessible; and everyone can take part in watching any of the colony's popular spectator sports which include horse racing, soccer, and field hockey.

Dining around

Gourmets love Hong Kong because it offers many choices in cuisines. Hong Kong residents love to eat, judging from the more than 19,000 restaurants ranging from elegant and expensive to simple and cheap. The Hong Kong Tourist Association's *Official Guide to Shopping, Eating Out, and Services in Hong Kong* includes a current listing of HKTA member restaurants.

Food for all tastes. Naturally, Hong Kong is famous for its Chinese cuisine, one of the most common being Cantonese cooking. However, you'll also find Chiu Chow, Shanghai, Peking, Szechuan, and Hakka cuisine. The Hong Kong Tourist Association's pamphlet *The Visitor's Guide to Chinese Food in Hong Kong* includes information on Chinese cuisine and recommended dishes, a primer on eating with chopsticks, and a list of Chinese restaurants in Hong Kong.

In addition to regional Chinese dishes, you'll find foods from Indonesia, India, Japan, Korea, Malaysia, Thailand, Vietnam, Burma, Europe, America, Mexico, Russia, and the Middle East. And the ubiquitous fast-food outlets serve everything from pizza and hamburgers to Chinese noodles.

Atmospheric variety. Hong Kong's dining spots are as varied in ambience as they are in range of cuisine. You can eat in a gourmet restaurant, a supper club, a quiet European bistro, a simple, family-style establishment, or even afloat on a sampan. At Lei Yue Mun in Kowloon, you pick your live seafood dinner from tanks and take it to a nearby restaurant to be cooked.

There are establishments featuring rooftop dining, including some that revolve. Here, along with an elegant meal and quiet music, you can gaze upon the twinkling lights of Hong Kong.

You'll find good restaurants in the Kowloon Peninsula (especially near the southern end), and in the Central, Wanchai, and Causeway Bay districts on Hong Kong Island. In fact, Causeway Bay has a whole street of restaurants to choose from; nearly two dozen Asian and European eateries line Food Street, located near the Excelsior Hotel.

A world of entertainment

Hong Kong's nightlife mixes Chinese and western entertainment. Chinese theater-restaurants offer Chinese cuisine and elaborate floor shows featuring traditional songs and dances. Many of the large hotels have chic supper clubs with western-style dinner/dancing, and hotel lobby lounges may showcase a pianist or combo during the late afternoon and evening hours. There are discos, jazz clubs, sing-along bars, and British-style pubs with dartboards. One tour package allows you to tour some of Hong Kong's nightspots on your own with admission and drink coupons for designated Hong Kong Tourist Association member establishments.

For culture. If you decide on an evening of culture, check the programs for City Hall in Central District and the Hong Kong Arts Centre and the Academy for Performing Arts in Wanchai. Entertainment possibilities include classical music concerts (the symphony season runs from September through July), plays, ballet, variety performances, and Chinese opera.

The Hong Kong Tourist Association presents free Chinese cultural shows weekly at the Cityplaza shopping arcade on Hong Kong Island and at New World Centre in Kowloon. Performances include Chinese folk songs, dances, instrumental music, acrobatics, puppetry, and opera.

The month-long Hong Kong Arts Festival, held annually in January–February, includes performances by local groups as well as groups from England, Scotland, and the United States. Entertainers from a dozen Asian countries participate in the biennial Festival of Asian Arts in autumn.

Taking a cruise or tour. When you tire of entertainment onshore, head for the harbor. Several evening harbor cruise tours serve cocktails, or cocktails and dinner, while you sail past the city's many multicolored lights. Some tours combine a cruise with a ride on the Peak Tram, a Hong Kong Island tram ride, or a bus tour through Kowloon. Still others might include dinner at a floating Chinese restaurant in Aberdeen, a visit to a nightclub for a European or Chinese floor show, or dinner at a revolving restaurant. For more information on evening tours, pick up a copy of the Hong Kong Tourist Association's pamphlet *Sightseeing.*

Recreational pursuits

Whether you prefer swimming, diving, golf, tennis, or hiking, Hong Kong has facilities to meet your needs.

Beautiful beaches. Beach-going is one of Hong Kong's most popular summer activities. On weekends, many people escape the city and head for the seashore.

The government has developed and maintains 39 beaches along Hong Kong's coast. Most include changing rooms, toilets, showers, refreshment stands, barbeque facilities, and lifeguards.

Golf. The Royal Hong Kong Golf Club welcomes visitors for weekday play (except on public holidays). Some of the major hotels have arrangements with the club for their guests to play, or you can obtain permission to play by calling the club for a booking. The club maintains a 9-hole course at Deep Water Bay (phone: 5-8127070) and three 18-hole courses at Fanling in the New Territories (phone: 0-901211).

You can also arrange to play at the Clearwater Bay Golf and Country Club on the Sai Kung Peninsula (ask about Hong Kong Tourist Association tours on Tuesdays and Fridays) and at the 18-hole golf course at Discovery Bay on Lantau Island.

Tennis. You'll find public courts at Victoria Park, Wong Nei Chung Gap Road, Bowen Road, and Kowloon Tsai Park. There is a fee for use of the courts; it's advisable to book ahead. There are squash courts in Victoria Park and in the Hong Kong Squash Centre on Cotton Tree Drive, Hong Kong Island.

Sports to watch

Spectator sports include horse racing, cricket, and association football (soccer). But you can also see yacht races in March, dragon boat races in June, an island walkathon in July, and tennis and lawn bowling the year around. Another daily activity that is fascinating to watch is *t'ai-chi ch'uan.*

T'ai-chi ch'uan. At dawn and dusk in many parks, gardens, and open spaces, young and old Chinese move through a series of graceful, balletlike exercises. Though these hypnotic movements resemble the dodging and feinting of shadowboxing, the men and women are actually practicing a 1,000-year-old tradition called t'ai-chi ch'uan. It combines graceful, natural body movements with techniques of breath control and concentration.

Horse racing. On race days during the mid-September to May season, Hong Kong horse racing fans head for the Happy Valley Race Track on Hong Kong Island, or the Sha Tin Race Track in the New Territories. The Royal Hong Kong Jockey Club sponsors horse races most Saturday afternoons, Wednesday evenings, and some Sundays during the season at one of these two tracks.

Since horse racing is a highly popular sport in Hong Kong, stands fill quickly on the race day. Announcements are made in Cantonese and English. The Royal Hong Kong Jockey Club has a limited number of guest badges available for the membership stands. These must be obtained from the club offices, adjacent to the Happy Valley Race Track, on the day before the race. There's also a horse racing tour package including transportation, guide service, guest entry to the membership stands, and a pre-race Chinese meal.

Other sports. Cricket aficionados gather to watch matches at the Hong Kong and Kowloon cricket clubs on Saturday and Sunday afternoons from November through April. The Hong Kong Cricket Club is on Wongneishong Gap Road and the Kowloon Cricket Club is on Cox's Road.

Soccer and field hockey matches are held at the Government and South China stadiums and at the Hong Kong Football Club. Soccer season is September through May; field hockey is played the year around.

EXPLORING THE NEW TERRITORIES

More and more of Hong Kong's people are flocking to newly built housing estates in the New Territories. Yet beyond these concrete, high-rise communities much of the New Territories remains rural, a region that includes duck farms, fish ponds, vegetable gardens, and rice paddies.

You can explore the New Territories on your own by bus, taxi, rental car, or train. Kowloon–Canton Railway trains leave frequently from the Kowloon station at Hung Hom (near the Cross-Harbour Tunnel) and travel through the New Territories to the border town of Lo Wu from 5:25 A.M. to 12 minutes past midnight daily. (Passengers not bound for China must disembark at Sheung Shui, one stop before Lo Wu.) There are also organized tours featuring various New Territories sights.

Sung Dynasty Village

The Sung Dynasty Village, a replica of an ancient Chinese community similar to those that flourished under the Sung emperors (A.D. 960–1279), lies on the southwestern coast of the New Territories. Tours to the village include transportation and a meal or snack.

Upon arriving at the village and passing through its ornate Chinese gateway, you'll immediately be impressed by the community's wealth of architectural detail. Intricate carvings decorate the columns and paneled walls of traditional Chinese dwellings and ceremonial buildings. The largest of these buildings is the Restaurant of Plentiful Joy where you can dine on cuisine that might have been served in the 10th century. Other village attractions include a woodcarving workshop, a temple, and a "rich man's house" furnished with authentic antiques. Along the streets you'll see fortune tellers, strolling minstrels, and members of a bridal procession, all in period costumes.

Other New Territories attractions

The New Territories offers an ever-changing scene of industrialized cities, ancient walled villages, rural farmland, market towns, miles of unspoiled beaches, duck and fish ponds, Buddhist temples, and museums.

Temples of interest include Taoist Ching Chung Koon Temple on Castle Peak Road. Dedicated to Lui Tung Bun, one of the Eight Immortals of Chinese mythology, it is famed for its bonsai collection. It's a steep uphill climb to the Ten Thousand Buddhas Monastery in Sha Tin. There are actually 12,800 Buddha statues.

Sam Tung Uk Museum in Tsuen Wan is a restored Hakka walled village originally founded in the 18th century by the Chan clan. It includes houses with period furnishings, a hall with ancestral altar, and exhibit rooms. Tai Po's Hong Kong Railway Museum features historic rail carriages dating from 1911.

Other sights include Luen Wo's traditional market and Plover Cove Country Park and Reservoir. Tolo Harbour, off the New Territories' northeast coast, possesses some of Hong Kong's most beautiful rural scenery. A ferry from Ma Liu Shui cruises the harbor, stopping at fishing villages.

THE OUTLYING ISLANDS

In addition to Hong Kong Island, the territory encompasses 235 islands—from small, uninhabited islets to larger, sparsely inhabited islands. Lantau, Peng Chau, Cheung Chau, and Lamma islands are easily accessible by regular ferry service from Hong Kong Island. There are also day and overnight tours to Lantau and Cheung Chau. For a change of pace, plan a visit to these islands dotted with tiny fishing communities, peaceful monasteries, and rural markets. Weekdays are the best time to visit these islands, which can be crowded on weekends.

Lantau, the largest island

Ten km/6 miles west of Hong Kong Island lies her big sister, Lantau Island. With an area of 142 square km/55 square miles, Lantau is twice the size of Hong Kong and the largest of the Hong Kong islands.

Lantau is a popular retreat for Hong Kong residents, particularly in the summer months. Beaches trim the shoreline and hiking trails span the rural valleys and mountains.

Ferries depart frequently from Hong Kong Island's Outlying Districts Pier for Lantau's Silvermine Bay. The ferry takes 50 minutes, making a stop at Peng Chau. On organized full-day tours, you can spend a whole day touring Lantau or you can combine a tour there with a stop at Cheung Chau.

From the Silvermine Bay Pier, public buses, minibuses, and tour buses travel to the island's major destinations. You'll find a map of the island on a board just ouside the pier exit.

Island attractions. Lantau's main road and bus route follows the southern shore, past the village and fine beach at Cheung Sha, the prison at Tong Fuk, and Shek Pik Reservoir. Tai O fishing village, on the northwestern shore, features houses built on stilts.

Overlooking the northwestern end of the island is Po Lin Monastery, high atop Ngong Ping plateau. The main temple has three bronze statues of Buddha. A huge Buddha, the largest in Southeast Asia, is currently under construction and will sit on a hill overlooking the monastery.

Visitors can enjoy a vegetarian lunch at the monastery, and even stay overnight on the monastery's hard wooden beds.

A tea plantation adjacent to the monastery offers opportunities for tasting locally grown teas and observing the harvesting of the leaves. There are also facilities for horseback riding and cycling.

To Peng Chau for porcelain

Tiny Peng Chau lies 1 km/¾ mile off Lantau's east coast. Many of the ferries to and from Lantau stop at Peng Chau. Though better known as a transfer point to the

TIME TO CELEBRATE

Multicolored lanterns bobbing in the breeze, golden lions and ferocious dragons cavorting, costumed dancers whirling to a lively tune—all these are sure signs that it's festival time in the Orient.

Colorful celebrations, an important part of the Oriental scene, herald religious observances, the planting and harvesting of rice, and historic events of all kinds. The pageantry of these events lends a special flavor to any journey to the Orient. Highlighted on this page are just a few of many festivals that visitors can sample.

Against the ultramodern background of Hong Kong's glass and concrete high-rises, sleek dragon boats skim the water in a lively race (right); the Dragon Boat Festival honors exiled scholar-official Ch'u Yuen, who deliberately drowned to protest government reforms in China. Participants in Japan's Takayama Matsuri Festival move a towering float from its shelter (bottom left). Fireworks burst with beautiful patterns of color (bottom right) during a celebration of Chinese New Year.

A CHINESE CUISINE PRIMER

Throughout the Orient you'll find delicious, tantalizing food prepared in a variety of ways with a host of intriguing ingredients, and Chinese cuisine may be the best of all.

Basically, Chinese food is divided into four regional styles: southeastern (Canton-style), northern (Peking-style), eastern or coastal (Shanghai-style), and southwestern (Szechuan- or Hunan-style). Different manners of cooking developed in each of these areas of China in accordance with locally-available ingredients and regional flavor preferences.

One of the most familiar Chinese cooking styles, Cantonese, features mildly seasoned fresh ingredients lightly steamed or stir-fried to retain natural flavors and juices. Menu selections include shark's-fin soup, crabmeat-and-corn soup, and stir-fried beef and vegetables. *Dim Sum*—a Cantonese smorgasbord of steamed and fried tidbits stuffed in flour wrappers or buns—is a lunchtime favorite with Hong Kong locals and a good way to sample a variety of specialties inexpensively. Such dishes as shrimp dumplings, steamed spare ribs, fried spring rolls, and steamed chicken buns may be selected from trays or trolleys brought to your table. The bill is totaled from the empty dishes you leave behind.

Northern or Peking-style dishes of meat, chicken, duck, pork, beef, or mutton are enhanced by sweet-and-sour sauces, wine-based cooking stocks, *hoisin* sauce, garlic, and sesame oil. Wheat rather than rice is the area's staple grain. Therefore, many dishes include noodles, dumplings, or bread. The area's most famous dish is the succulent Peking duck. Still another appetizing specialty is Mongolian hot pot, a fondue of meat and vegetables simmered in a rich stock at your table.

Shanghai, on the east coast, is known for its salty dishes flavored with a dark brown soy sauce. Most

dishes feature seafood; other specialties include drunken chicken—poultry simmered in rice wine.

Southwestern or Szechuan dishes are liberally laced with small red chile peppers. Specialties include chicken with hot pepper sauce, chile prawns, duck smoked with camphor wood and tea leaves, and *ban yui*, a peppery fish. The fiery aftertaste may be cooled by consuming noodles and bean curd.

Trappist Monastery on Lantau, the small (.53 square km/.33 square mile) island has a special charm. Cottage industries flourish and you can watch local porcelain craftspeople at work. Narrow lanes and no motor vehicles make the island inviting to walkers.

Peaceful Cheung Chau

Cheung Chau lies 6 km/4 miles southwest of Hong Kong Island. Only 3 square km/1 square mile in area, the island supports some 40,000 inhabitants, many of whom are fisherfolk living aboard junks in the harbor. Most of the residents of the hour-glass shaped island live in the town that occupies a flat, narrow isthmus. On the west side of

the isthmus is a protected bay; just five minutes away, on the east side, lies another bay edged by a stretch of sandy beach. Hilly land masses rise at either end of the isthmus.

Lamma Island, a picnickers' favorite

Lamma Island, off Hong Kong Island's southwestern coast, is a favorite picnicking area for boaters. Scattered along its north and south shores are a half-dozen quiet, isolated beaches.

Ferries from the Central District or from Aberdeen call at either Sok Kwu Wan on Picnic Bay on the island's eastern side or at Yung Shue Wan on the northwest side.

HONG KONG SIDE TRIPS

You can sample the cultures of two other countries on day trips from Hong Kong.

Macau, a 400-year-old Portuguese enclave, is only 55 minutes by jetfoil, 75 minutes by hydrofoil, or 2½ hours by ferry from Hong Kong. For more information on Macau, see pages 126–137.

To visit Shenzhen, a newly-developed Chinese border town, you can take a daily express train from Kowloon. Your tour includes stops at an art gallery, a kindergarten, and the Shenzhen Reservoir, as well as a Chinese lunch. Another tour allows you to spend several days in Guangzhou (Canton). For more information on travel to China from Hong Kong, check with the Hong Kong Tourist Association for a list of travel agents operating tours to China. Additional information on China can be found on pages 138–157.

KNOW BEFORE YOU GO

Below is some basic information to help you in planning a trip to Hong Kong.

Entry/exit procedures. You may visit Hong Kong for one month without a visa, but you will need a valid passport and may require proof of onward passage such as an airline ticket.

If you are arriving from an infected area, you must have an international health certificate showing inoculation against yellow fever and cholera. For further information on what inoculations are recommended, contact the U.S. Public Health Service prior to leaving home.

On departure, you pay an airport tax of HK $120.

Customs. Visitors may bring into the country, duty-free, 200 cigarettes, 50 cigars, or 250 grams (one-half pound) of tobacco; one liter of liquor; 60 milliliters of perfume; and 250 milliliters of toilet water. Prohibited items include firearms, ammunition, and such dangerous weapons as switchblade knives.

Currency. Hong Kong dollars are the official currency. Currency and traveler's checks can be exchanged at the airport, hotels, banks, or authorized money-changing stalls. Most shops and restaurants accept major credit cards; carry your passport for identification.

Health conditions. Hospital and medical services are excellent. Major hotels have either a resident physician or a list of recommended doctors. It's not advisable to drink the tap water outside the hotels.

Tipping. Many restaurants add a 10 percent service charge to the bill; this covers most tipping. Otherwise, the tip is 10 percent. Baggage porters receive HK $2 per bag, and taxi drivers get 10 percent of the meter total.

Language. Both English and Chinese are official languages of the colony; English is spoken in hotels and in most shops. Many of Hong Kong's Chinese inhabitants speak Cantonese or another Chinese dialect.

Time. The time difference between the U.S. West Coast and Hong Kong is 16 hours. When it's noon Sunday in Hong Kong, it's 8 P.M. Saturday in San Francisco.

Weather and what to wear. Subtropical Hong Kong can be quite hot and humid in summer and relatively cool in winter. The best time to visit is from September through January, when temperatures and humidity drop and days are clear and sunny. Temperatures average 23°C/73°F from late September to early December and 15°C/59°F from mid-December to the end of February. Between March and May, temperatures and humidity begin to rise. Summer begins in late May and lasts until mid-September, with average temperatures of 29°C/85°F and high humidity. This is also the rainy season; showers and thunderstorms usually occur in June and July. The typhoon season arrives in late summer and early autumn. Hong Kong is rarely hit directly by a storm, but heavy, buffeting winds occasionally close down the airport briefly.

If you're visiting Hong Kong during its hot summer months, bring lightweight clothing. Add a sweater for air-conditioned places, and an umbrella. Sweaters or light jackets are needed during the spring and fall months. Light woolens (even overcoats) are useful during the cooler winter months.

For more information. The Hong Kong Tourist Association's head office is in the Connaught Centre, 35th Floor, Hong Kong Island. The association's U.S. offices are located at 10940 Wilshire Boulevard, Suite 1220, Los Angeles, CA 90024; 421 Powell Street, Room 200, San Francisco, CA 94102; 548 Fifth Avenue, New York, NY 10035; and 333 N. Michigan Avenue, Suite 2323, Chicago, IL 60601.

In Hong Kong the U.S. Consulate is located at 26 Garden Road on Hong Kong Island.

MACAU

A Portuguese outpost in China's shadow, offering an exotic blend of Mediterranean architecture, Chinese marketplaces, banyan-shaded avenues, shuttered shophouses, lively casinos

A short distance southwest of Hong Kong lies tiny Macau, a 400-year-old Portuguese outpost on China's doorstep. The oldest permanent European settlement in Asia, Macau is a living museum in which the ancient cultures of Portugal and the Orient merge with the modern world.

From Macau's hilltop viewpoints you can look across Inner Harbour waters to the China mainland. Below the ruined facade of St. Paul's (São Paulo), you walk down narrow, Mediterranean-style cobblestoned streets past the open stalls of a Chinese marketplace. Above you, church spires and ornate temple roofs compete with modern apartment towers aflutter with bamboo poles of drying laundry.

GEOGRAPHICALLY SPEAKING

Like its neighbor Hong Kong, 64 km/40 miles to the northeast, Macau sits in the shadow of China. It's located on China's southeastern coast on the western shore of the Pearl River Estuary just 140 km/85 miles from Guangzhou (Canton). It includes a hilly peninsula, joined to China at its northern end by a narrow isthmus, and two small islands—Taipa and Coloane. The entire compact package totals only 16 square km/6 square miles.

The city of Macau occupies the peninsula. Narrow waterways separate Macau from Chinese islands immediately to the west. To the south, Taipa is linked to the

peninsula by a 3 km/1.8 mile bridge. Coloane is connected to Taipa by a 2 km/1.4 mile causeway.

Both of these islands provide heavily populated Macau with badly needed open space: tree-shaded country lanes, wide sandy beaches, wooded hills, and quiet farming and fishing communities. Macau's farmers cultivate only a small percentage of the produce needed by Macau residents. Junk-dwelling fisher folk help supplement this diet, together with a substantial food imports from China. Macau's Chinese housewives pass through the Barrier Gate (Portas do Cerco) daily to shop for produce across the border.

A TRADING CROSSROADS

The Portuguese arrived in Asia in the early 16th century. In 1513 Jorge Alvares, representing the tiny kingdom of Portugal, made contact with Chinese authorities in the Canton delta. Portuguese traders soon followed. About 1555, Portuguese began to settle in Macau, and in 1557 they made an agreement with Chinese authorities to establish Macau as a Portuguese trading center.

The agreement proved beneficial to both countries. Portuguese ships protected China's southern coast (and their own trade) from invasions by pirates, a common occurrence during this period. In return, Macau gained a virtual monopoly on trade between China, Japan, and Europe. Because the Chinese emperor had forbidden direct trade between China and Japan, the Portuguese served as the perfect go-betweens, reaping substantial profits from both countries. Macau also maintained a flourishing trade between Asia, Europe, and Mexico.

Like a ghostly sentinel, baroque stone facade of St. Paul's (once Far East's oldest Christian church) stands at top of broad granite staircase.

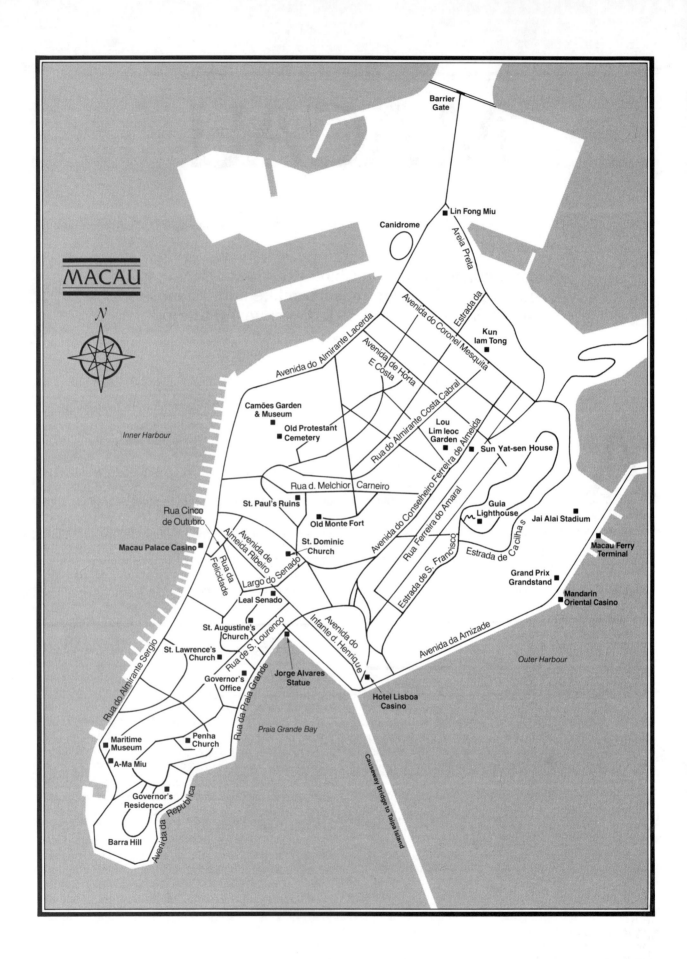

MACAU

Inner Harbour

Barrier Gate

Lin Fong Miu

Canidrome

Areia Preta

Estrada da

Kun Iam Tong

Avenida do Coronel Mesquita

Avenida do Almirante Lacerda

Avenida de Horta

E Costa

Camões Garden & Museum

Old Protestant Cemetery

Rua do Almirante Costa Cabral

Lou Lim Ieoc Garden

Sun Yat-sen House

Rua d. Melchior Carneiro

St. Paul's Ruins

Old Monte Fort

Avenida do Conselheiro Ferreira de Almeida

Guia Lighthouse

Jai Alai Stadium

Rua Cinco de Outubro

Avenida de Almeida Ribeiro

Rua da Felicidade

St. Dominic Church

Macau Palace Casino

Largo do Senado

Leal Senado

Rua Ferreira do Amaral

Estrada de S. Francisco

Estrada de Cacilhas

Macau Ferry Terminal

Grand Prix Grandstand

Mandarin Oriental Casino

St. Augustine's Church

St. Lawrence's Church

Rua de S. Lourenco

Avenida do Infante d. Henrique

Avenida da Amizade

Outer Harbour

Rua do Almirante Sergio

Governor's Office

Rua da Praia Grande

Jorge Alvares Statue

Hotel Lisboa Casino

Praia Grande Bay

Maritime Museum

Penha Church

A-Ma Miu

Causeway Bridge to Taipa Island

Governor's Residence

Avenida da Republica

Barra Hill

By the 1700s, China had opened its ports to other foreign traders. Because merchants were allowed to live in Canton only during the trading season (September through March), they spent the rest of the year living in affluence with their families on Macau.

Decline in trade

The trading port of Macau grew in prominence until the 19th century, when silt from the Pearl River began to build up in the harbor. Commerce dwindled, particularly after the British shifted their trade to the newly founded colony of Hong Kong on the eastern side of the Pearl River estuary. As Hong Kong's harbor gained commercial favor, Macau's importance as a port declined.

Macau today

Today, Macau's economy depends on profits from light industry (including textiles, garments, toys, and electronic goods), commerce, fishing, and tourism. It's also a leading gambling resort for Hong Kong residents.

Currently, Macau is a Portuguese territory with administrative and financial autonomy. Local authority rests with a governor, appointed by Portugal, and a 17-member legislative assembly. On December 20, 1999, Macau's administration will be transferred to China. Like Hong Kong, it will maintain its existing economic and social systems for another 50 years. As the Special Administrative Region of Macau, it will have a high degree of autonomy except in matters of foreign relations and defense.

THE ESSENTIALS/MACAU

Here are a few basics to help you plan a trip to Macau.

Getting there

You can reach Macau by sea via jetfoil, hoverferry, hydrofoil, high-speed ferry, jetcat (jet-propelled catamaran), or standard ferry. Most depart from the Hong Kong/Macau Ferry Terminal at Shun Tak Centre on Hong Kong Island.

Fast, popular jetfoils operate from 7 A.M. to 1:30 A.M. and take 55 minutes. High-speed ferries cross in 90 minutes, with five round trips daily between 8 A.M. and 10:30 P.M. Hoverferries, jetcats, and hydrofoils make the crossing in 65 to 75 minutes; standard ferries take just under 3 hours. Seats are reserved on all transportation.

Since weekends are especially busy, it's wise to book ahead. There's a surcharge for weekend trips.

Day and overnight excursions to Macau include visa fees, transit tickets, sightseeing, lunch, and accommodations (on overnight trips).

Accommodations

Macau offers a variety of accommodations; even the smallest hotels are clean, comfortable and usually air-conditioned. Hotels often add a 10 percent service charge and a 5 percent tourism tax to the bill.

Main tourist hotels include the Lisboa, Mandarin Oriental, Metropole, Presidente, Royal, and Sintra on the peninsula, and the Hyatt Regency Macau at Taipa Island Resort on Taipa. Wooden shutters, balconies, colonnades, and archways grace the Bela Vista on the peninsula and the Pousada de Coloane on Coloane Island, evoking old Macau. Pousada de Sao Tiago is constructed within the original walls of 17th-century Barra Fort on the peninsula's southern tip.

Travelers should make reservations well in advance for visits during major sports events, such as the Grand Prix, or on holidays, weekends, or festival days. Macau is a popular weekend and holiday destination for Hong Kong residents.

Getting around

Metered taxis are plentiful and inexpensive. Pedicabs (bicycle-powered trishaws) are also available and ideal for touring the less hilly areas of the city. Don't expect your trishaw driver to pedal you up the peninsula's steep hills. Be sure to settle on the fare before starting out. You can rent bicycles, motorcycles, and jeeplike mokes. There's bus service around the peninsula and to Taipa and Coloane.

Tours

There are city tours featuring peninsula attractions, and island tours of Taipa and Coloane.

Dining and entertainment

In Macau you can find restaurants serving Portuguese, western, Asian, and local Macanese cuisine. Macau's entertainment scene includes casino gambling, greyhound racing, jai alai games, Chinese opera, harness racing, and hotel floor shows (see page 136).

For more information

In Hong Kong, the Macau Tourist Information Bureau is located at 305 Shun Tak Centre, 200 Connaught Road, Central, Hong Kong Island. The Department of Tourism is at 1 Travessa do Paiva, Macau. There's also an information center at the ferry terminal in Macau.

MACAU'S PEOPLE

Of Macau's 400,000 people, 92 percent are crowded onto the territory's narrow, 5-square-km/2-square-mile peninsula. The rest live on Taipa and Coloane islands or aboard fishing junks. About 95 percent of Macau's people are Chinese. Portuguese and other Europeans make up the remaining 5 percent of the population.

The Portuguese have influenced Macau's cuisine and architecture. However, despite Macau's colonial overlay, its Chinese preserve their native traditions in theater, opera, food, festivals, and religion. Portuguese might be the official government language, but Cantonese is the language most widely spoken. (English is generally used in tourism, trade, and commerce.)

EXPLORING MACAU

Macau offers its visitors a unique blend of past and present, East and West. You can cover many of Macau's sights on a walking tour, relying on a taxi or pedicab only when traveling from one general area to another. Pick up a copy of *Macau Walking Tours* from the Macau Tourist Information Bureau. Self-drive *mokes* (small, jeeplike vehicles) can also be rented. Organized city sightseeing tours include 9-passenger "fun buses," replicas of 1920s English buses offering four different fixed itineraries.

Strolling the old streets

Within the historic part of the city, a major thoroughfare links the Inner and Outer harbours: the busy Avenida de Almeida Ribeiro. Branching off from this traffic-clogged avenue with its clutter of shop signs in Chinese, Portuguese, and English are numerous winding cobblestone lanes.

Strolling these narrow byways, you'll discover the colorful flavor of old Macau—pastel buildings decorated with baroque balconies, paint-worn shophouses with quaint wooden shutters, red and gold temples filled with incense smoke, and peaceful Christian churches.

Leal Senado. Located on Avenida de Almeida Ribeiro facing Macau's civic square, this impressive building houses the Macau Municipal Council and Library. Built in the 18th century in the style of a Portuguese manor house, Leal Senado is considered one of Macau's most outstanding examples of Portuguese architecture. You enter the building through a lobby area whose walls are decorated with blue-and-white Portuguese tiles and historic stone carvings.

Of religious importance. The 17th-century Church of St. Dominic (São Domingos), located on Rua de São Domingos northeast of Leal Senado, stands as another good example of Portuguese architecture. The church's cream-colored exterior is enhanced by decorative stucco moulding and long, green, shuttered windows. Giant carved doors lead to a pastel-colored interior graced by white pillars and an ornate, baroque altar. If the main entrance is locked, ring the bell on the gate next door.

Southwest of Leal Senado is St. Augustine's Church (Sto. Agostinho), whose present building dates from 1814. The statue *Christ Carrying the Cross,* which sits atop the marble high altar, is the focal point of the Procession of Our Lord of Passos (see "Festival Time In Macau," p. 133). In 1712, the Passos procession was canceled. When a food shortage followed, the local Chinese asked that the procession be reinstated.

Several famous landmarks

Two of Macau's most prominent as well as famous landmarks are the ruins of St. Paul's and the old Monte Fort (Citadel of São Paulo do Monte). Both overlook the city north of St. Dominic's.

St. Paul's. The ancient ruins of St. Paul's (São Paulo) stand like a ghostly sentinel at the top of a granite staircase. This stone facade and staircase are all that remain of a church designed by an Italian Jesuit and built by Japanese Christian exiles in the early 1600s. At the height of a typhoon in 1835, the church caught fire and was almost entirely destroyed. Supported by ten columns, the skyward-reaching, five-tier facade is elaborately embellished with carvings and statues of the Virgin, saints, angels, devils, a Portuguese sailing ship, a Chinese dragon, and a Japanese chrysanthemum.

Old Monte Fort. Built at about the same time as St. Paul's as part of the church complex, this fort's buildings were also destroyed by the 1835 fire that began in the fort's kitchens. Today, the fort is a public park offering panoramic views across Macau's rooftops to China.

From this fort, Macau's defenders successfully warded off a Dutch invasion in 1622. A cannonball fired from the fort found the Dutch powder supply, thereby securing Macau's victory.

The peninsula's southern tip

Macau peninsula's southern tip features several attractions worth a visit, including a shady boulevard, churches, a Chinese temple, and a maritime museum.

The Praia Grande. Once a favorite subject of 19th century artists, the Praia Grande retains elements of old-world elegance and charm despite the effects of typhoons, land reclamation, and urban renewal. Shaded by large banyan trees, this broad avenue borders the southeastern side of the bay.

At the northern end of the Praia, a monument honors Jorge Alvares, the first European to sail Chinese waters; its location marks the innermost part of the bay.

Incense smoke *drifts above A-Ma Miu's ornamental roof. Macau's oldest temple is dedicated to goddess of seafarers.*

Mediterranean-style buildings *nestle between high-rises in tiny Macau. Across the water lies China.*

A short distance southwest is the pink and pillared Governor's Office.

Macau's most fashionable church, St. Lawrence (São Lourenço), occupies a palm-filled churchyard atop a hill behind the Governor's Office. To reach the church, take Travessa do Padre Narciso inland to Rua de S. Lourenço. The white-trimmed church features twin towers, one housing a bell and the other a clock. Originally constructed in the 16th century, the church was rebuilt between 1801 and 1803. Inside, elaborate chandeliers hang from vaulted ceilings. Behind the altar, rays of colorful light stream through a stained-glass window.

Returning to Praia Grande and continuing southward along the bay you'll pass the elegant, rose-pink Governor's Residence, Palacio de Santa Sancha. Your best view of the palace is from the balcony of the Hotel Bela Vista.

Penha Church. Standing atop Penha Hill east of the Hotel Bela Vista, Penha Church is dedicated to the protectress of sailors, Nossa Senhora da França. The present church, attached to the Bishop's Residence, was built in 1935. The original chapel on this site was built in 1622 and rebuilt in 1837. In its early days, Penha Church was routinely visited by sailors before they departed on long sea voyages.

BEATING THE GAMBLING ODDS IN MACAU

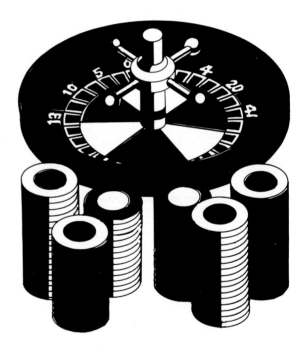

Gamblers by the thousands swarm to Macau—often called the Monte Carlo of the East—lured by the territory's 24-hour casinos. Each weekend and holiday, Hong Kong's residents speed over by jetfoil or hydrofoil, while visitors from neighboring countries wing into Hong Kong's airport aboard "gambler specials."

Popular places for betting are the Casino Lisboa in the Hotel Lisboa, the Macau Palace Floating Casino, the casino at the Jai Alai Palace, and the casino in Mandarin Oriental, Macau. Commonly played games are baccarat, bingo, blackjack, roulette, craps, keno, slot machines (called "hungry tigers" by the Chinese), French *boule,* and Chinese games including *fan-tan* and *dai-siu.*

If you choose to gamble, be careful. Learn the rules in advance or the smiling, demure lady croupier may prove your downfall. Macau's gambling rules differ slightly from those in Reno or Las Vegas. Ask the pit boss before you start placing bets on the wrong numbers.

If you want to watch Macau casino gambling, here are a few pointers:

Fan-tan. In this ancient game, the hand is often quicker than the eye. The object is to guess the number of white porcelain buttons—from a total of 60 to 100—remaining on the table after the croupier scoops them up by fours; you bet on numbers 1, 2, 3, or 4.

Players can win four different ways. Putting the money on *fan* or *lim* covers a single number at three-to-one odds; the latter gives insurance on a second number. Gamblers get even returns on two numbers with *gok.* The most complicated form of betting is *cheng;* with a single bet and two-to-one returns, the player loses if the opposite number wins, or he gets his money back if the side numbers win.

Dai-siu. Most interesting to craps devotees, dai-siu (big and small) is based on the throwing of three dice under a covered canister. Players wager on what they think the values will be when dice are uncovered. They can also bet on whether the combined roll will have a "big" or "small" value. If the same numbers appear (all twos or all threes), the gambler loses unless he has bet on three of a kind.

Boule. Similar to roulette, boule uses a spinning wheel but a larger ball. Instead of sweeping around the wheel, the ball bumps and jumps before settling into one of 25 numbered slots.

The minimum bet on all three games is P 10 or HK $10.

FESTIVAL TIME IN MACAU

You'll find both Portuguese and Chinese festivals and events celebrated in Macau. Dates for Chinese events vary from year to year, since celebrations are based on the lunar calendar. Check with the Macau Tourist Information Bureau for exact dates.

Chinese New Year. The most important Chinese festival of the year (usually in late January or early February) puts Macau in a joyful mood. Amid exploding firecrackers, dragon and lion dances continue through the night.

Yuen Siu (Lantern Festival). This festival marks the official end of the 15-day Chinese New Year season. Children carry multicolored lanterns through the streets during the celebration.

Procession of Our Lord of Passos. During this colorful religious festival held on the first weekend of Lent, the statue *Christ Carrying the Cross* is carried from St. Augustine's Church (Sto. Agostinho) through the streets to the city's cathedral. The following day, the statue is returned to St. Augustine's.

A-Ma Festival. During this April festival, Chinese gather at A-Ma Miu to pay homage to the goddess of seafarers. Religious ceremonies, Chinese opera, and firecrackers highlight the observance.

Feast of Tam Kong. In early May on the island of Coloane a procession in honor of Tam Kong, patron saint of fishers, is followed by a week-long celebration. The event is Coloane's most spectacular festival.

Procession of Our Lady of Fatima. With appropriate pomp and splendor, church dignitaries and townspeople join the May 13th street procession, following the statue of Our Lady of Fatima as it is carried from the Church of St. Dominic (São Domingos) to Penha Church.

Dragon Boat Festival. Dragon boat races are held each June in the Bay of Praia Grande. The local winner competes in the International Dragon Boat Races locally and in Hong Kong and Singapore.

Mid-Autumn Festival. This event, held in September or October, is also called the Moon Cake Festival. It celebrates the uprising against Mongol warlords by Chinese who hid secret messages in moon cakes. It's a time for families to gather outdoors to view the moon and dine on moon cakes.

New Year's Eve. A spectacular fireworks display lights up the sky over Praia Grande Bay on the evening of December 31.

A-Ma Miu. Macau's oldest Chinese temple stands amid huge boulders and gnarled banyan trees at the foot of Barra Hill, near the entrance to Inner Harbour. Dedicated to the seafarers' goddess A-Ma, the temple was built in the 1500s, then repaired and partially rebuilt in the 1800s. Still further repair work occurred after a recent fire destroyed part of the temple. A painting of a sailing junk decorates a boulder at the entrance.

Macau Maritime Museum. Located across the street from A-Ma Miu, this museum tells the story of Macau's rich nautical heritage. Displays focus on Portuguese and Chinese sea exploration, navigational techniques and instruments, cartography, hydrography, dredging, and fishing. Outdoors, floating exhibits at neighboring No. 1 Wharf include an ornate two-deck replica of a "flower boat" (ancient Chinese floating brothel), a fishing junk, and a *lorcha* (19th-century cargo vessel).

Guia Hill

The city's highest point, Guia Hill, is home to two interesting landmarks—a lighthouse and fortress.

Atop a peaceful, tree-shaded hill overlooking the Outer Harbour stands Guia Lighthouse. Built in 1865, the white, cylindrical lighthouse was the first maritime beacon on the China coast. Lit by kerosene until 1915, the lighthouse's beacon guided early tea clippers, fishing junks, steamers, and pirate ships safely into its harbor. Today, it still sends out a welcoming light to seafarers.

The fortress, with its massive turreted walls, was built between 1637 and 1638. Inside are military barracks.

Silvery fish *hang by tails in Macau market, awaiting purchase by chefs. Local cuisine includes Chinese, Macanese, and Portuguese favorites.*

On Macau tours into China, *destinations include birthplace of Dr. Sun Yat-sen, Republic of China's founder, plus visit to school and farming village.*

Still other sights

On the northern part of the peninsula you can visit Dr. Sun Yat-sen's Memorial House and several temples.

Memorial House of Dr. Sun Yat-sen. The founder of the Chinese Republic, Dr. Sun Yat-sen was one of the first Chinese doctors trained in Europe. A memorial house on Rua Ferreira do Amaral commemorates his work in Macau and displays memorabilia from the pioneering reformer's life. Built in mock-Moorish style, the building has high ceilings, archways, two-story columns, and balconies.

Kun Iam Tong. Built in 1627, this spacious Buddhist temple on Avenida do Coronel Mesquita, northwest of Dr. Sun Yat-sen's Memorial House, is dedicated to the Chinese goddess of mercy and is one of Macau's biggest temples. Of special interest to western visitors is the stone table in the temple courtyard, where the first treaty between the United States and China was signed on July 3, 1844. Temple halls are richly decorated and rows of porcelain figures adorn the ridgepole of the tile roof.

Lin Fong Miu (Temple of the Lotus). On Avenida do Almirante Lacerda, not far from the Barrier Gate, stands this elegant Chinese temple whose entrance is guarded by carved "temple dogs" (mythological beasts). A facade of intricate bas-relief carvings depicts stories from history and mythology. An inside courtyard features a lotus pond and frieze of writhing dragons.

Beautiful gardens

Even with limited acreage and a large population, Macau has space for gardens. Although small, these green areas provide restful havens from the hubbub of city life. One garden even has a museum to explore.

Camões Garden and Museum. Set on a small hill on the peninsula's western side, this attractive garden with its inviting ferns and banyan trees provides a quiet retreat for Macau residents, especially on warm days. A grotto-like, rocky nook contains a bronze bust of Luíz Vaz de Camões (1524–1580), Portugal's celebrated poet.

The garden grounds were part of the house once occupied by the chairman of the British East India Company. The whitewashed 1770s building is now the Camões Museum. Displayed inside is a Han Dynasty bronze temple drum, Ming pottery and porcelain, Qing Qing enamelware, traditional Chinese furnishings, ancient weapons, and paintings. The museum is located on Praca Luís de Camões.

Next to the Camões Museum is the 19th-century Old Protestant Cemetery, now used more as a garden than a graveyard. There's a small Anglican chapel, a shaded sunken garden, and gravestones with inscriptions revealing a little of the early history of Macau and the South China coast.

Garden of Lou Lim Ieoc. Located on Estrada de Adolfo Loureiro, this formal garden resembles the landscapes often depicted in classical Chinese paintings. You enter by walking a winding path past ornamental "mountains." A bridge with nine graceful curves spans a lotus-filled lake. The architecture of the main pavilion is a combination of both Chinese and European styles and features a tiled roof whose upturned eaves are supported by Corinthian columns.

OUTLYING ISLANDS

Like Hong Kong's outlying islands, Macau's islands of Taipa and Coloane offer sandy beaches, forested hills, and traditional villages. At one time the only way to reach these islands was by ferry. Today a bridge links Taipa to the peninsula, and Coloane can be reached from Taipa by a causeway.

Easy access to Taipa and Coloane from the mainland has opened these southerly Macau islands to development. There are hotels on both islands, and Taipa has a harness racing track. In addition, the island is the site of the University of East Asia campus.

Other Taipa attractions include the Taipa House Museum, a 1900s colonial-style mansion with large verandas and louvered wooden shutters. It's the first of five buildings to be restored along the banyan-shaded waterfront *praia* (promenade) near Taipa Village. The home has been furnished as it would have been when inhabited by Portuguese families in the early 20th century. The century-old Our Lady of Carmel Catholic Church overlooks the praia.

Rural Coloane, with its secluded coves and forested hills, was a haven for pirates when Macau was the center for trade between China and the West. Today, it's a quiet retreat for visitors.

Included among attractions are Coloane Park, a large expanse of gardens and ponds with a big walk-in aviary filled with colorful birds. Popular beaches include crescent-shaped Cheoc Van and Hac Sa, a wide strip of black sand bordered by a grove of pines. Nearby is Hac Sa Sports and Recreation Complex with its Olympic-size pool, sports field, and children's playground.

You can easily visit Taipa and Coloane on an organized tour from downtown Macau, take a regularly scheduled bus, or drive there yourself.

SHOPPING AT A GLANCE

Macau shops contain local and Portuguese crafts, goods from China, and the usual array of free port merchandise—transistors, tape recorders, watches, and electronic wares. Though many of the store items have price tags, bargaining is a generally accepted practice. Shops are open from 10 A.M. to mid-evening.

Items for sale

Most of Macau's stores are small, family-owned operations. The main shopping area is located along Avenida do Infante D. Henrique and Avenida de Almcida Ribeiro and neighboring side streets. Here you'll find stores selling Portuguese wines and liquors (Hong Kong customs allows you 1 bottle duty free), porcelain, cameras, sportswear, decorative patio and fireplace tiles, beadwork, and hand-knitted woolens.

The area's Chinese shops offer carved camphor and teakwood chests, Chinese wines, gold charms, jade, pearls, and linens. Macau's "flea market" occupies the lanes around the Rua das Estalagens (near St. Paul's Ruins).

Purchasing jewelry

Numerous small jewelry shops display ready-made jewelry or can make pieces to order. If you are considering purchasing gold products in Macau, use caution. Eighteen-karat gold jewelry does not contain 75 percent gold here; ask what the percentage of gold is, not just karat weight.

In cooperation with the Department of Tourism the Goldsmith and Jewellers Association has produced a jewelry shopping brochure listing reputable jewelers. These shops can be distinguished by an identifying decal in their windows. When shopping for jewelry, gold, cameras, watches, or electrical goods, it's important to get a warranty card plus receipt of purchase.

What not to buy

The United States restricts the import of products made from animals and plants it has officially listed as endangered or threatened. The fact that these items are sold abroad doesn't mean they'll be allowed into the United States. See page 9 for more information.

MACAU DINING

Macau's hotels, *pousadas* (inns), and restaurants offer a pleasing array of Portuguese, Chinese, Korean, Thai, Japanese, and European dishes as well as local Macanese specialties.

Many entrees are served in simple Portuguese country style—meat, poultry, and fish, garnished with potatoes, tomatoes, and black olives. Stewing is a favorite method of cooking many items, including lobster. One traditional Portuguese dish is *bacalhau*, dried cod baked, grilled, stewed, or boiled. Soups include *caldo verde* and *sopa alentejana*, both containing meat, vegetables, and olive oil.

The spices of India and Africa add tantalizing flavor to many of Macau's local dishes. Popular favorites include African chicken (grilled chicken served with a spicy sauce seasoned with peppers) and piquant prawns baked or grilled with peppers and chiles. Brazil's contribution to Macau's eating experience is *feijoadas*, a stew of kidney beans, pork, potatoes, spicy sausage, and vegetables simmered in a spicy sauce. A variety of Portuguese red and white wines and sparkling *vinho verde* are available to accompany the meal.

ENTERTAINMENT AND RECREATION

For many visitors Macau's gambling casinos are its main attraction. Giant neon signs advertise the casinos and on weekends thousands of Hong Kong residents pass through their doors to try their luck.

Gambling aside, Macau's after-dark activities generally move at a much slower pace than those of Hong Kong. Several of Macau's hotels feature Chinese floor shows, imported club acts, and Portuguese folk dancing. Some cabarets and nightclubs offer dance music.

Spanish jai alai players compete nightly at the city's Jai Alai Stadium, which faces Outer Harbour. Played according to rules much like those of squash, jai alai is considered the world's fastest game. A player hurls a hard ball from a basketlike glove called a *cesta*. The ball, traveling at speeds of up to 150 miles per hour, bounces once, then smashes off the far wall. The opponent must catch the fast-moving ball on the fly with his cesta and return it.

Greyhound racing begins at 8 P.M. four nights a week at the Canidrome, on Avenida do Almirante Lacerda near the Barrier Gate.

The Macau Trotting Club holds harness races at its oval track on Taipa Saturday and Sunday afternoons, with additional midweek races in summer. Transportation to the track is available by coach from the Lisboa and Hyatt Regency hotels.

During November the Macau Grand Prix motor races draw spectators and entries from around the world to the territory.

Courts and equipment for badminton and tennis are available. For more information, contact the Department of Tourism.

INTO CHINA

A number of travel options are available for those wishing to visit neighboring China. You can take a single- or multiday group tour originating in Macau, or you can join a tour group from Hong Kong during its Macau stopover.

You can organize either type of China excursion in Hong Kong (see page 125), or arrange one in Macau through a travel agency that operates China tours. The tour operator will take care of filing visa applications for participants; in advance of your trip, you will need to fill out a visa application form and provide the tour agent with a passport-size photo.

The cost of the tour usually includes visa fee, group transportation, hotel accommodations (on multiday tours), meals, and a guided sightseeing program.

One-day tours

These short bus tours into China feature neighboring Guangdong Province's Zhongshan County. After passing through the Barrier Gate, you travel through the new high-rise developments of Guangdong's Zhuhai Special Economic Zone. Beyond this, the countryside becomes a blend of ancient walled farming villages, rice paddies plowed by conical-hatted men and their water buffaloes, and duck-filled ponds. The tour includes a stop at Cuiheng Village, Dr. Sun Yat-sen's birthplace; a visit to his Memorial Middle School; lunch in Shiqi with a chance to explore its bicycle-filled streets; a walk through a traditional farming village; and a visit to a village school.

Multiday excursions

Multiday tours can include stays in one or more cities. A 2-day excursion from Macau spends a night in Shiqi. A 2-day tour from Hong Kong takes a day trip into China after staying over in Macau. From Hong Kong there are 3-day trips that include nights in Macau and Shiqi, and 4-day trips featuring overnights in Macau, Foshan, and Guangzhou.

KNOW BEFORE YOU GO

Here are some practical details to help you plan your trip to Macau.

Entry/exit procedures. Only a valid passport is required for the citizens of the United States and many additional countries. Residents of other countries can obtain a visa, if needed, from Portuguese consulates overseas or in Hong Kong, or upon arrival in Macau. Group tours from Hong Kong to Macau usually include visa arrangements and fees. Departure and re-entry forms (and your passport) are necessary for British customs in Hong Kong upon your return from Macau.

You may need an international health certificate showing inoculation against yellow fever and cholera if you are coming from an infected area. For further information on what inoculations are recommended, contact the U.S. Public Health Service prior to leaving home.

On departure from Hong Kong you pay a tax of HK $15. No tax is levied by the Macau government upon departure.

Customs. Visitors are not usually subjected to customs inspection, but you must observe Hong Kong regulations when returning there (see page 125).

Currency. The Portuguese *pataca* is the official currency; however, Hong Kong dollars are freely accepted in Macau.

Health conditions. Most medicines and toiletries are readily available, and many doctors speak English.

Bottled water is provided in hotels and restaurants. It's not advisable to drink the tap water.

Tipping. Light tipping is the rule. Most hotels and restaurants add a 10 percent service charge and a 5 percent tourism tax.

Time. The time difference between the U.S. west coast and Macau is 16 hours. When it is noon Sunday in Macau, it's 8 P.M. Saturday in San Francisco.

Weather and what to wear. Macau's mild, subtropical weather is influenced by monsoons from the southwest and northeast. The best time to visit is from September to early December or late March to early May. Sea breezes do help to cool Macau during the hot months (May to October) when temperatures average 28°C/83°F with high humidity; this is also the typhoon season. During the ideal visiting seasons daytime temperatures average between 18°C/65°F and 24°C/75°F. Nights can be chilly. Winters can be cold. Appropriate dress for Macau is informal, but not too casual. Lightweight suits and dresses are good for the summer months. Light woolens are suitable for the winter.

For more information. You can address questions about Macau to the Government of Macau, Department of Tourism, 1 Travessa do Paiva, Macau. In Hong Kong, the office is at 305 Shun Tak Centre, 200 Connaught Road Central, Hong Kong Island. In the United States there are Macau Tourist Information Bureaus at 3133 Lake Hollywood Drive, P.O. Box 1860, Los Angeles, CA 90078; 608 Fifth Avenue, Suite 309, New York, NY 10020; and P.O. Box 22188, Honolulu, HI 96822.

CHINA

A long-isolated region revealing a world of misty
pinnacles, rural villages, industrious communes,
crowded city streets, traditional art forms,
smiling children

Isolated from the eyes of the western world for more than a generation, the People's Republic of China didn't unlock its doors to tourism until the late 1970s. At first, tour itineraries included only a few cities. Today, much of this vast land is open to exploration by both group and independent travelers.

Visitors soon discover that China presents many faces—city streets brimming with bicyclists and pedestrians; quiet rural villages edged with lush, green rice fields; museums filled with ancient art treasures; misty mountain pinnacles reminiscent of scroll paintings; schoolrooms full of smiling children; and public gardens with pavilions, lakes, and winding walkways. These are only glimpses of China's kaleidoscopic scene.

A VAST, VARIED COUNTRY

Covering some 10 million square km/4 million square miles, China is the largest country in Asia and the third largest in the world (after the U.S.S.R. and Canada). It stretches over 5,000 km/3,100 miles from the East China Sea westward to the mountainous borders of Nepal, India, Pakistan, and the U.S.S.R. From the rugged Russian frontier marking its northern boundary, China extends roughly 5,500 km/3,400 miles to the South China Sea.

The "Middle Kingdom"

China's geographical relationship to the rest of the world helps to explain why the Chinese have called their land "the Middle Kingdom"—heart of the universe.

For centuries China was isolated by immense natural barriers. Its northern boundary is protected by the desolate Siberian and Mongolian plateaus and the Gobi Desert. To the west, high mountain ranges and the Sinkiang Desert separate China from the U.S.S.R., Afghanistan, and Pakistan. The mighty Himalayas form the southwestern border, isolating China from India, Nepal, Sikkim, Bhutan, and Burma. From the high mountain valleys, rivers flow south into neighboring Laos and Vietnam. Only on China's northeastern border with Korea was travel by land possible.

The lay of the land

Forming a natural east-west dividing line, the Qin Ling (Tsinling) Mountains and the Huai River separate the country into north and south China. North of this dividing rise elevated flatlands, edged by a smooth, regular coastline. Vast deserts, dramatically punctuated by high mountains, characterize the northwestern part of China. Extensive forests and fertile farmlands enrich China's northeast; wheat and other grains are the principal crops.

To the south lie seemingly endless hills and valleys, broken by rivers and lakes that interfere with easy communication or transport between localities. On steeply terraced hillsides along China's southern seaboard, rice grows in abundance. The rocky and ragged coastline curves around protected harbors where China's fishing people live aboard boats.

Mountains. More than two-thirds of China is above 975 meters/3,200 feet; only 14 percent lies below 488 meters/1,600 feet. Among China's many mountain

*China's Great Wall snakes across hilly
countryside. Built in 3rd century B.C., it
tops most visitors' itineraries.*

ranges are the Himalayas, which include the world's highest peak, Mount Everest (Qomolangma)—on the border between China and Nepal), at 8,848 meters/29,028 feet. At the other extreme, China dips to one of the lowest points of the world, the Turfan Depression (Turpan Pendi), 130 meters/426 feet below sea level.

Rivers. China's land mass slopes from west to east, draining the waters of its great rivers—the Yangtze (Chang Jiang) and the Yellow (Huang He)—into the East China Sea. The latter river transports vast amounts of fine yellow topsoil, blown from the northwestern deserts, which in the past frequently caused the river to silt up and overflow.

The country's largest and most important river is the Yangtze, 6,300 km/3,915 miles long and supporting one-third of China's population in its basin. A vast network of irrigation ditches, canals, and tributary rivers branches out along its length, watering both northern wheat fields and southern rice fields. Over the centuries, the Yangtze has also served as a strategic water highway for steamships, junks, and sampans.

The Grand Canal (Da Yunhe), dating as far back as the 7th century, links the Yangtze to the Yellow River. By the 13th century, the canal ran some 1,931 km/1,200 miles from Hangzhou (Hangchow) north to Beijing (Peking), carrying grain, silk, and porcelain as tax payments to the emperor. Widened and dredged, the canal is still in use today.

Vegetation and animal life

Much of China has been under cultivation for centuries, with rice and wheat as the major crops. Grapes, kumquats, oranges, peaches, pomegranates, pineapples, bananas, coconuts, and sugar cane are grown in the south-

ern provinces. Tea remains an important crop in the southern and southwestern provinces.

Giant pandas still roam the forest bordering Sichuan (Szechwan) province, though their numbers are growing scarce. Other rare species include the snub-nosed monkey, white-lipped deer, and Yangtze crocodile. China has some 420 species of reptiles and 1,150 species of birds.

A HISTORY OF TURBULENCE

A country of awesome antiquity, China has a recorded history of some 4,000 years. Neolithic remains dating from 6000 to 4000 B.C. have been found throughout China. The fossilized remains of one famous resident, the Peking Man, date back 400,000 to 500,000 years. The Yellow River basin is recognized as the cradle of Chinese civilization—the oldest known continuing culture in the world.

Dynasty follows dynasty

With the establishment in 2200 B.C. of the Xia (Hsia) Dynasty near Anyang, the first Chinese state came into being. Continuing until 1700 B.C., this agricultural civilization began a series of 22 dynasties that ruled China for the next 4,000 years.

During the Shang (Yin) Dynasty (1700–1122 B.C.), which also ruled the Anyang area, Chinese writing was first developed. Written records were cast in bronze or inscribed on tortoise shells and bones. This dynasty introduced a class system of nobles, servants, workers of the land, and artisans.

In 1122 B.C. the Shang was overthrown by Zhou (Chou) rulers, who established their first capital near Xi'an (Hsi-an) but later moved east to Luoyang (Lo-yang). Under the Zhou Dynasty (1122–221 B.C.), central power weakened and the country became divided into several kingdoms. The ruling feudal lords of these kingdoms began to bicker, each hungry for more power and wealth. Their quarrels, between 475 and 221 B.C., resulted in the "Warring States" period of Chinese history. Iron casting, developed earlier for agricultural tools, was diverted to weapon making.

The empire's unification. During the Qin (Ch'in) Dynasty (221–207 B.C.), China was unified under her first emperor, Qin Shi Huangdi. He organized the country into administrative regions, inaugurating the Chinese empire. During this period, family units became strengthened and China's civilization matured to one of sophistication. Roads were built, money was standardized, and the famous Great Wall was constructed.

Civilization evolves. Finally, the Qin Dynasty was overthrown by the Han Dynasty (206 B.C.–A.D. 220). During

A QUESTION OF SPELLING

Why is Peking now *Beijing* and Canton called *Guangzhou*? China has adopted a new phonetic system—called *hanyu pinyin*—designed to help non-Chinese pronounce Chinese words correctly, and it has resulted in some spelling changes.

In this book, we've included both the new spelling and, in parentheses, the old when we mention a place for the first time. After that, the place name will be in hanyu pinyin. In referring to such familiar names as Yangtze River, Yellow River, and Grand Canal, we've mentioned their Chinese translation in parentheses.

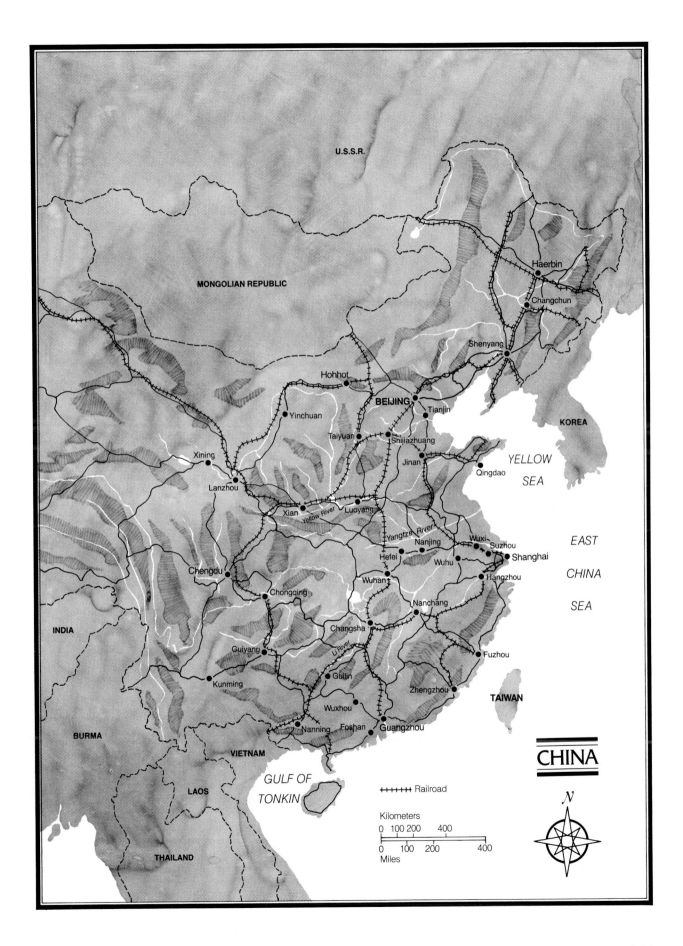

U.S.S.R.

MONGOLIAN REPUBLIC

Haerbin

Changchun

Shenyang

KOREA

Hohhot

BEIJING
Tianjin

Yinchuan

Taiyuan
Shijiazhuang

Xining

Jinan

Qingdao

Lanzhou

YELLOW
SEA

Xian
Yellow River
Luoyang

Yangtze River

Nanjing

Wuxi
Suzhou

EAST

Hefei

Wuhu

Shanghai

Chengdu

Wuhan

Hangzhou

CHINA

Chongqing

Nanchang

SEA

INDIA

Changsha

Guiyang

Li River

Fuzhou

Guilin

Kunming

Zhengzhou

TAIWAN

Wuxhou

BURMA

Nanning
Foshan
Guangzhou

VIETNAM

LAOS

GULF OF
TONKIN

THAILAND

CHINA

+++++ Railroad

Kilometers
0 100 200   400

0   100   200   400
Miles

N

China   **141**

Bridge spans canal *at entrance to Beijing's Forbidden City, once home for emperors. Compound includes palaces, temples, courtyards, and gardens.*

Sleek-lined international hotels *in Beijing and other major cities now provide China visitors with luxury accommodations.*

this period China grew increasingly civilized, becoming a worthy rival of the Roman Empire. Agriculture, irrigation, and the use of iron tools developed sufficiently to support a nation of 57 million Chinese at the beginning of the Christian era. Scientific advances included the manufacture of paper and the use of the seismograph to record earthquakes. Porcelain, silk brocades, and fine wool were produced and trade routes opened.

But when the Han Dynasty fell in A.D. 220, China's unity and organization disintegrated once again.

Country divides. During the next 350 years, China split into the Three Kingdoms, which later regrouped into the Southern and Northern dynasties. Led by Yang Qian, the Northern Dynasty reunified China and began construction of the Grand Canal. After Yang's assassination, an army officer named Li Shih Min founded the Tang (T'ang) Dynasty, consolidating China's second empire into the largest in the world.

Urbanization and cultural advances. China flourished during the early Tang period (618–907). Xi'an and Luoyang became major population centers, with more than a million people each. Great achievements brought literature, art, ceramics, and architecture to new heights. But centuries-old agrarian troubles persisted. Peasants, lacking land of their own, roamed the country, and the seeds of revolt began to sprout.

China split again during the Five Dynasties and Ten Kingdoms rule from 907 to 979. Midway through this period, Beijing was founded by the "barbarian" Khitan. After order was reestablished under the Song (Sung) Dynasty (960–1279), China expanded its trade, urbanization, and technical skills. Despite intermittent wars, peaceful intervals lasted long enough for the development of private schools, printing (400 years before Gutenberg's birth), and the abacus, the world's first adding machine.

Improvements in navigation led to increased maritime trade. Permanent communities of Koreans, Persians, and Arabs were established in the ports of Guangzhou (Canton), Hangzhou, and Quanzhou. But once again decay followed progress; court corruption and restive landless peasants made China prey for Mongolian invaders.

Invaders from the north. In 1213, horsemen of Genghis Khan swept out of the north, capturing Beijing two years later. By 1241, southern Russia, Persia, and Hungary were in the hands of the "barbarians." In 1279, Genghis's grandson Kublai Khan captured Hangzhou, the Song capital, where he founded the Yuan (Mongol) Dynasty (1279–1368) and exercised control over most of Asia.

But by oppressing the Han (China's predominant racial group) and favoring Mongolian people with appointments to official positions, the Mongols planted the seeds of their own destruction. A series of famines finally sparked a peasant uprising, led by Zhu Yuanzhang. After successfully overthrowing the Mongol rulers, he declared himself Emperor Hong Wu in 1368 and founded the Ming Dynasty.

Ming Dynasty restores traditions. During the Ming reign (1368–1644), the capital was moved from Nanjing (Nanking) to Beijing. The Forbidden City and many of Beijing's great temples were built, and the Great Wall was repaired. Maritime trade flourished, and the Ming rulers established relations with some 30 countries.

While Europe stood on the brink of the industrial revolution, China gazed backward, trying to restore the ancient traditions destroyed by the Mongols. Some 11,000 volumes of rare books were collected (most of them to be destroyed 200 years later when westerners sacked the Forbidden City). But the reestablishment of traditional life brought with it the rise of corrupt officials and wealthy landowners.

Concessions to foreign powers. When the Manchus breached northern China's Great Wall in 1644, Beijing again fell under barbarian control. In southern China, resistance against the Manchus continued, led by Cheng Ch'eng-kung (also known as Koxinga). In 1661, however, he and his followers fled to Taiwan.

The Qing (Ch'ing or Manchu) Dynasty (1644–1911) was the last imperial dynasty. It oversaw a decadent period that culminated in submission to foreign powers, with devastating damage to national pride.

Through trade concessions and force, the Japanese, Americans, British, and other Europeans opened China to the West. While Christian missionaries traversed the land trying to convert China's 400 million "pagans," the British navy took Hong Kong Island and, following the Opium War (1839–1842), opened five other Chinese ports. After the second Opium War (1856–1860), 11 additional ports were opened and Kowloon was ceded to the British.

Taiping Rebellion. From 1850 to 1864, a civil war known as the Taiping Rebellion tore China apart. Though the rebels supported the Christian movement and the building of a democratic society, western powers supported the Manchus (to ensure trade concessions), so the Taiping Rebellion was doomed. Twenty million people died during this civil war.

Sino-Japanese War. Thirty years later, China suffered defeat in the 1894 Sino-Japanese War and, as a consequence, surrendered the island province of Taiwan and the Penghu Islands (Pescadores) to Japan. On the mainland, Japan and the western nations scrambled for railway concessions, naval bases, and commercial ports. They divided China into "spheres of influence," thereby breaking up the country.

Boxer Rebellion. Reaction to foreign domination was inevitable. In 1900, a movement of revolt against foreigners caught fire. Supported by the Empress Dowager Ci Xi, groups of Chinese nationalists known in the West as Boxers staged an uprising, surrounding and laying siege to Beijing's foreign legations for 55 days. A combined force from seven western nations and Japan eventually rescued the diplomats, missionaries, and their families. During the fracas, the Forbidden City was burned.

A republic is born. On October 10, 1911, Dr. Sun Yat-sen established a provisional government in Nanjing and founded the Republic of China. But internal conflicts and warfare continued to tear the country apart. The following year, as one far-reaching consequence, the Chinese Communist Party was born.

Sun Yat-sen attempted to unify China by joining forces with the Communists and admitting them to the Guomindang (Nationalist Party). He set up a military academy near Guangzhou and named a Russian-trained officer, Chiang Kai-shek, as president, and Zhou Enlai (Chou En-lai) as dean. Upon Sun's death in 1925, Chiang Kai-shek succeeded to the party's leadership and became head of the republic.

Over an 11-year period beginning in 1926, Chiang's government attempted to exterminate the Communists led by Mao Zedong (Mao Tse-tung). In 1934, after several unsuccessful attempts, government troops outnumbered and surrounded Mao's Red Army. Mao and 90,000 of his followers managed to escape, beginning the epic 6,000-mile Long March across mountains and rivers to northwest China.

Sino-Japanese War (1937–1945). During this period of unrest, the Japanese controlled northern and eastern China, and Chinese Nationalists and Communists joined forces to defeat Japan. Following Japan's surrender, Chiang—backed by American aid—regained control of northern China, but the internal power struggle continued despite American efforts encouraging a coalition government.

In 1948 the Communist-led People's Liberation Army drove Chiang's nationalist forces from the north, capturing Beijing without a fight. On October 1, 1949, Mao Zedong proclaimed the People's Republic of China, and Chiang and a million of his followers fled to Taiwan.

The People's Republic of China

First business for the Communists was to launch an aggressive program of industrialization, at the same time restructuring the war-ravaged nation along socialist lines. During the First Five-Year Plan (1953–1957), all industry and commerce was nationalized, all agriculture collectivized. The development of heavy industry took top priority.

In 1958 the "Great Leap Forward" was launched in an attempt to speed up and modernize the country's economy. Emphasis was placed on governmental decentralization and local decision making. Housewives joined the labor market, and rural people's communes were established with further collectivization of property.

Cultural Revolution. In 1966 the Mao Zedong-inspired Cultural Revolution was launched. Chinese Red Guards—university students joined by some of their professors—were the backbone of this revolution. Attempting to purge the country of "bourgeois" elements, they sought stricter adherence to Mao's thinking. Once again, chaos and violence plagued China.

During the late 1960s, social rule was transferred to revolutionary committees, made up of People's Liberation Army members and the Communist Party. Under this new coalition of soldiers, peasants, and workers, the country resumed its march toward economic recovery.

Relations with the West. Cold-war relations between China and the West began to thaw slightly in the 1970s, as Chairman Mao Zedong and Premier Zhou Enlai sought reconciliation with the United States. In 1971, the People's Republic of China was admitted to the United Nations, and during the next year trade opened between the U.S. and China.

More political turmoil. The year 1976 brought the deaths of two leaders of the revolution and the post-1949 government: Mao Zedong and Zhou Enlai. Momentous changes followed.

Shortly after Mao's death, the "Gang of Four"—Jiang Qing (Mao's widow), Wang Hongwen, Yao Wenyuan, and Zhang Chunqiao—were arrested, accused of conspiring to overthrow the government. After this purge, Hua Guofeng was named chairman of the Chinese Communist Party and Deng Xiaoping was appointed vice premier, vice chairman of the party, and chief-of-staff of the People's Liberation Army.

Full diplomatic relations were established between China and the United States on January 1, 1979; a U.S. embassy opened in Beijing, and consulates in Guangzhou, Shanghai, Shenyang, and Chengdu (Chengtu).

China's government today

Under the 1978 Constitution, the Chinese Communist Party (CCP) and its leadership is the leading political force in the country, making political, economic, and social policy decisions. The state government is responsible for coordinating national economy and overseeing foreign affairs. Its governing body, the State Council, is headed by a premier nominated by the CCP.

Administratively, China now consists of 22 provinces, 5 autonomous regions, and 3 independent municipalities: Beijing, Tianjin (Tientsin), and Shanghai. Under the provinces come municipalities and districts (or counties in the countryside).

CHINA'S PEOPLE

China's population exceeds 1 billion. Visitors quickly notice the teeming crowds—on foot or bicycle, people seem to swarm over sidewalks and roadways. China's rice bowls—the Yangtze River Delta, Sichuan Basin, Pearl River Delta, and Hunan Basin—hold the country's heaviest population clusters. Many of these people are peasants, forming the backbone of China's agricultural economy.

The country has 56 nationalities, with the predominant racial group (94 percent) being the Han Chinese—their name taken from the Han Dynasty that reigned more than 1,000 years ago. The other 6 percent are minority racial groups who have settled most densely in the deserts, mountains, and steppes that fringe the mainland. Many minorities retain their own customs, languages, religions, folklore, and colorful dress.

City and country lifestyles

Though conditions have improved for those who work the land, the life of a farmer peasant is still an arduous one. The people's communes (collective units for agricultural and industrial production) have been abolished, but most agricultural land is still collectively owned, with pay divided according to individual output. People are encouraged to farm small plots for their own household use and to supplement their income by selling the produce at market.

City dwellers work 8-hour days, 6 days a week, in factories and offices. High-rise buildings are beginning to appear on the city scene, but the prevailing structures are still three- to four-story buildings or more traditional *pingfang* (one-story houses with three wings enclosing a courtyard). Housing is in short supply in China, and apartments are very small.

Bicycles are more prolific in China than automobiles. Bicycle riders of all ages fill city streets and country roads. Bicycles are even used for the transportation of goods such as sacks of rice or mattresses.

Dress. For decades, both men and women wore what westerners call the "Mao suit"—loose-fitting jackets and pants of gray or blue. Today colorful dress frequently appears, especially in urban areas. Many women wear bright or pastel skirts and blouses, especially in summer, and men often dress in white or light blue shirts and dark trousers. China's children have always worn colorful prints and patterns.

Recreation. The Chinese have long understood the benefits of physical exercise and sports. Today, thousands exercise early each morning, often in massive formation. Older people prefer the slow, graceful movements of t'ai-chi ch'uan, while the young participate in more vigorous, organized classes. Even jogging has become popular there.

Other popular sports are basketball, soccer, cycling, badminton, volleyball, table tennis, swimming, track and field events, ice skating, and hockey.

Religion. China once had three great ethical movements: Buddhism, Taoism, and Confucianism. Christianity, including Catholicism and Protestantism, was introduced to China in the 19th century. Religious activities were prohibited during the Cultural Revolution, but have now resumed. The constitution of the People's Republic provides for religious freedom.

Education for all

Prior to 1949, 80 percent of the population was illiterate, but today that number has been reduced to less than 10 percent. Youngsters begin their schooling at age 7 with primary education (lasting 6 years), and then go on to middle school for another 6 years.

After middle school, there are two educational possibilities: college or technical school. Both require passing stiff entrance examinations. Only 5 percent of those graduating from middle school are accepted for further formal education.

PLANNING YOUR TRIP

A number of international air carriers, including China's CAAC (Civil Air Administration of China), now fly into the country from the United States. Flights across the Pacific Ocean from the West Coast usually include a stopover in Tokyo or Hong Kong. European-based international carriers offer flights from the U.S. East Coast to China by way of their European home bases. Main points of entry into China are Beijing, Shanghai, and Guangzhou.

Tours. Although independent travel is now allowed in China, most travelers still prefer to explore China on a group tour. The length of stay can range from 2 days to 4 weeks, and group size can vary from 12 to 50 people. The itinerary is fixed, with planned daily sightseeing packages. The cost of the tour includes transportation, 3 daily meals, sightseeing with guide and interpreter, and accommodations.

More than 200 cities and areas are now open to tourists. Popular destinations include Beijing, Xi'an, Shanghai, Guangzhou, Guilin (Kweilin), Nanjing, Wuxi (Wuhsi), Suzhou (Soochow), Hangzhou, and Kunming. Still other group tours venture farther afield to include Silk Road highlights, Tibet, and a cruise through the Yangtze River gorges. There are even special-interest tours for artists, wildlife enthusiasts, archeology buffs, and cyclists.

Some tour operators also handle independent travel to China, arranging the trip through the China International Travel Service. This organization makes all final arrangements (transportation, accommodations, meals, sightseeing) for group and individual travel within China. These packages can offer airfare and hotels only, or everything including a guide. Independent travelers are advised to avoid the peak travel season: April, May, September, and October.

Cruises. Some first-time visitors to China might prefer a cruise along China's coast, with a chance to explore diverse ports-of-call and the country beyond on land excursions. With a cruise, there's the convenience of comfortable shipboard accommodations, western cuisine, and the blessing of having to unpack just once.

Via Hong Kong. From Hong Kong you can fly into China, take a train, or go by hovercraft (up the Pearl River to Huangpu). There's also boat service to Guangzhou, Xiamen Island, Shantou, and Shanghai. Tours into China from Hong Kong are also available and range from just a few days to several weeks.

Be flexible. Once you're inside China, details of your tour become the province of the China International Travel Service, not the foreign tour operator.

The key to enjoying a China tour is to remain flexible. The day-to-day details of a trip may not be confirmed until arrival. Hotels can change, as can flights, depending upon availability of space in both. Flight delays are common.

Occasionally, tourists find the activity-packed itineraries somewhat strenuous, especially during China's hot summer months, and some find accommodations less luxurious than they might wish. This is changing with the addition of more deluxe and first-class hotels.

Seeing life and culture. China tours are no longer restricted to a mundane roster of model factories and communes. Today, itineraries have broadened into the country beyond, and are likely to include historical sites, local points of interest, museums, arts-and-crafts institutes, and schools, as well as factories and technical institutes.

Getting around inside China

Within the country, visitors usually travel between distant points by air, with CAAC being the major Chinese airline. Shorter trips may be by train, offering fascinating glimpses of China's varying landscape. First or "soft" class is comfortable, cooled in summer by powerful fans or occasionally air-conditioned. There are also dining cars.

City transportation. Most cities have good bus and trolley systems. Beijing offers a subway system, and Shanghai's is under way. But take care: if you can't read Chinese, you may find public transport bewildering. Ask your guide to write out your destination, and show the note to someone who can alert you at the right stop. And remember, subways and buses—like city sidewalks—will be crowded.

If you plan to take taxis, you will need your destination written out, along with the name of your hotel (for your return). Taxis, ordered through your hotel, have fixed fares calculated per kilometer. Rental cars are now available, though driving is not recommended for visitors.

Exploring on your own. There are no rules requiring that visitors be accompanied by a guide at all times. During free time, you can go shopping or just take a stroll on your own. You'll find the Chinese people warm and friendly, eager to try out the English now widely taught on radio and television. People are likely to approach without shyness—and soon you may find yourself knee-deep in a discussion of cultural differences while a good-natured crowd gathers to observe and contribute. Shop on your own and you may attract a similar crowd, one of whom may volunteer to act as your guide, helping you find the items you're shopping for.

New hotels expand accommodations

A number of large, modern hotels have been built in major Chinese cities in recent years—or are now under construction. There's also been an effort to refurbish the country's older hotels.

Hotel accommodations are assigned for most travelers by the China International Travel Service. However, travel agents or tour operators in the United States can often book confirmed accommodations at first-class hotels in major cities.

Hotel dining rooms serve Chinese and western food, and room service (primarily for drinks and snacks) is available. Other services include laundry, barber and beauty shops, gift shops, postal facilities, and a currency exchange desk. Some of the newer hotels even have health clubs, swimming pools, and coffee shops.

Dining in China

Your tour price includes three meals a day, generally served at your hotel at designated times, your table and menu selected for you in advance. Unless you arrange in advance for a Chinese breakfast (usually noodles in some form), the morning meal will be western-style eggs, toast, and coffee. But lunch and dinner will be Chinese.

It's fun and worth the additional expense to venture away from your hotel dining room at least once. In large cities, good restaurants feature specialties from many different provinces; you'll also find numerous small local restaurants favored by the Chinese. Though most diners use chopsticks, western cutlery is available on request.

Intricate ivory carving *requires patience and skill. Each region specializes in different craft; Shanghai is center for ivory.*

Beijing shopper *selects family's evening meal from streetside market stall. Freshness is paramount.*

Usual dining hours for the evening meal are from 7 to 9 P.M., though restaurants in hotels catering to international visitors may have extended hours.

Entertainment scene

Night life in China is anything but wild. However, some of the new, major city hotels now have discos, complete with flashing strobe lights. There are also bars and cafes.

Highlighting the entertainment scene are Chinese cultural performances. Peking Opera—with its songs, pantomimes, dancing, acrobatics, and elaborate costuming—heads the list. Drama is also popular, with new works appearing in major cities. Apart from drama, theaters offer musical and dance performances, ballets, acrobatics, and puppet shows.

Shopping tips

You're sure to be pleased at the range of goods you can take home from China. But if you see something you like, don't wait for comparison-shopping—buy it, since you may not see the same type of goods in another store.

Where to shop. A boon to shoppers is a nationwide campaign to revive traditional arts and crafts. At workshops and factories, you can watch people at work and purchase goods produced on the premises.

Each region offers its own art and craft specialty. For example, Hangzhou and Suzhou are renowned for excellent silk goods, Tianjin for carpets, Guangzhou and Changsha for ceramics, and Beijing and Shanghai for cloisonné. Look for these items at local stores and workshops.

INSIDE THE FORBIDDEN CITY

In the days when emperors made the Forbidden City their home, commoners and foreigners who ventured into the sacred compound without permission could expect execution. Today, a journey through this majestic remnant of traditional China, nestled in the heart of Beijing, entails no such risk. Now open to all as the "Palace Museum," the Forbidden City is no longer forbidden pleasure.

The journey begins with passage through the red-brick archway of Tian'anmen (Gate of Heavenly Peace) under the gaze of a huge Mao portrait. Continuing north, you cross a moat to reach Wumen (Meredian Gate), the actual entrance to the Forbidden City. Surrounding the compound are high brick walls punctuated with tile-roofed towers at each corner.

First built by the Ming emperor Yong Lee in the early 15th century, the Forbidden City covers some 101 hectares/250 acres and has been rebuilt several times. Its six palaces, roofed in yellow tile, were constructed in a line down the center of the enclave. Gardens lie behind the palaces.

Long shielded from curious eyes—Chinese as well as western—the Forbidden City contained the private quarters of the emperor and empress, the apartments of concubines, the imperial palace, various other palaces and temples, libraries, and the imperial art collection extolling China's great history. Altogether, the Forbidden City encompassed some 9,000 rooms.

Covered corridors lead visitors to the Hall of Supreme Harmony, the Hall of Perfect Harmony, and

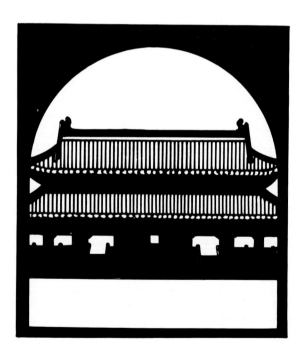

the Hall of Preservation of Harmony. Constructed of lacquered wood and topped with the imperial yellow tiles, these halls display art treasures from China's dynasties.

Every large city in China has a Friendship Store (Youyi Shangdian), existing solely for tourists' convenience. At Friendship Stores, all prices are fixed, and they're marked in Arabic numbers. Salespeople speak English, and often other foreign languages as well. In major cities, you'll also discover department stores, markets, and numerous small shops. Most large stores and Friendship Stores are open 7 days a week from 8 A.M. to 8:30 P.M.

What's for sale. Choice Chinese mementos include jade jewelry, lacquerware, rugs, cloisonné, silk fabric and garments, embroidered linen napkins and tablecloths, handpainted porcelain, signature chops, and other artwork—paintings, handcarved figurines, scenic silk prints, woodblock prints.

What not to buy. The United States restricts the import of products made from animals and plants it has offi-

cially listed as endangered or threatened. The fact that these items are sold abroad doesn't mean they'll be allowed into the United States. For more information on restrictions, see page 9.

BUSTLING BEIJING

Located in northern China at the northwest edge of the North China Plain, Beijing lies about 153 km/95 miles inland from the East China Sea. The capital city and home to some 9.3 million people, Beijing is the administrative, political, communication, and cultural center of the country.

Visitors arriving by plane land at Beijing International Airport, about 29 km/18 miles northeast of the city center. The drive to town takes about 45 minutes.

CHINA'S GREAT WALL

The still-massive Great Wall once wound its way across 6,035 km/3,750 miles of rugged northern China terrain, from the east coast at Shanghaiguan to the edge of the Gobi Desert in China's far west. The wall, on which 23 centuries have taken their toll, has been partially restored, and a short excursion from Beijing will lead you to the stroll of a lifetime—a walk on the Great Wall of China.

The wall, originally a series of lesser walls and fortresses, was fused into a continuous barrier during the Qin Dynasty of the 3rd century B.C. Dotted by 25,000 watchtowers, it was intended to prevent nomadic "barbarian" tribes in the north from invading the farms and villages to the south. The wall was so wide that five cavalrymen could ride abreast while patrolling. Though time and nature have diminished it, the wall remains massive and clearly identifiable.

For your walk on the wall, you go through an arch cut into the wall itself, then ascend a ramp to the top of the wall. Joined by other tourists and Chinese visitors, you can walk along the wall for about 457 meters/500 yards. At a watchtower midway in your walk, windows cut into the walls provide sweeping vistas of the hills of northern China. Since the wall follows the contours of the land, parts of it are steep and stairs have been installed. Once you reach the end of the section open to the public, you pause to let your eyes follow the ruins of the wall as it stretches to the horizon. Then you turn and retrace your steps.

In summer, be prepared for morning fog, and if you go on a Sunday, expect to encounter crowds. In winter, dress for Siberian cold.

Trips to the Great Wall are included in area sightseeing tours from Beijing, a trip of about 56 km/35 miles.

Rural farm villages, *complete with thatch-roofed dwellings and barnyard fowl, lie beyond China's teeming cities. Farmers work hard to feed country's 1 billion people.*

Sail-propelled junks *bring a Chinese landscape painting to life on the Li River near Guilin. Cruising China's rivers adds another dimension to touring in country.*

A bit of background

After Ming emperors moved their capital from Nanjing to Beijing, in the 1400s, they lavished their seat of power with a wealth of palaces, pavilions, and parks. Emperors of the Qing Dynasty brought their own architectural glory, and many of Beijing's historic palaces, pagodas, temples, gardens, and other vestiges of prerevolutionary times date from this period.

Old Peking consisted of two walled cities: a square-shaped area to the north, slightly overlapping a rectangular area to the south. The northern portion became known as the Inner City; within this enclave lay the Forbidden City. The southern portion, with its crowded Chinese population, became known as the Chinese city. A moat surrounded both walled cities.

Modern buildings now overshadow the capital city's earlier architectural wonders. However, such architectural treasures as the Forbidden City have been preserved.

Beijing highlights

For a good sampling of Beijing, plan to see such city sights as the Forbidden City (see the special feature on page 148), Tian'anmen (Gate of Heavenly Peace) Square, and the Temple of Heaven—and leave some time to shop, too.

Tian'anmen Square. Located between the northern and southern cities, vast Tian'anmen Square lies in the center of Beijing. It was here that Mao Zedong proclaimed the People's Republic of China in 1949. Fronting this immense area, the world's largest public square, is the city's main east–west thoroughfare, Chang'an Avenue. Bordering the square is Tian'anmen (Gate of Heavenly Peace), a massive stone gate built in 1417 and restored in 1651.

Facing Tian'anmen Square on the west is the Great Hall of the People, housing a huge banquet hall and a 10,000-seat theater. On the east side of the square are the Museum of Chinese History (covering China's past, from its origins until 1919) and the Museum of the Chinese Revolution (covering the post-1919 period).

Mao Zedong Memorial Hall stands on the south side of the square facing the gate. And in the middle of Tian'anmen Square rises the 37-meter/120-foot-high Monument to the People's Heroes.

Temple of Heaven. About 3 km/2 miles southeast of Tian'anmen Square, within the Chinese city, stands the imposing Temple of Heaven, a complex covering a square mile. A broad avenue, 732 meters/800 yards long, links three main structures: the Hall of Prayer for Good Harvests, the Imperial Vault of Heaven, and the Circular Mound Altar of Heaven. In early times, the emperor would leave the Forbidden City to come here on the eve and day of the winter solstice to pray for good harvests.

Other points of interest. More interesting sights than can be adequately described in this brief guide are scattered throughout Beijing. They include the National Art Gallery, the Beijing Museum of Natural History, Nationalities Cultural Palace, the Lu Xun Museum, the Beijing Zoo (where you'll meet China's famous giant pandas), and such outstanding structures as the Temple of True Remembrance, the Lama Temple, and the Temple of the White Pagoda. Parks include Zhongshan Park, west of the Forbidden City, and People's Cultural Park, east of Tian'anmen Square.

Shopping centers. In addition to the Friendship Store (considered the best one in China), you can shop at the Beijing Department Store on Wangfujing, the city's main shopping street. Dongfeng Market, located across the street from the department store, sells everything from books and clothing to bakery goods.

Beijing side trips

Outside Beijing lie several more attractions worth the short drive required to see them. Presented here is information on three of them. Turn to page 149 for a special feature on the country's most famous landmark, the Great Wall of China.

Marco Polo Bridge. About 16 km/10 miles southwest of Beijing, a white marble bridge—first described in glowing detail by Marco Polo—spans the Yong Ding River. Though the 12th century bridge has been rebuilt many times, this 235-meter/771-foot-long marvel retains many of its original details, notably the carved pillars, each topped by a small lion. Stone elephants and other animals guard its approaches.

Summer Palace. About 11 km/7 miles northwest of Beijing stands the former imperial summer palace (Yiheyuan). The original summer palace, built in the 12th century, was burned by British and French troops in 1860. Empress Dowager Ci Xi rebuilt the palace in 1888.

Covering some 267 hectares/660 acres, the complex of pavilions, temples, and galleries clusters around vast Kunming Lake, rimmed on three sides by green hills. The entire area, hilly and wooded, is enclosed by walls.

A long covered walkway—its pillars and cross beams painted in romantic scenes—follows part of the lake's north shore. Midway, an arch marks the route to the buildings atop Longevity Hill, among them the Fragrance of Buddha Pagoda and the Sea of Wisdom Temple. The hilltop offers fine views over the lake. Tranquil gardens laced by winding paths cover the hill's northern slope. At the western end of the covered walk, you'll see the Empress Dowager's famous marble boat.

A lake ferry departs nearby, cruising to an island in the southern part of the lake. Two bridges are noteworthy: a 17-arch bridge that links the island with the lake's eastern shore, and the Jade Girdle Bridge on the western side of the lake.

The Thirteen Ming Tombs. Lying in a natural amphitheater surrounded by hills 48 km/30 miles north of Beijing, the Ming Tombs are underground burial sites constructed for 13 of the Ming emperors. Visitors approach the tombs through an arched red gateway and travel along a road lined with magnificently carved animals and other figures. On Sundays and public holidays, the tombs are a favorite picnic destination.

Only 2 of the 13 tombs have been excavated. The largest and best preserved is that of Chang Ling. The tomb of Ting Ling (Emperor Wan Li) is an underground palace entered by descending a grand staircase and passing through a huge marble gate. Possessions of the emperor and his two consorts are on display. Four stories underground you'll finally reach the burial vault.

SHANGHAI, CHINA'S FAMOUS SEAPORT

Renowned as China's most westernized city, Shanghai rambles along the Huangpu River, 19 km/12 miles south of the Yangtze River's mouth. With about 11 million people crammed together into its 6,100-square-km/ 2,355-square-mile area, Shanghai ranks as China's larg-

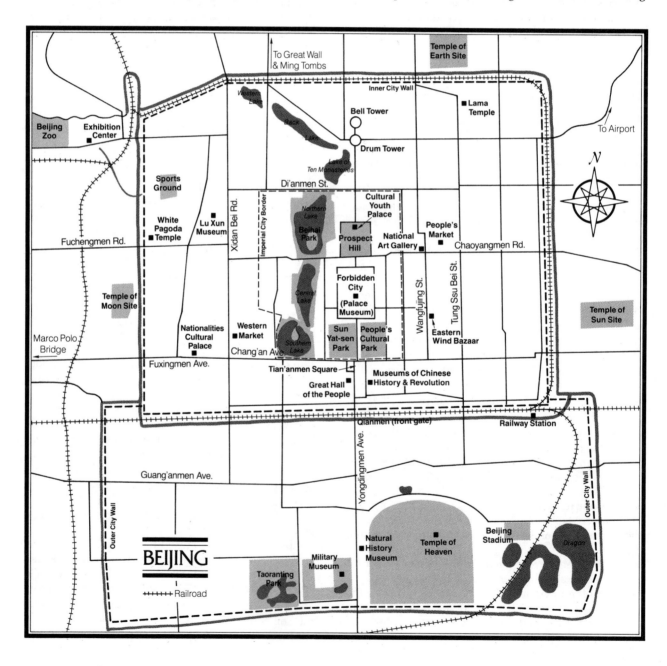

est city. It's a leading seaport and a bustling industrial and commercial center as well.

You can reach Shanghai by train or air—it's a 2-hour flight from either Beijing or Guangzhou. Some cruise ships also stop here.

For centuries a lively trade center, Shanghai saw a great increase in trading activity after the First Opium War (1839–1842); at that time, China was forced to grant trading concessions to western nations, and foreigners took control of the city's commerce and customs regulations. You can still see the western-style buildings erected during this era, especially along Zhongshan Road between the Wusong River and the old Chinese city. Known as the Bund, this tree-shaded section of thoroughfare skirting the Huangpu River was the exclusive domain of foreigners after they took power. The Tudor-style Shanghai clock tower, an important landmark, overlooks the Bund.

Exotic sights

Narrow, labyrinthine alleys twist through Shanghai's oldest section, the old Chinese city. Located south of Jinling Road, this tiny and crowded enclave packs in a variety of small stores, bustling markets, noodle shops (restaurants), and a bazaar brimming with handicrafts. At the north end lies Yu Yuan Garden with its hills, pavilions, winding paths, lotus-filled ponds, teahouses, and a magnificent zigzag bridge spanning a small lake.

Just north of the old Chinese city, at the corner of Yan'an and Henan roads, the Shanghai Museum of Art and History displays a vast collection of antique bronzes, ceramics, prints, and life-size terra-cotta statues excavated from Emperor Qin Shi Huangdi's tomb in Xi'an (see page 156). Stroll a little further to the People's Park, a haven of greenery in the city's center.

Excursions into the city's outskirts take visitors north to Lu Xun Memorial Park to see mementos of China's honored revolutionary writer, and south to Longhua, with its ancient pagoda and temple.

Shopping and entertainment

Among the more than 400 shops along Nanjing Road, Shanghai's major shopping street, you'll find the Number One Department Store, offering an impressive array of consumer goods. The large, three-story Friendship Store is located on the Bund.

For entertainment, treat yourself to folk dance programs, opera, films, and circuses.

GUANGZHOU, THE SOUTHERN GATEWAY

A major gateway to China for many international visitors, Guangzhou spreads along the northern edge of the Pearl River, 145 km/90 miles northwest of Hong Kong. From Hong Kong, you can easily reach Guangzhou by train, hovercraft, or plane.

This semitropical city is lively with trade activity. Each spring and autumn, the Chinese Export Commodities Fair (formerly the Canton Trade Fair) invites numerous foreign businesses to exhibit their wares.

Beyond these commercial opportunities, this city of wide, tree-lined boulevards offers yet other attractions. You can sample its excellent cuisine, notably the superb local seafood. Savor, too, Guangzhou's beautiful parks, and absorb the beauty of the Huaisheng Mosque and the Liurong (Six-Banyan-Tree) Temple with its nine-story pagoda. Stroll through the Guangzhou Zoo, enjoy outdoor entertainment at the Cultural Park, or visit an agricultural commune.

Guangzhou's two main shopping streets are Beijing and Renmin roads—but don't overlook the Friendship Store on East Huanshi Road.

OTHER PLACES TO EXPLORE

With the growing number of Chinese cities open to visitors, tour operators have expanded their itineraries to include more destinations. In this section, we present a brief review of some of the cities you might visit. We've put them in alphabetical order for easy reference.

Guilin, a traditional landscape

Some of China's most breathtaking scenery borders the Li River in the vicinity of Guilin, about 300 air miles northwest of Guangzhou.

Nature has eroded the region's soft limestone into a splendid array of upraised hills (called karsts), unusual mountain caves, and strangely shaped rocks. Clear lakes and rivers abound. In the mist and rain, the moist air becomes a transparent curtain, shading the landscape into a dreamlike, gray-blue panorama of floating mountains and cascading waterfalls.

Visitors to Guilin can explore the area's many hilly parks, as well as stalactite- and stalagmite-laden caves. A half- or full-day boat trip carries you down the Li River from Guilin. As you cruise past cave-pocked cliffs, naturally sculpted limestone rocks, bamboo groves, and an occasional whitewashed village, you'll share the river with small fishing boats. You return to Guilin by bus.

Hangzhou, paradise on earth

One of China's loveliest, most scenic resort areas lies 161 km/100 miles south of Shanghai near the southeastern coast. A million residents live in Hangzhou, a city the Chinese call "paradise on earth" because of its canals, waterways, bridges, weeping willows, pavilions, and famous West Lake (Xi Hu). Marking the southernmost point of the Grand Canal, the city lies on a sand bank between West Lake and the winding Qiantang River, not far from the East China Sea.

Hangzhou's primary attraction is West Lake, some 486 hectares/1,200 acres scenically enclosed on three sides by hills. West Lake was originally a shallow bay adjoining the Qiantang River. As its outlet silted up, it gradually became an inland lake.

Two ancient dikes divide the shallow lake into three irregular sections. Trees, gardens, and footpaths rim the lake's 14-km/9-mile shoreline dotted with temples, pagodas, and fountains. Gondolalike boats glide across its serene surface.

Much of Hangzhou's prosperity comes from silk and tea production. Its silk industry was established in the 7th century. At a local factory you can learn about silk production, and purchase fabrics and decorative household articles. The Friendship Store in Hangzhou also has a selection of silk products.

A big regional crop is Longjing (Dragon Well) green tea. Arrangements can be made for a visit to a tea plantation commune.

Kunming, city of eternal spring

Situated at an elevation of 1,890 meters/6,200 feet, this city offers a mild subtropical climate and flower blossoms year-round. With a population of nearly 2 million including members of a number of China's ethnic minority groups, this city is the capital of Yunnan Province.

Attractions include Dianchi Lake overlooked by the temple-studded Western Hills. At the summit of one hill is Dragon Gate, a group of caves and statues carved by hand out of the rock. The job took 72 years.

The towering, karst-like peaks of the Stone Forest lie 126 km/78 miles southeast of Kunming. Centuries of wind and rain have created the 80 hectares/200 acres of bizarre limestone formations.

Luoyang, an ancient capital

Ancient and historically renowned, the city of Luoyang dates back to China's earliest history. Located about 362 km/225 miles southwest of Beijing, it served as the empire's capital and cultural hub several times over the centuries. Today, activity revolves around industry and agriculture.

Landmarks of antiquity include two Han Dynasty tombs and a museum housing archeological finds from the area. South of town, where the Yi River cuts a 549-meter/600-yard channel between high cliffs, you can prowl through the Longmen Buddhist Caves.

Nanjing, the southern capital

Counterpart to Beijing, China's "northern capital," Nanjing is known as its "southern capital." It served as capital of all of China as early as A.D. 229 and as recently as 1938.

Nanjing rises from the south bank of the Yangtze River, some 998 km/620 miles southeast of Beijing. The city's 3 million residents take pride in Nanjing's greatest modern achievement: the two-level, 1.6 km/1-mile-long road and rail bridge spanning the Yangtze River. Before the bridge's completion in 1968, no overland route existed between the lower Yangtze River valley (Nanjing and Shanghai) and Beijing.

A heavily industrialized city, Nanjing nevertheless retains vestiges of its ancient past. Artifacts at the Nanjing Museum on East Zhongshan Road illustrate 5,000 years of Chinese history.

The area's other attractions include the tomb of the first Ming emperor and the Sun Yat-sen Mausoleum. You can also study portions of the ancient city wall.

The Silk Road, ancient East-West route

Some China tours now visit Central Asian towns once connected by caravan trails used to transport exotic goods of the East to the Roman and Byzantine empires. Silk Road tours might include Xi'an (where the Silk Road began), Lanzhou (an important oasis), Dunhuang (site of the Mogao Caves decorated with priceless Buddhist art), Turpan (with a neighboring ancient walled town), and Urumqi (the most landlocked city in the world).

Suzhou, city of canals and gardens

Sometimes called "Venice of the East," picturesque Suzhou lies 84 km/52 miles (a 3-hour train trip) west of Shanghai. Dominating the city are the Grand Canal and numerous smaller waterways, spanned by as many as 300 humpbacked bridges.

Suzhou boasts some of China's most beautiful gardens. Scattered throughout the city, they were designed primarily for the pleasure of wealthy scholars and officials, many of whom retired here after service at the emperor's court. Gardens feature pavilions and galleries, artificial hillocks and rock piles, lakes (stocked with fish and water lilies and spanned by lovely bridges), islets, and clumps of bamboo and trees.

A short distance northwest of the canal-encircled city is Tiger Hill (Huqiu), a manmade hill that is the site of a pre–Song Dynasty pagoda.

Suzhou is known for its silk and top quality embroidery. You can visit a silk embroidery center, where traditional and revolutionary designs are adapted to tapestries and other products, as well as silk weaving and printing mills.

Visitors can take a cruise on the Grand Canal between Suzhou and Wuxi. Completed in the 7th century, it was the first and still is the longest manmade waterway in the world. It extends 1,804 km/1,121 miles, connecting Beijing in the north with the Yellow River and Hangzhou in the south.

Chinese culinary skills *include artistic presentation of food. This appetizer course looks too beautiful to eat.*

Sun paints rosy glow *on Tianjin street as bikers and farmer head to work. Horse-drawn cart carries winter cabbages to market.*

China 155

AN ANCIENT EARTHENWARE ARMY

They stand in ghostly silence in an underground vault, an army of terra-cotta warriors ready to defend their emperor's nearby tomb. They were buried here more than 2,000 years ago, upon the death of China's first emperor, Qin Shi Huangdi. Uncovered accidentally by a well-digging team in 1972, this life-size earthenware army is one of China's most astounding archeological finds.

No two warrior statues are alike, causing archeologists to speculate that each was fashioned in the likeness of an actual member of the emperor's honor guard. The warriors, completely outfitted with weapons, chariots, and horses, were placed in battle formation, facing east toward Qin's old enemies.

The vault—originally roofed with massive wooden timbers and covered with earth—was looted and burned 4 years after Qin's death, and most of the weapons were taken. The vault's charred supporting timbers gave way, and the remaining contents became buried in earth.

Excavation has been slow. Many of the figures were damaged during the cave-in, but missing pieces have been found nearby, easing reconstruction. Many of the reconstructed warriors have been replaced in the vault, while others stand on display in a nearby museum (and in other museums throughout the country). A hangarlike roof covers the excavation site, and visitors can observe the painstaking archeological process from a raised walkway.

Archeologists believe the area (32 km/20 miles east of Xi'an) to be rich in treasures as yet undiscovered.

Another vault nearby has yielded more terra-cotta figures—and to the west of the current digs, Qin Shi Huangdi's mausoleum, an untouched funerary city, may house even more archeological splendor.

Tibet, roof of the world

Still other China tours have ventured into Tibet, with itineraries including Xigaze (home of Tashilhunpo Monastery) and Lhasa (with the magnificent Potala, former home of the Dalai Lama). However, tourist entry into Tibet is sometimes restricted.

Wuxi, a lake resort

Northeast of Nanjing, on the rail line to Shanghai, is the industrial and resort city of Wuxi. Its biggest attraction is Lake Tai, one of China's five largest lakes. You can meander among its islands on a boat excursion.

Several outstanding gardens in Wuxi include Jichang Garden in Xihui Park, and Li Garden, a wonderland of rockeries, colorful flora, and arched bridges.

Artisans at work can be seen at Huishan Clay Figure Workshop; a local silk factory also offers tours.

Xi'an, former trade center

Capital of China during the course of 11 dynasties, the city of Xi'an sits in the fertile Wei River Valley, 845 km/525 miles southwest of Beijing. During its pinnacle period in the Tang Dynasty, the city was called Chang'an. Then one of the wealthiest and largest cities in the world, it profited from its location on the Silk Road, the main trade route between East and West. Today, even with a population of 2.5 million, modern Xi'an hardly fills the old Tang city limits.

The discovery of Emperor Qin Shi Huangdi's burial site with its army of life-size terra-cotta figures (see the special feature on this page) has made Xi'an an important stop on a China visit. Other sights to see include the 43-meter/141-foot Small Goose Pagoda and 64-meter/210-foot Big Goose Pagoda. Xi'an also offers several museums and parks, and portions of the old city wall are visible.

Yangtze River, cruising the gorges

Still other tours include some of China's major cities plus a multiple-day cruise on the Yangtze River. Embarkation/debarkation points are usually Chongqing and Yichang. In addition to the passing scene of riverside villages and towns, this cruise includes the drama of the spectacular Yangtze River Gorges with their perpendicular cliff walls, towering, mist-shrouded mountains, and magnificent vistas at every river bend.

KNOW BEFORE YOU GO

Here are some important details you'll want to know as you plan your trip.

Entry/exit procedures. Before they can enter the People's Republic of China, citizens of the United States and other countries recognized by the Chinese government need a valid passport and visa obtainable through application to a Chinese consulate (in Chicago, Houston, New York, or San Francisco) or embassy (in Washington, D.C.). Two photos are required, along with a $7 fee.

People traveling to China with a group will travel under a group visa. Tour participants submit a visa application, along with their passports and photos, to the tour operator or travel agent, who handles all further processing.

If you are arriving from an infected area, you must have a health certificate showing inoculation against yellow fever or cholera. Currently, it is recommended that travelers get a gamma globulin shot before travel to China due to the risk of hepatitis in certain areas. For further information on what other inoculations might be recommended, contact the U.S. Public Health Service before leaving home.

Customs. Upon entering China, each traveler fills in a customs declaration stating the amount of money, including traveler's checks, in his or her possession (you can bring any amount of foreign currency into China). Also declared are items of value, such as watches, cameras, jewelry, and so forth. You may bring in two cartons of cigarettes (or cigars or tobacco in reasonable quantity) and two bottles of liquor.

Currency. The Chinese currency is the *renminbi*, whose basic unit is the *yuan*, divided into 10 *jiao*. Renminbi can only be purchased and exchanged in China. Import and export is prohibited. Unspent Chinese currency must be reconverted upon departure.

Internationally recognized traveler's checks are accepted in China, and major credit cards are also accepted in some places.

Health conditions. Hospitals and medical services are good in China's cities, and many doctors speak English. All villages have paramedical personnel.

Some medicines and toiletries are available in the larger hotels, but you should take along any special medicines, including a diarrhea remedy. Drink only bottled mineral water (widely available) or water that has been boiled (for example, the tea water you'll find in a thermos in your hotel room).

Tipping. In a word—don't. Throughout China, tipping is neither expected nor allowed.

Time. The time difference between the U.S. west coast and Beijing is 16 hours (Beijing time applies to all of China). When it's Sunday noon in Beijing, it's 8 o'clock Saturday night in San Francisco.

Weather and what to wear. China's climatic conditions vary greatly from north to south. The best seasons to visit are spring and autumn.

The northern provinces experience marked seasonal variations, ranging from the freezing mark in winter to over 27°C/80°F in the summer, with high humidity. The south is subtropical, except for a brief winter; in Guangzhou, temperatures remain around 21°C/70°F for 10 months a year, reaching almost 32°C/90°F in midsummer. It rains often in the south in summer. Average annual rainfall is about 60 inches.

You'll be most comfortable if you dress conservatively and informally during your visit, except for occasions such as cocktail gatherings and banquets.

Language. China's official national language is *putonghua* or "common language," a derivative of the Beijing dialect (also referred to as Mandarin). Regional native dialects are also used. If you're curious about spelling changes in place names, such as Beijing (Peking), see page 140.

For more information. Residents of North America should contact the China National Tourist Office (333 W. Broadway, Suite 201, Glendale, CA 91204 or 60 E. 42nd Street, Room 465, New York, NY 10165) for more information on travel in China. The national headquarters of the China International Travel Service is at 6 East Chang'an Avenue, Beijing, China. The Hong Kong branch office is at 6th Floor, Tower II, South Sea Centre, 75 Mody Road, East Tsim Sha Tsui, Kowloon.

INDEX

Iron and paper lanterns *add festive note to celebration at Japan's Miyajima Shrine.*